THE REPUBLICANS

The Republicans

From Lincoln to Bush

Robert Allen Rutland

University of Missouri Press
Columbia and London

University of Missouri Press, Columbia, Missouri 65201
Printed and bound in the United States of America
All rights reserved
5 4 3 2   00 99 98

Library of Congress Cataloging-in-Publication Data
Rutland, Robert Allen, 1922–
        The Republicans : from Lincoln to Bush / Robert Allen Rutland.
        p.   cm.
        Includes bibliographical references (p.   ) and index.
        ISBN 0-8262-1090-2 (pbk. : alk. paper)
        1. Republican party (U.S. : 1854–   )—History.   I. Title.
JK2356.R87   1996
324.2734—dc20   96-23180
                                                                          CIP

∞™ This paper meets the requirements of the
American National Standard for Permanence of Paper
for Printed Library Materials, Z39.48, 1984.

Designer: *Mindy Shouse*
Typesetter: *BOOKCOMP*
Printer and binder: *Thomson-Shore, Inc.*
Typeface: *Sabon*

To the Memory of
H. R. "BOB" HALDEMAN
The most loyal Republican I ever knew

Contents

Preface

Over a decade has passed since I decided to write histories of our major parties for the lay reader who might want to know what each party stood for in a world reeling from the media blitz. In 1979 I finished *The Democrats: From Jefferson to Carter,* as the cold war was plenty hot and the national debt was still under one trillion dollars.

In the interval, the presidential primaries have become all-important for the party not holding the White House, the cold war has ended, and the national debt has soared like an out-of-control space satellite. Yet, the Republic survives and we have a world that still accepts the American dollar as its currency of preference.

Things are never as bad as they seem at first glance. Although I have been a Democrat all my life, I consider it a historian's duty to seek and tell the truth, and my training at Vanderbilt University was rather old-fashioned, in that I was taught to be a narrative historian, not a political analyst. How many times did Professor William C. Binkley say to us quivering graduate students: "Let the facts speak for themselves!"?

So that is what I have tried to do in *The Republicans: From Lincoln to Bush.* My research has made me admire Lincoln tenfold, made me realize how historic currents can take control of a man or a party, and forced me to acknowledge the cyclical nature of American political popularity.

If I have done my work properly, readers will understand that political parties are created to exert power and lead the nation in a particular direction. Our pluralistic society is the envy of decent men and women the world over; a large segment of the globe is still dominated by forces that prefer bullets to ballots. We can feel good about our Constitution and our political parties, knowing that nothing man contrives is perfect, but when it comes to the political spectrum, the Founding Fathers and the Americans who have followed them have shown mankind that peace and dignity are not mere dreams for mortals.

This is no "message" book, but I hope readers will conclude that a toleration for the other person's opinion is the best option we Americans have during our elections. Majority rule is still king; and both Democrats and Republicans can be thankful that one vote still counts. Long live the two-party system!

Acknowledgments

Credit must go to the University of Missouri Press and the director, Beverly Jarrett, for prodding me to fulfill a promise made long ago to write this book. Jane Lago, the sharp-eyed editor at Missouri, was helpful at every stage of production. The reference staff at the McFarlin Library, University of Tulsa, and Jean Grabill of the Tulsa City-County Central Library made the work much easier and prevented many errors from creeping into the pages when my back was turned. The patience and excellent suggested revisions of Tid Kowalski also deserve recognition. To all of you, my profound thanks!

THE REPUBLICANS

CHAPTER ONE

Fusion Out of Confusion

"Many a Republican has made his pilgrimage and stood in devout reverence on the spot pointed out to him as the birthplace of his party," Wilfred Binkley observed. "Not all of them, however, have stood at the same place." Some were in Ripon, Wisconsin; others bared their heads at Jackson, Michigan; while some have mistakenly felt a tug at their hearts in Hodgenville, Kentucky. Exactly where the Republican party was born is a matter of mild dispute, but never in American history has a political party come into being so rapidly, moved so successfully, and held on to its title so tenaciously as the Republican party that first struggled for recognition between 1854 and 1855.

Yet, in the beginning, there was no Republican bandwagon, and few public men were eager to enroll in the fledgling party. "Terminology counted for less than what was happening," historian David Potter surmised as he sorted through the evidence related to Republican origins. On only one fact can nearly all agree: the obnoxious Kansas-Nebraska Act of 1854 inflamed the North and made the old Whig and American (Know-Nothing) parties collapse as new allegiances were speedily formed to stop the spread of slavery. Passed by a Congress dominated by Senator Stephen A. Douglas and southern standpatters, the Kansas-Nebraska Act overturned the Missouri Compromise that had kept the lid on sectional political animosities since 1820. Neither Senator Douglas of Illinois nor President Franklin Pierce of New Hampshire had the slightest idea that the act was a time bomb that would eventually cause the creation of a new political party to challenge the Democratic party (usually called the Democracy at that time), which had dominated the American scene since Jefferson's election in 1800.

Among the forgotten ironies of our political history is the central role of Thomas Jefferson in the founding of both the modern Democratic party and the modern Republican party. As the Democratic-Republican candidate for president in 1796 Jefferson wove a political philosophy, and after his election in 1800 he implemented his program of civil liberties, low-key (and low-tax) national government, and equality before the law for all citizens. With many twistings and turnings, twentieth-century Democrats still pay homage to their founding father: Thomas Jefferson.

And so do Republicans, for when their party was in search of a name as the notion of a "Fusion" party emerged in 1854–1855, the various splinter groups coalesced under the Republican banner first raised by Jefferson. *They* would bring the nation back to the ideals and goals of Jefferson himself, as first enunciated in his Declaration of Independence. Bedrock to the basic Republican ideology was the idea that slavery was wrong, that "all men are created equal," as Jefferson said, and if America stood for anything it stood for political equality for every citizen.

When the ardent antislavery editor Samuel Bowles spread his gospel in the *Springfield Republican,* he did not have to change the newspaper's name—the one chosen by his father in 1824 was perfect for the new circumstances. Lincoln, when he dropped his Whig loyalties to become a Republican, thought it "both curious and interesting that Jefferson's birthday was celebrated in Boston on April 13, 1859, while those claiming political descent from him have nearly ceased to breathe his name everywhere." As the slaveholders shunned Jefferson for his idealism, Lincoln observed, the Republican party had embraced Jefferson's principles as "the definition and axioms of [a] free society."

The Democrats of his day, Lincoln said, "hold the *liberty* of one man to be absolutely nothing," when that man was enslaved by a man of property. "Republicans, on the contrary, are for both the *man* and the *dollar;* but in case of conflict, the man *before* the dollar," he added. And of course, that situation reminded Lincoln of a story. He had once witnessed a brawl involving two drunks, both wearing heavy coats. The fight, "after a long and rather harmless contest, ended in each having fought himself *out* of his coat, and *into* that of the other." In the switching of ideals from the Democrats to the Republicans, he added, the two parties "have performed about the same feat as the two drunken men."

"But soberly," Lincoln continued, "it is now no child's play to save the principles of Jefferson from total overthrow in this nation." Lincoln confirmed the Republican elevation of Jefferson to the role of patron saint. Had not Jefferson written the Northwest Ordinance, with its prohibition of slavery above the Ohio River? The ordinance was enacted by Congress on July 13, 1787, and Republicans would make the anniversary of its passage a day for celebration and rallies.

So in the whirlwind created by the Kansas-Nebraska fracas, the American people stuck with the old two-party system they had inherited from their British forebears. A seedling planted in presidential campaigns by antislavery enthusiasts in 1848 became a sturdy sapling in 1856 and a mighty oak in 1860. A powerful Democratic congressman who later became a Republican stalwart recalled that in 1844 the Democrats had denied Martin Van Buren the presidential nomination because he opposed the annexation of Texas, a slave state. "Slavery upon which by common consent no party issue had been made was then obtruded upon the field of party action" as Van Buren's supporters "resented what they considered southern efforts to force pro-slavery views on the party as a whole." Gideon Welles, a Democrat who converted to Republicanism and served in Lincoln's cabinet, recalled that the 1844 fight led to the "ultimate downfall of the Democratic party . . . [thereafter, national parties] took a sectional or personal character."

After 1844, national politics turned mean, and after 1848 they became downright nasty. From Andrew Jackson's time the Democrats had favored a broader suffrage and low tariffs and had shown a penchant for the underdogs in society—immigrants,

3

dirt farmers, small merchants—while Whigs drew their support from the propertied classes North and South. Both parties tended to show more loyalty for a leader (Jackson, Clay, Polk) than for a cause. Indeed, party platforms were often a nuisance to the Whigs, so much so that they decided political planks only created splinters. They nominated military heroes, totally omitted the usual platforms, and still won the 1840 and 1848 contests.

Nonetheless, there was no lack of splinter groups, for the Free-Soilers came up with a candidate in 1848, and right behind them came the Prohibitionists, the Abolitionists (in the Liberty party), a vigorous but unorganized band of zealots who wanted mails and railroads stopped on Sundays, and the xenophobic Know-Nothings. Horace Greeley, the Whig editor of the influential *New York Tribune*, stoked the fires of encouragement for these minorities. Soon the *Tribune* attained a weekly circulation of 200,000 and Greeley's name became a household word in New England and the Midwest. These obstreperous single-issue groups appealed to the puritan strain in many Americans who wanted to change the world's habits. A law prohibiting the sale of ardent spirits, passed in Maine in 1851, encouraged other moral crusaders to enter the political arena. Fiercely Protestant, most of these parties were "agin" sin and more, whether it was whiskey, slavery, Sabbath-breaking, Catholic immigrants, or a combination thereof.

The Compromise of 1850 barely gave everybody a temporary breathing spell. California was admitted as a free state, but the South demanded, and got, a fugitive slave law that stuck in the craw of abolitionists and plenty of Democrats who lived above the Mason-Dixon line. Not long thereafter, death took Daniel Webster and Henry Clay, Whigs who had more loyalty to the Union than to a political party. Gone too was John C. Calhoun, who had more loyalty to his states' rights principles than to either a party or the Union itself. Thus powerful forces for compromise or moderation were removed along with the southern spokesman whose intellectual potshots were a safety valve for proslavery apologists.

It was just when the Democratic party seemed at high tide that the issue of slavery in the western territories of Kansas and Nebraska suddenly began to dominate the political agenda. America's political spectrum would never be the same.

The Kansas-Nebraska Act galvanized the North in the spring of 1854, creating a salutary opportunity for the Democrats' opponents. Two groups jostled for the lead—the antislavery elements in the North and a fast-growing band of political activists who formed a secret order pledged to defeat all foreign-born or Catholic candidates for office. The antislavery men (remember, all voting was done by white males) took such titles as anti-Nebraska Democrats (or anti-Nebraska Whigs), or spoke of a People's or Union party, while the secret politicians promised to answer only "I know nothing" when questioned about their order. Technically, they were originally the Order of the Star-Spangled Banner, and later, the Know-Nothings. In Boston's environs, the Know-Nothings dramatically surged forward in the polling places, applauded by the blue bloods who feared the influx of Irish immigrants. Patrick Kennedy of County Wexford in Ireland, the grandfather of John Fitzgerald Kennedy, arrived in Boston as the tension rose and typified the "foreigners" that rabid Know-Nothings wanted to disfranchise.

Undoubtedly both groups touched responsive chords in the North, for a variety of reasons, but initially it was the Know-Nothings who seemed most destined to challenge the Democrats. They won an upset election in Philadelphia, then built a strong organization in New England that was prepared to challenge Democrats at all levels in the fall elections.

The Democrats were vulnerable, even before the Kansas-Nebraska Act became the litmus test of loyalty. Democrats beholden to southern factions had squelched a homestead law that would have given small farmers public lands at low cost, and a law creating a subsidized railroad linking the Mississippi to the Pacific was similarly bottled up in committees dominated by Democrats. Suddenly, the schism created by the Kansas-Nebraska Act caused the Democrats to shoot themselves in the foot, for now they were committed to thwarting liberal programs and forced into a reactionary stance.

In passing the Kansas-Nebraska bill, the dominant congressional Democrats split badly along sectional lines, with the 88 northern Democrats in the House of Representatives divided 44 to 44. In the congressional elections that followed, northern Democrats lost 66 seats, whittling the total House Democratic delegation to a mere 83, as Republicans captured votes from disenchanted Democrats in Michigan, Wisconsin, Ohio, and New England and gained a 108-seat majority. The devastated Democratic party was in danger of becoming essentially a sectional party serving southern interests.

The fall elections in 1854, however, did not cause all the factions aroused by the Kansas-Nebraska Act to form a coalition. Prior to passage of the Kansas-Nebraska Act, bands of aroused anti-Nebraska Democrats, Whigs, and Free-Soilers had met at Ripon, Wisconsin, on February 28 in an effort to organize opposition to the pending bill. Illinois antislavery men tried to form a Republican party at mass meetings in Rockford and Ottawa, and early in July a "Fusion" meeting was held in Jackson, Michigan, to call for use of the Republican banner as a legacy of the Jeffersonian tradition. Informal meetings by congressmen in caucus rooms or Washington boardinghouses showed the need for a national organization to direct opposition. An informal meeting of anti-Nebraska representatives took place shortly before the despised bill passed. Someone suggested that a new "Republican" party be formed, but nobody followed through with an explicit program, and the idea died as the bill became law.

Meanwhile, the Know-Nothings had been busier and more focused than the nascent Republicans, particularly in Massachusetts, where they virtually removed the opposition from the state legislature, gaining 63 percent of the vote; they scored lesser victories as well in Pennsylvania and New York. Further triumphs in California, Maine, New Hampshire, and Connecticut caused the *New York Herald* to suggest that the Know-Nothings might capture the White House in 1856.

But in an era when the mails were slow and the pace of life not regulated by electronic images, there was a widespread reluctance by disillusioned but loyal Whigs and Democrats to hurry into forming a new party. Such cautious Whig leaders as Senator William H. Seward saw the Democrats' legislative blunder as an opening for revival of their ailing party. Henry J. Raymond, editor of the *New York Times*, choked with rage over the new law but advised friends that "Nothing would more certainly ruin the general cause [of antislavery] than such a formal disbandonment [*sic*] of the Whig party." In Illinois, when a committee tried to form a state Republican party, it received no encouragement from Lincoln, even though he was anxious to run for the Senate. "I suppose my opposition to the principle of slavery is as strong as that of any member of the Republican party," Lincoln wrote, "but I had also supposed that the *extent* to which I feel authorized to carry that opposition . . . was not at all satisfactory to that party." Still proud of his Whig badge, Lincoln wanted only to denounce any violation of the Missouri Compromise, and he considered anything beyond that too radical for his Whiggish instincts.

Lincoln was being careful because he was ambitious. "I have really got it in my head to try to be United States Senator," Lincoln confessed after he brushed with Douglas in a scorching debate at Springfield. Lincoln ran as a Whig for the vacant seat late in 1854 but lost his early lead, and the post went to Lyman Trumbull, an anti-Nebraska Democrat. In Ohio, Salmon P. Chase, a Free-Soil Democrat in the Senate, was afraid to make any leap into the dark but wanted a "Fusion" movement to have obvious Democratic ties. Senator Seward of New York, worried about reelection, told friends he was not excited about the Republican movement, disdained any connection with the nativist Know-Nothings, and thus seemed content to end his days as a Whig of the old school.

Seward changed his tune in 1855 when his mentor, Thurlow Weed of Albany, decided it was time to abandon the Whig ship. "The necessity of getting in line with other states is imperative," the New York kingmaker told Seward as he struggled with Fusion advocates for a graceful way to create a viable party in New York. Their solution was to call both Whig and Republican conventions to meet on the same day, in the same city, in an orchestrated scheme to merge dissenters into a single organization. A confused delegate asked Seward which convention he should attend and was told that it made no difference. "The delegates would go in by two doors," he explained, "but they would all come out through one."

The result of these maneuverings, as historian William Gienapp noted, was that New York's shrewd Weed was able to forge a party that forsook the troublesome secrecy of the Know-Nothings by a specific resolution as it focused on the main mission: curbing slavery. A weak effort by angry Whigs to resurrect their party a few weeks later failed miserably.

Conversion from Whig or Know-Nothing to Republican was still not a booming business, despite the tantalizing hopes of antislavery men who looked to the 1856 presidential election as a gateway to the promised land. An uneasy congressional coalition of anti-Nebraska Democrats, Free-Soilers, Republicans, and Whigs invited all comers to a national convention scheduled in Pittsburgh on Washington's birthday in 1856 to create a national party. Corridor gossip said it would be called the Republican party. Horace Greeley (who claimed the name *Republican* was his idea), finally cast his lot with the upstarts. Greeley showed up alongside anti-Nebraska Democrats and Know-Nothing stalwarts who balked at directions from old-line Whigs. Timid delegates spoke of a People's or Union party, however, so there was no agreement on a name for the proposed new party. Finally, the delegates sidestepped efforts to push a nativist program and united mainly in their opposition to the extension of slavery. They adjourned with a call for a June national convention in Philadelphia where they could nominate a presidential candidate. The delegates returned home with more hope than confidence.

Amid the hand-wringing of cautious Whigs who feared an alliance with the amateurish Republicans and Know-Nothings, unconnected events on May 21, 22, and 24 focused attention on the nation's festering schism. Persistent clashes in Kansas between proslavery and abolitionist marauders had erupted in a pitched battle. Only one man was killed (by falling bricks, not a bullet), but free-state supporters publicized the incident as "the sack of Lawrence." Northern newspapers inflamed public opinion overnight. Then on the next day a South Carolina congressman entered the Senate chamber in the nation's Capitol and caned Senator Charles Sumner, a Massachusetts Republican, into bloody insensibility. Sumner would not take his seat again for two and a half years. Instantly, he became a martyr for outraged Republicans.

Citizens North and South barely had time to ponder these bizarre happenings when the telegraph lines carried the news on May 24 that the fanatical abolitionist John Brown and his followers had killed a proslavery member of the Kansas territorial legislature and several hapless farmers, apparently as revenge for the Lawrence raid. This incident was magnified into a conspiratorial plot by southern newspapers, while Brown was praised by northern abolitionists for his attack on "border ruffians." Terror seemed amok in the land, particularly in the columns of Greeley's *New York Tribune,* and the three events together heralded a summer of discontent as the presidential race of 1856 loomed in a time of growing tension.

Restive Whigs and turned-out Know-Nothings were not as concerned about Greeley's reports from "Bleeding Kansas" or Sumner's limp body as they were with the potential patronage in the event of a Democratic debacle. Except for brief intervals, the Democrats over a fifty-year period had filled territorial posts, clerkships, customs offices, and postmasterships by the thousands. To public men who believed the point of politics was patronage, the idea of breaking the Democratic lock on the public rolls was more enticing than the vague talk of cheap homesteads or a Pacific railroad. But to the zealous antislavery partisans, most of them amateurs at the game of politics, there was only one issue to be resolved in the coming presidential election—the containment of slavery as embodied in the Missouri Compromise and upset by the Kansas-Nebraska Act. At the same time, Know-Nothings kept up their din about the threat of Catholic immigrants to the national welfare.

Lincoln, still wary of leaping into any new political connection, saw a big difference between the antislavery partisans and the Know-Nothings. "How can anyone who abhors the oppression of negroes be in favor of degrading classes of white people?" he asked. "As a nation, we began by declaring that 'all men are created equal.' We now practically read it 'all men are created equal, except negroes.' When the Know Nothings get control, it will read 'All men are created equal, except Negroes and foreigners and Catholics.' "* Lincoln understood the strength of the Know-Nothings, but he feared the dangers latent in nativism.

Thus despite the appeal of Know-Nothingism, only the Republican party stood as a bulwark against the extension of slavery, and both parties were riddled with opportunists who cared little about slavery, yet needed a political base. American history exemplified the fact that every politician must have a party.

No member of Congress embodied this opportunism more than Nathaniel P. Banks of Massachusetts. Banks, a onetime Democrat who turned Know-Nothing before he won a House seat in 1854, had a foot in both camps. The majority in the Congress elected in the fall of 1854 was no longer Democratic but rather a nondescript conglomerate of Republicans, parvenu anti-Nebraska men, and Know-Nothings who hesitated to act jointly when the important business of choosing a Speaker faced them. Ultimately, after two months of haggling, the newly elected Republicans decided they would support Banks until the end, and at last Banks emerged as Speaker of the House. His narrow victory, with a vote of 103 to 100, presaged more trouble for the Democrats. It represented a triumph for the congressmen whose main allegiance was to an antislavery bloc, by whatever name. More significant, Banks's victory meant that the Republicans had shown their strength by blocking the Democrats' efforts to name their man to the powerful Speaker's post.

But was Banks a "closet" Republican? Northern Know-Nothings convened while the memories of Sumner and Kansas were fresh and nominated Banks as their presidential candidate, as a foil for the Republican nominee and to thwart the plans of the standpat Know-Nothings (who had nominated former president Millard Fillmore). Banks was pledged to step down in favor of the man chosen by the Republicans at their June convention. A conglomerate of political hacks and has-beens crowded the scene as supporters of Seward, Chase, Supreme Court Justice John McLean, and Sam Houston jostled for position at the June

---

*Quoted in David Potter, *The Impending Crisis, 1848–1861* (New York: Harper and Row, 1976), 253.

Republican convention. Old Senator Thomas Hart Benton's son-in-law, General John C. Frémont, was soon a front-runner with the convention insiders despite the fact he had recently been a Democratic senator from California. Speaker Banks claimed he had discovered Frémont and first touted him as the Republican party's best hope in 1856. Banks's own credentials as a Republican were still shaky, so it took a newspaperman with longtime experience in national political intrigue to boost Frémont's stock as a candidate. Francis P. Blair, a veteran Democrat who once edited the *Washington Globe*, was looking for an anti-Nebraska Democrat with minimal political liabilities. Although he was a come-lately choice, Frémont filled the bill. He was handsome and still in his forties, and professional politicians winked at his weaknesses in the face of his boyish charm. As a caustic wit observed, Frémont exhibited "all of the qualities of genius except ability."

Skillfully, Banks and Blair planned their boomlet for Frémont. Early in 1856 scattered northern newspapers endorsed Frémont as a candidate, and Banks's House colleagues signed on as Frémont men. Schuyler Colfax, a former Whig now turned Republican, had a growing midwestern following. He compared Frémont (who was now popularly known as "the Pathfinder" because of his western explorations) to Andrew Jackson as one who could stand up to the southern slavocracy. By implication, Jackson had threatened to hang traitors, and so would Frémont. The bandwagon was beginning to lurch forward.

Weed and the New York Republicans looked on the Frémont boomlet without dismay, for there was a sense of bad timing that kept them from pushing Seward forward. The Democrats had held their nominating convention in early June and chosen James Buchanan, a Pennsylvanian whose views on most issues were vague. The Democrats drew a line in the sand, however, with their platform plank endorsing the Kansas-Nebraska Act as a safe-and-sane solution to the slavery controversy. Senator Douglas's attempt to have the concept of "squatter sovereignty" endorsed fell by the wayside as too controversial, for the Democrats were afraid to alienate any northerners who had not left the fold. Senator Hannibal Hamlin, a Democrat from Maine, was still disgusted. "The old Dem[ocratic] party is now the party of slavery," he thundered as he switched his allegiance to the Republicans.

Several weeks before the Republican convention, Greeley had second thoughts about Frémont. Early on, Greeley had lauded Frémont in the *Tribune* as a worthy carrier of the new party's banner, but after a visit with Frémont's supporters Greeley balked. "All would be well if F[rémont] were not the merest baby in politics," he told a friend. "He don't know the ABCs," Greeley confessed after watching Frémont in action. Greeley, always ready to turn on a dime, thought about abandoning Frémont and endorsing Banks in the *Tribune;* but something happened to change Greeley's mind, for on June 5 the *Tribune* publicly proclaimed its support for Frémont.

After that, there was no stopping the Frémont forces. The only mystery surrounded the choice of Frémont's running mate, and here Lincoln's name was injected by his Illinois friends. On the first ballot Lincoln had 110 votes, but in a prearranged deal William L. Dayton of New Jersey was nominated on the second ballot. Lincoln hid any disappointment but confided to Senator Trumbull: "It would have been easier for us, I think, had we got [Justice] McLean." Still hewing a conservative line, Lincoln distrusted Frémont as a potential radical who would alienate the old Whigs with irresponsible statements. In fact, McLean had been placed in nomination, then his name was withdrawn, and in the ensuing confusion somehow Frémont was nominated by a unanimous ballot.

Before adjourning, the Republicans adopted a platform that denounced slavery as "a relic of barbarism" and insisted that slavery could not exist in any territory of the United States because of the "due process" clause in the Fifth Amendment. For good measure the delegates called for passage of a homestead act and laws to create a Pacific railroad. Conservatives feared that the statement on slavery needlessly antagonized old-line Whigs and others in the Fusion camp. But for the moment, an aura of harmony settled on the delegates as they headed home.

Although Greeley talked about a clean campaign, devoid of any mudslinging, he spoke nonsense. Candidates conducted front-porch campaigns, but their partisans held rallies, arranged bonfire parades, and waged a war of words in weekly and daily newspapers throughout the land. At the time, former president Fillmore seemed a formidable candidate, and so the prospect of a three-ticket race caused some observers to speculate that the final outcome would rest in the House of Representatives. In fact, Fillmore faded fast as the summer wore on, while Frémont basked in his popularity. Simultaneously, his backers demonstrated, on paper, how Frémont could be elected, even though he would not win a single southern state.

Pennsylvania, always a question mark in a close contest, loomed as the chief battleground. There Republicans lacked the power of state patronage and hoped that a heavy infusion of Republican newspapers, plus rallies where the jug passed freely, might accomplish an upset. Indiana was also leaning toward Buchanan, and impassioned pleas to shore up Republican strength there generated heavy mailbags but fewer votes. New England looked safe for Frémont, as did the upper Midwest.

In the final weeks of the campaign a bombshell of sorts fell into the Republican camp when Preston Brooks, the young man who had caned Sumner in the Senate, toured the South as a kind of conquering hero. News stories of Brooks's reception at the quaintly named village of Ninety-Six, South Carolina, were widely printed in the North to show the arrogance of the "Slavocracy." Brooks's speech, in which he promised to raise a force to invade Washington and seize "the Treasury and the Archives of the Government" if Frémont was elected, created a sensation. Brooks openly declared that secession of the South from a Yankee-dominated federal government would be a blessed option, in the event of a Republican victory. The *New York Times* denounced Brooks for threatening the Union and the sacred tenet of majority rule. "The opportunity was seized and used for the proclamation of sentiments of treason and rebellion against the Federal Government," the *Times* complained. On the bottom line, the southerners' rhetoric posed a threat against the Union "unless they could be permitted to *control* the General Government in their own way, and for the exclusive attainment of their own ends."

Republican editors took up the chant to frighten the opposition. No less an expert than Millard Fillmore read the reproaches in the northern press and made his own pronouncement. If Frémont won the presidency, Fillmore said, he would "owe his election entirely to the troubles in Kansas and the martyrdom of Sumner." The Republicans, he added, "ought to pension Brooks for life."

Angered by Brooks's triumphant tour and secessionist threats, Greeley was ready to explode. But his wrath was soothed by the cash-register bell as his *Tribune,* by now the avowed campaign organ of the Republican standard-bearer, scored impressive gains in circulation. During the summer of 1856, Greeley added 66,000 new subscribers until his weekly *Tribune* was mailed to 280,000 readers from Maine to Minnesota. When Democratic newspapers claimed Frémont was a Catholic and former slaveholder, Greeley rushed to defend the Pathfinder against such slanders. When Democrats predicted a Buchanan landslide, Greeley lined up his own list of projected results in the *Tribune,* showing that Frémont had the upper North and Buchanan all of the South. As Greeley saw it in the summer, the crucial states were Pennsylvania, New Jersey, and Indiana. Greeley thought Frémont would win all three and become the first Republican president in history.

The rumor of Frémont's Catholicism hurt his chances in the areas where Know-Nothings had been strong. "The Catholic story is doing much damage," Thurlow Weed admitted. When Greeley issued a denial of the canard, amused Democrats hailed the editor's "fishy" story. In truth, Frémont was an Episcopalian, but he handled the incident clumsily, and his managers had good reason to keep him under wraps as much as was decently possible.

Lincoln took to the hustings on Frémont's behalf and discounted the brash southern talk of secession. At Galena, Lincoln told the crowd that "all this talk about dissolution of the Union is humbug—nothing but folly." But with his ear to the ground, Lincoln knew that Frémont was still too far ahead of the conservative Illinois voters. Pennsylvania voted in October, and Buchanan carried his home state, as well as Indiana and New Jersey; by Greeley's own calculation, that was the election.

In his hometown newspaper Lincoln read that Buchanan and Fillmore both ran ahead of Frémont in Illinois. Frémont's name was not on the ballot in most southern states, and he had only a trickle of votes in four slave states. So besides his northern toehold, Buchanan had the southern bloc and 174 electoral votes to Frémont's 114 and the 8 votes of Maryland for Fillmore. For disconsolate Republicans, this was not a victory, but it was a good start. No campaign ever had a better slogan than "Free Speech, Free Soil, Frémont!" Frémont was finished as a presidential hopeful, but the men who had nominated him were not. The Whig party was dead, the Know-Nothings were dying, and all of the talent, wealth, and experience of their party members now shifted to the upstart Republicans. Indeed, some of the survivors were elated by the closeness of the Democrats' triumph. Indiana went for Buchanan, but former Whig Schuyler Colfax saw a silver lining as he compared their battle to the encounter on Bunker Hill, "where those who finally retreated won the victory."*

Clearly, it was not a time to weep but a time to sow. The Republican harvest would not be long in coming.

---

*Quoted in George H. Mayer, *The Republican Party, 1854–1964* (New York: Oxford, 1964), 47.

CHAPTER TWO

Taney Tosses a Torch

The Bible used by James Buchanan for his presidential oath on March 4, 1857, had barely been encased when a new storm broke on the nation's political horizon. Chief Justice Roger B. Taney, who administered Buchanan's oath, sat in solemn stillness when the Supreme Court made public its ruling on March 6 in the case of *Scott v. Sanford*. At dinner that night, Buchanan might not have alluded to the case, but for the next three years the name of Dred Scott would be part of American conversation, becoming a milestone in American history.

If the Republican party needed a shot in the arm, this was it. The Dred Scott decision helped project slavery back into the middle of the nation's political debates, forced southern apologists to hail a judicial blunder as a great legal triumph, and gave northern opponents of slavery a new weapon in their battle to contain and eventually destroy the "peculiar institution."

For years the case had wound its way through the state and federal court system, starting with a slave's petition for freedom on the ground that his residence in a free state and free territory had released him from bondage. Scott's master had died in 1843, but his master's widow had remarried (to a Massachusetts man, who was elected to Congress as an antislavery Know-Nothing!). More litigation led to a Missouri court ruling that Scott was, despite his residence in Illinois and the Wisconsin Territory, still a slave. This decision in 1854 did not settle the matter, for in 1856 the case had become a legal cause célèbre when it finally was placed on the Supreme Court docket. Scott's status, as a black man, was in question, and so was the constitutionality of antislavery statutes passed by the territories.

As every thinking voter in the United States then knew, the Kansas-Nebraska Act said that Congress was not empowered to restrict slavery in either of the western territories named in the act as they moved toward statehood. From the rubble heap of the Missouri Compromise, Congress passed the buck to the high court. If the idea of squatter sovereignty was valid, a territory along either the Rio Grande or the Canadian border could approve a constitution permitting slavery, or denying it, just as its eligible voters decided. That was Senator Douglas's stock-in-trade, but the Scott decision said differently. If Congress could not touch on slavery in territories, could it permit territorial legislatures to restrict slavery?

Rumors leaking from the high court's chambers in 1856 indicated the justices were seeking a judicial loophole that would allow them to say succinctly that Scott's freedom was a state matter not proper for a federal court's jurisdiction. And that would be that—the Missouri Compromise was dead—but so what?

During the weeks before Buchanan took office, the court's mood shifted. Five of the nine justices were southerners, and few legal minds expected them to give any aid-and-comfort to the antislavery supporters following the case. They were right, as Marylander Taney proved when he delivered the long, tortured opinion that would soon shake Capitol Hill like an earthquake.

In short, Taney (and five other justices, only one a northerner) held that blacks could not be citizens nor become citizens, that blacks "had no rights which the white man was bound to respect," and to make matters clear beyond doubt, that the Missouri Compromise was unconstitutional. Scott was still a slave, because Congress had no power to interfere in the property of a citizen "without due process of law." In practical terms, the decision seemed to mean that the entire western domain was open to slavery.

This was a novel ruling, and its impact was immediate in legal circles, lawyers' offices, and the White House. Buchanan hailed the decision as a final answer to the vexing question of slavery in the territories. In fact, it was nothing of the sort, though it took some time for the damage it had done to become apparent. For the moment, farmers in Ohio did not stop plowing to read the decision, nor did schoolteachers in Vermont interrupt classes to talk about the Scott matter. Like an oily rag smoldering in an untidy closet, the Scott decision caused no immediate harm. But it smelled bad and it did not go away.

Greeley had sulked around his Manhattan office after the fall elections, afraid he had backed the wrong horse. Greeley "feared that Republicanism would prove to be a flash in the pan," historian Jeter Isley noted. The Dred Scott decision gave Greeley new grounds for optimism. The whole business was a conspiracy, Greeley decided, trumped up by proslavery gang members in Washington who were lickspittles to southern arrogance. War! the *Tribune* declared, in a scathing editorial: "It is a war upon free labor, it is a war upon non-slaveholders, whom the Court seeks to deprive of the power to protect themselves against the competition of slave labor, and to deliver over, bound hand and foot, to the absolute control of a slaveholding Oligarchy." Once again the bonfire rallies paraded through the villages and towns of the North, but with a difference. This time the outrage over the Scott decision was organized and directed by the Republicans who had been battle tested the preceding autumn.

Taney was the chief target of the editorials and speeches disseminated by print shops from Zanesville to Boston. The aging onetime slaveholder (who was a Catholic to boot) was pictured as a moral leper leading a band of associate justices, most of whom held from one to nine slaves. Indeed, one justice had owned a rice plantation with perhaps forty blacks under his overseer's lash.

Southern congressmen hailed the decision as settling the slavery question with finality. Toasts were offered in Charleston salons, in the French Quarter, and wherever Buchanan's backers gathered in joviality at what appeared to be a final ruling on the right to extend slavery wherever the Stars and Stripes flew.

Lincoln, moving with more speed toward center stage, had already taken his cue from the last State of the Union message by Franklin Pierce. Speaking to a Republican banquet in Chicago in December 1856, Lincoln chided the president for forgetting that Buchanan had been elected by less than a majority of the votes cast. "Our government rests on public opinion," Lincoln said. "Whoever can change public opinion, can change the government. . . . All of us who did not vote for Mr. Buchanan . . . are a majority of four hundred thousand." Really warming to his task, Lincoln pleaded for his fellow Republicans to "come together, for the future. . . . We *can* do it. The human heart is with us—God is with us." Gone was all the hesitation shown during the Kansas-Nebraska fight. Lincoln was rolling up his sleeves.

A citizens' rally in Lincoln's hometown gave him the opportunity to blast the Scott decision. Almost as Lincoln spoke, the election returns from the Kansas territory were being counted, and it was far from certain as to whether the new state would have a free or a slave constitution. Lincoln also knew that suspicious antislavery voters in Kansas had boycotted the election, claiming it was a sham effort to legalize slavery. Douglas had insisted that "free state Democrats" would vote in Kansas, but few had been found, and Lincoln could not resist a poke at the Democrats by saying that if a single "free State Democrat" should appear in Kansas "I suggest that it might be well to catch him, and stuff and preserve his skin, as an interesting specimen of that soon to be extinct variety of the genus, Democrat."

Then Lincoln got down to business. The Dred Scott decision insisted that blacks had no part in forming the United States, when in fact (Lincoln said) Negroes were more active in the country during its formation than they were at the moment. In 1776 and 1787 five states allowed free negroes to vote, he noted, but in 1857 "all the powers of earth seem rapidly combining against him." Lincoln said he spoke for himself, not the Republican party, when he expressed the need for efforts to return blacks to Africa, and he predicted, "We shall find a way to do it, however great the task may be." Meanwhile, good Republicans insisted "with whatever of ability they can, that the negro is a man; that his bondage is cruelly wrong, and that the field of oppression ought not to be enlarged." As he often did, Lincoln concluded on a cash-and-carry note: "The plainest print cannot be read through a gold eagle; and it will be ever hard to find many men who will send a slave to Liberia, and pay his passage while they can send him to a new country, Kansas for instance, and sell him for fifteen hundred dollars, and the rise."

Lincoln rarely made such bold statements without calculating beforehand the probable effect. In his attack on the Scott decision, Lincoln was trying to make Douglas look like a hapless anomaly in the Democratic party, while tying the Republicans to the fate of slavery in the vexed nation.

The Republicans were moving pretty fast anyway. In the northern states where legislatures began deliberating early in 1857, the new party had scored substantial gains, enough to elect Zachariah Chandler to the Senate from Michigan, Preston King from New York, and the formidable Simon Cameron from Pennsylvania. The Republicans would not control the next Senate, but they would have enough seats to give the Democrats pause. With Seward ready to serve as a minority leader, the sectional forum took on a different coloration.

Buchanan's tenure in the White House made the Republicans' job easier than it looked. A pensive fifty-eight-year-old bachelor, Buchanan was a northerner only by birth. His friends and associates—even the men at the Cincinnati convention who rigged his presidential nomination—were all southerners. As their captive, Buchanan thought the troublesome problems in Kansas and Nebraska could be solved by appointing strong-willed administrators to oversee the transition from territory to state. A downturn in the marketplace in 1857, when cotton prices dipped, was not too worrisome for the president who promised that slavery would not be imposed in the territories unless the inhabitants voted in favor of the "peculiar institution."

The so-called Panic of 1857 caused some banks to fail and shifted the spotlight away from slavery for a few months. In that interval, the issue of a protective tariff as a Republican panacea was discussed in party councils. Many northern manufacturers were tired of the Democrats' low-tariff policies and blamed depressed prices on the lack of a tariff barrier. William Cullen Bryant, the *New York Post* editor who had become a convert to Republicanism, still clung to his free-trade principles and urged

Republicans to reject calls for a protective tariff. Bryant's call for a commitment to free trade was, events proved, a mere cry in the wilderness. Pennsylvania iron manufacturers were keen for a higher tariff, and in a bow to these interests some Republicans (as historian Eric Foner noted) soft-pedaled their earlier flirtation with free trade. Greeley was never one to speak softly, however, and he blamed the recession of 1857 on the low-tariff policies of the Democrats. The busy editor placed in his mental file a marker for "protective tariff," as he searched for issues that would show the Republicans were not simply wedded to a single issue: slavery.

The *Tribune* editor was not alone in seeing that the practical implication of the Scott decision was that, from the Missouri border westward, the national domain was open to slavery. Looking at the map, Republicans saw a vast battleground where the future of slavery would be decided by political maneuvering, not bullets. The majority ruled, and the business of Republicans was to attain a majority in Congress, and then capture the White House. When Republicans in the Congress tried to make laws out of their party platform by introducing legislation to give settlers pieces of the public domain at bargain prices, their bill passed the House but lost by one vote in the Senate. A year later, Senate Republicans mustered more strength and passed the Homestead Act and sent it to Buchanan's desk, but the president listened to his southern advisers and vetoed the popular bill, in part because of fears that it would help create more free states.

The Minnesota Territory was ready to move toward statehood, but the specter of Kansas placed everything on hold. Slavery seemed to provide the backdrop for nearly every piece of legislation or administrative order. Buchanan's cabinet was loaded with southerners who brazenly opposed any subsidized construction of a railroad favoring a northern route to the Pacific. Buchanan's pals wanted a southern route that would link New Orleans with the Pacific Coast and incidentally help solidify any support in the Arizona and New Mexico territories for slavery. All these maneuvers exacerbated the feelings of northerners. Most offended, perhaps, was Senator Stephen Douglas, who was fair-minded (and profit-minded) enough to favor a western railroad with an eastern terminus in Chicago.

In short, there was much on the country's mind besides the Scott decision and Kansas. But at the nation's capital there was a sectional tilt to nearly every piece of legislation that dealt with commerce, transportation, banking, or national defense. Jefferson Davis, Pierce's hardworking secretary of war, was typical of the cabinet officers appointed after 1850. Davis took pains to see that surveys were made of a railroad route through an inhospitable and sparsely populated Southwest. To railroad men and Senator Douglas, such a scheme was the height of folly, a travesty when practicability was being preached by investors who wanted profits, not votes. Undaunted, Davis switched from the cabinet to the Senate and steadfastly affirmed the need for a southern Pacific route.

Nobody could argue that such a railroad would be profitable, but southerners had a different set of values. Balanced against their prejudice toward a southern route was the fact that nearly $400 million had been invested in American railroads by 1857, with most of the tracks laid in the North and paid for by dollars resting in northern banks. In 1850 those banks had been Whig controlled, but in 1857 the money managers in Buffalo, Boston, Cleveland, and Chicago were (or soon would be) Republicans. Only in New York City, where the Democrats held healthy majorities, were the bankers and merchants still openly friendly with Buchanan and his southern supporters.

The nation was still a country of farmers, with over 70 percent of the population living close to a barn or in towns of less than three thousand. And it was with the agrarians in the North that the Republicans began to make headway in earnest. They were aided and abetted by Greeley with his weekly *Tribune* mailed at low rates and sold for a dollar a year to subscription clubs springing up in Iowa, Wisconsin, and Minnesota as well as the upper reaches of Vermont and Maine. From the time Greeley endorsed Frémont until the Scott decision, the nearsighted but perceptive editor was thinking in terms of the presidential election of 1860. Early on, Greeley began to whittle away at the opposition by assuring his readers the slavocracy was trying to capture the national government, lock, stock, and, barrel, and thus keep slavery embedded in the United States at a time when nearly every other Western nation was abandoning human bondage as a forsaken, discredited economic device and an abomination to human decency.

Given hindsight, why did the Republicans not sweep on to victory after victory from 1857 forward until they entered the White House in full triumph in 1860? The chief explanation perhaps is that the American people were and remain innately conservative. As a nation of farmers, Americans took comfort in doing things as their grandfathers had done—including voting. Urban Americans have continued this conservative tradition, except when the future looked cloudy because of a war or a depression. Only when cash is scarce and jobs disappear will the American electorate take the risk of voting for a liberal candidate or a party committed to drastic action.

Indeed, Americans have never liked change for change's sake, and they were not ready to declare in 1857 that the constitutional endorsement of slavery was both a human tragedy and a political blunder. For every Congregational minister outside Boston who was condemning slavery there was a Presbyterian or Baptist counterpart in Richmond who could find a biblical passage justifying human bondage; for every cotton broker in Memphis who was more interested in his profits than in his conscience, there was a Lawrence capitalist who did not care whose labor brought cotton into his mill as long as his ledgers were awash in black ink. Most politicians understood this, but the "conscience" Whigs who despaired in 1850 when the Fugitive Slave Act brought violence to Boston were no longer in a minority on Boston's Beacon Hill. The mood of the nation had shifted dramatically in 1854, and the shifting political sands were still blowing when proslavery forces decided that Kansas would be the testing ground that would settle the labor status of the western public domain. Slave or free? That was the simple question.

Instead of moving ahead steadily at the polls, the Republicans found tough going in local elections where slavery was not an issue but school boards were. In Ohio, Illinois, Indiana, and Pennsylvania, Democrats began to regain their strength. In Pennsylvania, Senator Cameron and his friends ate crow when their candidate for governor was badly beaten. Only north of the Connecticut River, where the former Know-Nothings either retreated or converted to Republicanism, did the new party have reason to celebrate.

And then came Kansas.

In his inaugural address, Buchanan had promised that Kansas was going to be free or slave as the residents there alone would decide. To implement his promise he appointed a native Pennsylvanian who had been a Mississippi senator, Robert J. Walker, to carry out his pledge. Nothing went according to plan. Kansas's free-state residents believed the June election for delegates to a statehood convention was rigged, so they refused to vote. With only proslavery men voting, only 2,200 out of 9,000 eligible voters cast ballots, and they elected delegates who were ready to write a constitution that would permit slavery in the new state.

The election was legal but farcical. The new governor tried to be fair and succeeded only in alienating the free-staters (still not firm Republicans) and southerners who thought he was bending too far backward to accommodate pro-northerner elements. In his inaugural address, Walker had intimated that geography was hostile to the notion of slavery in Kansas and suggested that proslavery forces might move their sights down to the Indian Territory, where slavery already was practiced among the Five Civilized Tribes living there. Critics called this approach by Buchanan's appointee "vile hypocrisy" and began to undercut Walker in the president's councils. Walker's friendly overtures to the free-state rump government, which set up its "capital" in Topeka, did nothing to mollify Democrats in Georgia and Mississippi, where state conventions adopted resolutions censuring the hapless governor.

Meanwhile, the Kansas delegates, legally elected and set to meet in September, realized that the way was open for them to convene and prepare a proslavery constitution that could be sent to Washington as the final step toward statehood. Fast losing all his credibility, Walker talked the convention delegates into postponing their meeting until after the October elections for a new territorial legislature. He was buying time, or so he thought. But the legislative elections proved to be fraudulent, and as he sorted through them and threw out the corrupt votes, the result was a majority for the free-staters.

Eastern newspapers, led by Greeley's *Tribune,* duly reported all these machinations in excruciating detail. At heart, Greeley suspected Walker might be able to make good on Buchanan's promises, and if that was the case, Kansas would soon be in the Union as a slave state. This would vindicate Douglas's prediction that "squatter sovereignty" would work, and weaken the Republicans who claimed that anything short of a prohibition against slavery in the new territories (or states) was unacceptable.

To Greeley's great relief, his cause (and the Republicans') was aided by the Kansas convention. Meeting in Lecompton in October, the delegates wrote a document similar to the other state constitutions with a two-house legislature, executive branch, and judiciary. Nothing unusual there—but they inserted clauses excluding free blacks from entering the state (the free-staters wanted such a provision, too), and they left the matter of slavery dangling. A referendum was scheduled to determine whether the constitution, in its final form, would permit the practice of slavery.

Nobody was pleased. The antislavery men claimed they had been betrayed, because the referendum offered only a limitation on slavery, not outright denial. Blacks brought into the state or living there when statehood became a reality might be kept in bondage until a specific date, as some free-staters pointed out. What's wrong with that? white southerners asked, for that was the practice in Kentucky, Missouri, and Illinois and could work in Kansas, too. What about children born to slaves? The Lecompton constitution took care of that—they would be the property of the parents' owners.

Walker took sick leave and washed his hands of the whole business, but Buchanan listened to his southern pals and decided to go for it. He endorsed the Lecompton plan as a "final solution" to the Kansas problem, accepted Walker's resignation, and apparently believed the thunderous applause rising from South of the Potomac and Ohio boundaries. Senator Douglas was stunned, but Democrats controlled the Senate and approved the Lecompton constitution in late March. A deal was needed to stop the enabling legislation in the House, and a compromise was shaped that would hold up the statehood process while another vote was held in Kansas. Radical antislavery men in the Republican ranks condemned the deal, and one, Joshua Giddings from Ohio, was so upset that he suffered a paralytic stroke. But this new approach won in the House to confound Buchanan and his southern friends.

They had one more ace up their sleeves. An administration friend introduced new legislation that dangled a carrot before the Kansas voters. Introduced by Representative William English of Indiana, this bill gave Kansas a bribe in the form of a huge land grant if voters approved the Lecompton plan but continued Kansas's territorial status if the plan was turned down. This strategy backfired when the Kansas voters, with the free-staters back at the polls, turned the mishmash compromise aside and voted overwhelmingly to reject the Lecompton constitution.

During the debates over the Kansas problem, southern rhetoric escalated. Frustrated and angry, the cotton-state Democrats revived their threats of secession and warned their northern colleagues. In defense of slavery, which Senator James Hammond of South Carolina extolled as a boon to the cotton-producing states, the ultimate insult was offered. Northern workers, Hammond insisted, were worse than slaves, they were in fact the "mudsills" of society. Republicans would not let him forget that remark, but they were treading on shaky ground because the Kansas dilemma was creating fissures in their own party structure.

Senator Douglas had fought Buchanan on the Kansas bill, and he opposed approval of the Lecompton plan, causing a split within the Democratic ranks. Douglas's courage in standing up to the president and his party made him popular with a strange mixture of former Whigs and Democrats. Strangest of all, Horace Greeley suddenly had a bee in his bonnet—why not boom Douglas for the presidency in 1860? When Banks, no longer Speaker but still a man to be reckoned with, joined in praising Greeley's idea, the reaction in Republican circles was a mixture of disbelief and dismay. Then Congressman Colfax of Indiana, the ex-Whig turned Republican, said he liked Douglas, too.

Panic did not ensue, but the notion that Douglas should be elected on a squatter-sovereignty platform disgusted the Free-Soilers inside and outside Congress. After all, the Republicans had declared in 1856 that their guiding principle was: No extension of slavery. Wasn't that what the Kansas-Nebraska fracas was all about? Wasn't any compromise with slavery a deathblow aimed at the destruction of the Republican party?

Against this background, Douglas came up for reelection in Illinois. Aware of the hatred he faced from the Buchanan wing of the Democratic party, Douglas focused on the state legislature, where he would have to garner enough support to win his once-safe Senate seat again. Illinois Republicans, undaunted by Douglas's popularity in the state, turned to Lincoln and nominated him early on, a break with tradition since senators were usually chosen *after* the legislative campaigns. The stage for an epic battle was set.

Lincoln's political life was on the line, and he knew it. In April 1858 he told a close friend that "an old line whig lawyer . . . told me to-day that *he himself had seen* a letter from one of our republican congressmen, advising us all to go for the reelection of Judge Douglas." Days later, Lincoln again reported to Elihu Washburne that Joseph Medill, publisher of the *Chicago Tribune,* was "in great alarm at the prospect . . . of Republicans going over to Douglas, on the idea that Douglas is going to assume steep free-soil ground." As the Republican state convention approached, Lincoln heard that Greeley was ready to endorse Douglas and attributed the powerful editor's defection to poor judgment rather than an underhanded deal. Ever charitable, Lincoln said Greeley probably wanted "Douglas re-elected over me or any other republican" because of a perception that the Democratic senator's "experience, and *ability,* if you please, would more than compensate for his lack of a pure republican position" and help the party more than the election "of any one of our better undistinguished pure republicans."

Lincoln thought Greeley's position was pure hogwash, but he recognized that the *Weekly Tribune* was so popular in Illinois that Greeley's benign approval of Douglas would "continue to be, a drag upon us." But Greeley be damned, Lincoln must have reasoned, as he heard rumors of a plot by Democrats and weak-kneed Republicans to derail the Lincoln boomlet in Springfield. On the eve of the convention Lincoln encouraged a supporter to be of good cheer. "It is a trick of our enemies to try to excite all sorts of suspicions and jealo[u]sies amongst us," Lincoln warned, as he appealed for steadfast support.

That support was made manifest when the Illinois Republican convention in mid-June 1858 nominated Lincoln for the Senate. As the convention wound down, Lincoln came prepared with a dramatic address that would propel him into the national spotlight. After this "house divided" speech Lincoln's stature grew overnight. For both those who heard him and those across the nation who read the speech, there was an implicit message: Lincoln was no country bumpkin of a lawyer, but a man of uncommon commitment to an unpopular idea. He was "Honest Abe."

The "house divided" speech of June 16, 1858, was in a sense the real beginning of the Republican party, for thereafter the former fusion alliance regrouped under a unified banner that told voters everywhere there could be no compromise, that the Union could not be destroyed, but slavery would. Above all other ideas, Lincoln said, stood the simple dictum: " 'A house divided against itself cannot stand.' I believe this government cannot endure, permanently half *slave* and half *free*. I do not expect the Union to be *dissolved*—I do not expect the house to *fall*—but I *do* expect it will cease to be divided."

The telegraph lines carrying Lincoln's message eastward had been in place for over a decade, but his words alone were electrifying for northern minds and infuriating for southern ones. Perhaps not one professional politician in ten shared Lincoln's commitment to the principle that slavery was "in course of ultimate extinction," but the temporizing was over. Some men in the Republican party, like Banks or Chase, would have run on a railroad ticket if the results would lead to the high office they coveted. Others, such as Greeley, constantly thirsted for victory, so they calculated that if Douglas could win, why quibble over the legal niceties of "squatter sovereignty"? Victory, to the political opportunist, is the sweetest morsel on the table.

After June 1858 Lincoln would not back down, and the drama of the next two years proved that he spoke for most of the North when he said there would be no more compromising, no more half measures in the name of unity. Then, Lincoln predicted, "The result is not doubtful": "We shall not fail—if we stand firm, we shall not fail."

Soon Lincoln was involved in the stirring debates with Douglas that sparked excitement as their words hummed across the nation. The Freeport meeting in late August, where Lincoln asked Douglas if there was any legal way "the people of a United States Territory" could "exclude slavery from its limits" before statehood, was a decisive moment. His friends begged Lincoln not to pose the question, insisting Douglas could answer the question in a way that would make his reelection a certainty. Lincoln believed the question left Douglas on the horns of a dilemma that would ultimately ruin his chances to win the White House.

Plainly, Lincoln was worried because there was so much admiration for Douglas cropping up in Republican circles. So Lincoln wanted to take the contest for the Senate onto higher moral ground. Thus the real issue would become one of right versus wrong, and Lincoln wanted the Republican party to stand on the side of the angels. In the last debate, Lincoln made the good-versus-evil point as strongly as he could. The Republican party, Lincoln said, regarded slavery "as being a moral, social and political wrong," and to clarify matters the party would "*make provision that it shall no longer grow*. . . . That is the real issue. That is the issue that will continue in this country when these poor tongues of Judge Douglas and myself shall be silent. It is the eternal struggle between these two principles—right and wrong—throughout the world."

When the votes for the legislators who would pick a senator were counted a few months later, Lincoln lost to Douglas. But by that time Lincoln's name was circulating in Republican strongholds from Augusta to St. Paul. Lincoln's position was forthright, so that any other aspiring Republican leader would have to be measured by where he stood, or did not stand, in relation to Lincoln.

Greeley thought Lincoln had done well, but not well enough. The *Tribune* editor backed away from the Illinois contest, however, as he became embroiled in New York politics. Greeley decided he deserved the gubernatorial nomination from the fusionists, but Thurlow Weed had other plans. A split between the powerful Weed and Greeley widened. A "safer" Republican was nominated for governor, and Greeley pouted as he plotted ways to weaken Seward, whom he regarded as Weed's puppet senator. The state election returns that fall registered huge Republican gains. In Illinois, Lincoln's backers won a majority of the total vote, but Douglas's men still controlled the legislature, so the "Little Giant" would go back to the Senate as an anti-administration Democrat. Greeley gleefully reported Douglas's triumph, for he saw it as a wedge that would divide the Democrats in the 1860 presidential race. Douglas "must either be nominated," the *Tribune* noted, "or the Democratic party practically retires from the contest, surrendering the Government to the Republicans."

Beyond Illinois, the Republicans made remarkable gains in every free state except California. Twenty-five anti-Buchanan congressmen would be coming to Washington from New Jersey, New York, and Pennsylvania.

Lincoln had lost his race for the Senate, but the Republicans were celebrating a string of victories in other northern states. The spotlight quickly shifted to the 1860 presidential race. Meanwhile, rancorous Democrats smarted from the news reports that made it clear their party was in disarray, North and South, over the same question that Taney had thought was finally settled in 1857.

CHAPTER THREE

~

The Rail-Splitter Triumphs

Over the years the mythology surrounding Lincoln and the Republican party has obscured the shaky beginnings and strange alliances that created the fusionists of 1856–1860. Partly out of expediency, they had chosen to call themselves "Republicans." The rise of Lincoln's popularity following the debates with Douglas should not negate the fact that in 1859 Lincoln was probably content to be regarded as a good vice presidential candidate to balance a ticket headed by either William H. Seward, Salmon P. Chase, or Edward Bates.

Who was Bates? Greeley's favorite candidate—that's who Bates was. No one else had taken the former Whig from Missouri seriously until Greeley (angry with Weed and Seward) began extolling the obscure Bates in columns of the *Tribune*. Bates, who had recently freed his slaves, also had chaired the Know-Nothing convention of 1856 that nominated Fillmore for president. His conservative credentials were almost impeccable, yet only an eccentric like Greeley could have thought Bates a viable candidate for Republicans to embrace.

By this time, Seward was disgusted with Greeley but afraid to make an open break. Weed also hoped to keep Greeley on his side, but then the editor confused his friends and foes alike with an editorial stating that Seward was too radical to be a presidential candidate in 1860. Then in the next breath Greeley predicted Seward's candidacy to be only a matter of time.

In his own backyard, Lincoln was still something of a hero. After the state legislature made Douglas's reelection official, Lincoln bestirred himself to publish his speeches. Admirers assured him that a pamphlet containing his arguments would help the Republican cause generally, and his own ambitions in particular. Senator Chase, ever eager to keep his fences mended, wrote Lincoln a letter expressing regret at his loss to Douglas, thus offering Lincoln a chance to go on record as being a good loser. Lincoln replied, "Had we thrown ourselves into the arms of Douglas," as Greeley had suggested at one point, "the Republican cause would have been annihilated in Illinois, and, as I think, demoralized, and prostrated everywhere for years, if not forever." By fighting the good fight, Lincoln added, "the Republican star gradually rises higher everywhere."

To local Republicans, Lincoln counseled caution. When a state Republican convention was set to meet at Ossawatan in May 1859, Lincoln advised a leader to avoid any signs of "deference to Douglasism, or to the southern opposition element. Either would surrender the *object* of the Republican organization—the preventing [of] the *spread* and *nationalization* of Slavery. This object surrendered, the organization would go to pieces."

No longer shy about his Republican credentials, Lincoln looked ahead to 1860 and told his neighbor that Illinois Republicans should not seek to smoke the peace pipe with the South. "There are many men in the slave states . . . any one of whom I would cheerfully vote to be either President or Vice President provided he would enable me to do so with *safety* to the Republican cause." Lincoln believed any backing off from the proposition that slavery had to be contained in the South would do irreparable damage to the Republicans in the looming presidential race. "Lowering the Republican Standard," he warned, " . . . will result in gaining no single electoral vote in the *South* and losing every one in the North."

Joseph Medill, owner of the *Chicago Tribune*, began to pay more attention to Lincoln as the year wore on, and during the late summer and fall, as Lincoln accepted speaking engagements in Iowa, Ohio, and Wisconsin, the *Tribune* gave full coverage to the Rail-Splitter's remarks and helped spread the image of the Springfield lawyer as a man of humble origin. Born in a log cabin in Kentucky, Lincoln was self-educated and strong enough to split rails all day and still win a friendly wrestling match in the evening. His brief service in the Black Hawk War was also noted, without Lincoln's own footnote that the so-called war had been pretty much a joke. A war is a war, and a veteran is a veteran, as some later presidential candidates would learn to their sorrow.

The Republicans in Congress tried to elect another Speaker but were denied the powerful post when a best-selling book critical of the South, *The Impending Crisis of the South* by Hinton Helper, emphasized the polarization of opinion already well under way. Helper matched the venom of the southern fire-eaters by suggesting that the poor whites in the South ought to rise up against those who, in Helper's view, were oppressing them: the planter class. John Sherman of Ohio, a leading spokesman for Republicans, endorsed Helper's book and tried to raise money for distribution of more copies. And if that was not bad enough, John Brown carried out his lunatic raid in Virginia in October 1859, and a few Republican newspaper editors hailed the convicted traitor as a hero. Brown's summary trial and execution were hailed as proof of swift justice, but in Boston the screeds of William Lloyd Garrison and other abolitionists were aimed at making Brown into a martyr.

Late in 1859, after Kansas voters had patched together a constitution, Lincoln traveled to the troubled territory to speak on the eve of an election for territorial officers and a delegate to Congress. Appearing in five Kansas towns, Lincoln made no effort to defend John Brown (who was executed almost as Lincoln spoke) and urged Republicans to use the ballot box instead of a rifle. At one whistle-stop Lincoln turned to the southern hecklers with a warning. Lincoln's biographer Benjamin Thomas wrote: "Lincoln declared that the South, too, must learn the lesson of John Brown. . . . if the South should undertake to destroy the Union, 'it will be our duty to deal with you as old John Brown has been dealt with.' "

Some dates seem to be fixed in the nation's historical memory as defining years—1776, 1860, 1941. Events in those years marked them as times of changes that affected the United States forever. As 1860 opened, John Brown's body was "moulding in his grave," but the sectional din took on a higher pitch because it was an election year. Speculation on the presidential race was so rife in February 1860 that the possibility of a bloody Democratic convention did not seem remote. The Douglas people believed the time had come to give the "Little Giant" his due. Buchanan was not interested in a second term, but his southern friends vowed they would go to any length to deny Douglas the nomination at their Charleston convention.

Republicans had their problems, too, as Sherman's endorsement of the Helper book sent his race for the speakership into a tailspin. An old Whig moderate from New Jersey was finally settled on as a compromise, in order to deny Democrats the powerful post. Meanwhile, a group of former Whigs and Know-Nothings had sent out a call for a Constitutional Union party to meet in May. No Republican of any standing encouraged them, but Senator John Crittenden gave them his blessing and awaited theirs.

Part of every political campaign, from 1789 to the present, is the preparation of biographies for the leading contenders. These help supporters know the man they are supporting and understand his position. During the Christmas season in 1859 Lincoln's friend Jesse W. Fell had expressed an eagerness to publish such a tract to help Lincoln's presidential chances. Republican newspapers in the Midwest had begun to discuss Lincoln as a "dark horse" who might become their party's nominee if one of the favorites stumbled on the home stretch. Lincoln's "Autobiography" was characteristically modest and brief, notable for his confession that his election as captain of the Black Hawk War volunteers "gave me more pleasure than any I have had since." He barely mentioned his one term as a congressman but made a significant admission near the end of his story. "I was losing my interest in politics, when the repeal of the Missouri Compromise aroused me again," Lincoln confessed. "What I have done since then is pretty well known." The blossoming of dogwoods in southern Illinois coincided with publication of Lincoln's tale of his fifty-one years as a U.S. citizen.

Other Republican hopefuls were not idle. Chase talked like he was a candidate for the Republican nomination, but in fact he was self-nominated in the same way that presidential hopefuls begin their quest in the age of television. Seward was trying to live down the radical label pinned on his coattails after he made his "irrepressible conflict" speech, which suggested that a sectional war was inevitable. The newspapers teemed with speculation. Many editors assumed Douglas was a shoo-in for the Democratic nomination but saw a feed bag full of potential candidates on the Republican side.

Greeley returned from his trip to California, issued his famous "Go West, young man, go West" advice, and used the *Tribune* to douse the flames of enthusiasm sputtering for Chase and blazing for Seward. Both were too radical, Greeley avowed. In an often-quoted statement (sent to a reader, but not printed in his newspaper), Greeley confessed he was tired of losing: "I want to win this time, yet I know the country is not Anti-Slavery. It will only swallow a little Anti-Slavery in a great deal of sweetening. An Anti-Slavery man *per se* cannot be elected; but a Tariff, River-and-Harbor, Pacific Railroad, Free-Homestead man, *may* succeed *although* he is Anti-Slavery." Greeley began his boomlet for Bates, convinced the Republicans would swallow the old man despite a mealymouthed public letter Bates released to the press.

Lincoln may have thought Greeley's boost for Bates was a smoke screen for his real plan: the nomination of Douglas by both the Democratic and the Republican conventions to give a united front against whomever the southern Democrats chose. Lincoln knew that all Illinois Republicans were not supporting him as a "favorite son" at the Republican convention, so he wrote his former campaign manager in the senate race with a plea for help.

"I am not in a position where it would hurt much for me to not be nominated on the national ticket," Lincoln told Norman Judd, "but I am where it would hurt some for me to not get the Illinois delegates. . . . [His opponents] are most bitter against me; and they will, for revenge . . . lay to the Bates egg in the South, and to the Seward egg in the North, and go far towards squeezing me out in the middle with nothing. Can you not help me a little in this matter, in your end of the vineyard?" Clearly, by early February 1860 Lincoln had been bitten by the presidential bug.

"I will be entirely frank," he wrote a friend, "the taste *is* in my mouth a little."*

Before the month was out, Lincoln's stock in the presidential race leaped upward because of a single speech made in New York City. Lincoln had been invited to speak at Henry Ward Beecher's Brooklyn church in the fall of 1859. But by the time Lincoln accepted and rode the train eastward a group of young Republicans had made new arrangements for their sponsorship of the talk and rescheduled it for the auditorium in Manhattan's Cooper Union building. Anti-Seward Republicans were behind the move, and they treated Lincoln to much pomp and ceremony as he arrived at the Astor Hotel. Snow started to fall, but the weather failed to dampen the Republicans' enthusiasm as 1,500 crowded into the hall and saw Horace Greeley sitting on the platform as part of the welcoming committee. By his presence, Greeley let it be known that he was through with Weed and Seward, and *probably* ready to dump Bates and back Lincoln. But with Greeley, one never knew.

Lincoln was not in his best form as he began his remarks, but as he warmed to the challenge, he hurled bolts at Douglas, the Democrats, and the southerners who were blinded by slavery. Lincoln insisted that the Republicans were not radicals and challenged southerners to prove their insinuations. "When you speak of us Republicans, you do so only to denounce us as reptiles, or, at best, no better than outlaws." And, he added, "sectional" outlaws at that. "You say we are sectional. We deny it," Lincoln said as he quoted Jefferson to show that the greatest southern leaders had, early on, favored some kind of gradual emancipation.

Reports from Charleston and elsewhere in the South of secessionist sentiment drew Lincoln's wrath. The fire-eaters were threatening to leave the Union if an antislavery president was elected. The South wanted to make all the rules and have the nation abide by them, or else. Lincoln scorned the threat: "But you will not abide the election of a Republican president! In that supposed event, you say, you will destroy the Union. . . . That

---

*David Herbert Donald, *Lincoln* (New York: Simon and Schuster, 1995), 241.

is cool. A highwayman holds a pistol to my ear, and mutters through his teeth, 'Stand and deliver, or I shall kill you, and then you will be a murderer!' "

Coercion would not do, Lincoln warned. Then he turned to the Republicans, with a word of advice. "It is exceedingly desirable that all parts of this great Confederacy shall be at peace, and in harmony, one with another. Let us Republicans do our part to have it so." He ended with the quotable aphorism: "Let us have faith that right makes might, and in that faith, let us . . . dare to do our duty as we understand it." The audience went wild.

Lincoln, clean shaven and six feet four inches tall, worked through the crowd and went on to speeches in New Hampshire (the occasion was a trip to visit his son Robert, a student at Phillips Exeter Academy) and Providence, Rhode Island; then he drew more crowds for talks at New Haven, Hartford, and smaller cities in Connecticut. The *New York Tribune* followed Lincoln's triumphant and somewhat spontaneous tour of New England with growing approval. Greeley was now openly contemptuous of Weed, and Weed repaid Greeley in kind by keeping him off the New York delegation to the Republican nominating convention. Greeley responded by latching on to the Oregon delegation as a substitute. This gave him a pass to the convention floor, where he could help foment support for Bates, Chase, or possibly Lincoln.

The Democrats were having their troubles. Southerners at the Charleston convention, angered at Douglas's strength and believing that the idea of squatter sovereignty was now an antislavery ploy, finally adjourned in late April without making a choice. A second meeting was set for Baltimore in May. While Democrats of any persuasion fumed, the Constitutional Union party convened in Baltimore and named John Bell, a conservative senator from Tennessee, as its presidential candidate. The delegates eschewed any effort to create a platform; instead, they simply declared the party stood for "the Constitution and Union" and went home.

Now it was the Republicans' turn. Anxious to show Chicago off as a city on the move, Republicans and booster friends had enticed the national party to select the Illinois metropolis for the 1860 convention site. Chicago was doubling its population every three years and was a rail junction of burgeoning proportions with 110,000 inhabitants and growing by the hour. Medill and his civic-minded buddies raised $5,000 to build a temporary "Wigwam" for the delegates arriving at the train stations in a whoop-it-up mood. Chicago then boasted that it had nearly a thousand saloons. Cynics added that there was at least one bawdy house for every five bars. Perhaps it was true.

For Republicans it was party time, as they crowded into the 100-by-180-foot hall built for an audience of 10,000. It was draped with more bunting and gilt eagles than the dazzled delegates had ever seen before. The great seals of the attending states were hung from the rafters amid evergreen wreaths. Bands inside and outside the huge hall tooted popular favorites, hucksters sold badges, and flags streamed from the pillars in gala abundance.

On the surface, the Seward men were in control. Governor Edwin D. Morgan of New York, Weed's handpicked chairman of the general meeting, had the power to recognize or ignore obstreperous delegations. Optimism reigned as the 465 delegates bustled into their seats on May 16, ready to name the man they believed would be the nation's next president. The Republicans sensed that their candidate would be in the White House come March 1861. But they had no clear idea of who that man would be as Morgan rapped his gavel and called them to order.

The platform committee had done its job by omitting any reference to slavery as a blight on the land but denying the validity of "squatter sovereignty." There were planks for a Pacific railroad, for a homestead law, for a protective tariff, and for the admission of Kansas as a free state. Nearly every delegate could relate to one of the planks, and the whole platform was a grab bag of promises that the delegates solemnly believed would become law after they won the fall elections.

Perhaps no delegation was noisier than that of the Illinois Republicans. Meeting a week earlier at Decatur, they beheld two fence rails that were—so a sign said—made by Lincoln and Thomas Hanks in 1830. Lincoln acknowledged that the rails *might* be his handiwork, but the crowd did not care. Lincoln was their rail-splitting candidate and as a favorite son deserved their twenty-two votes. Thus they made sure that a nominating speech would be made and that the Illinois delegation would not split its vote but observe the unit rule.

Supporters for each of the main candidates had set up a hotel headquarters and welcomed delegates to bars where bourbon, cigars, and spittoons made a glorious combination for serious talk. Lincoln's friends rented space at the Tremont House, and Judge David Davis, a three-hundred-pound giant of a man, ran the campaign from his smoke-filled rooms. Although Senator Seward arrived in Chicago as the front-runner, his break with Greeley had hurt, as had his "irrepressible conflict" speech, which made Seward appear to some Republicans as far too radical to win the support of either the border states or midwestern voters who were not strong antislavery men. Bates, Chase, and Senator Simon Cameron of Pennsylvania all had some following, but none had supporters as devoted or as noisy as Lincoln's Illinois band.

Lincoln had been in Chicago back in March, tending to his legal business, when he heard from Ohio that Republicans in the Buckeye State preferred him over Chase as their nominee. "My name is new in the field," Lincoln replied, "and I suppose I am not the *first* choice of a very great many. Our policy, then, is to give no offence to others—leave them in a mood to come to us, if they shall be compelled to give up their first love." With magnanimity, Lincoln cautioned the Ohioans not to offend Chase, "because he gave us sympathy in 1858, when scarcely any other distinguished man did." How could you not like this man?

Seward's friends became restive as signs of disenchantment appeared. The Seward headquarters at the Richmond House exuded confidence, but at caucuses for the key Pennsylvania and Indiana delegations, Seward's support was dwindling, particularly after the Republican gubernatorial candidates from both states said they were fearful that Seward's radicalism was a drag on the whole ticket. A groundswell appeared to be in the making when the New Jersey delegates agreed to cast a token vote for their favorite son on the first ballot, then switch to Lincoln *if* Pennsylvania made a similar move.

Although the "smoke-filled room" is often castigated as a blight on American history, let it be said that sometime around midnight on May 18, Judge Davis sat in a room with a bluish haze surrounding the gathered Republicans and cut a deal. Davis promised the Pennsylvanians that if they would switch to Lincoln after a complimentary vote for Senator Cameron, their man would be in the Lincoln cabinet. Around breakfast time, the Pennsylvania delegation formally voted to support Lincoln after a first-ballot vote for their favorite son, and a wasted second-ballot vote for ancient Judge McLean.

To keep the Wigwam full of Lincoln men, Fell found a cache of admission tickets that were handed out to supporters of the Rail-Splitter. When he first reached Chicago, Greeley paid little attention to Lincoln and directed his efforts on behalf of Bates until it became clear the cause was hopeless. After two days of wheeling and no dealing, Greeley was ready to give up. Late on May 17 he sent a telegram to his New York office predicting the collapse of the "Stop Seward" movement. Greeley thought Seward was picking up steam and headed for victory. Balloting was to start on May 18, and a discouraged Greeley tried to catch a few hours of rest as he awaited the inevitable triumph of the senator who was now his archenemy.

An hour after the Pennsylvania caucus, the convention was formally opened for the main business of nominating a presidential candidate. When Seward's name was dropped, his backers screamed and paraded around the Wigwam with fervor; but their noise was only a prelude for the Lincoln men. The din following Judd's nomination of "Honest Abe" was described by an eyewitness: "A thousand steam whistles, ten acres of hotel gongs, a tribe of Comanches, headed by a choice vanguard from pandemonium, might have mingled in the scene unnoticed." Lincoln was still in Springfield, waiting in the *Springfield Journal* offices for news. The telegraph operators were standing by.

In short order similar demonstrations greeted the nominations of other favorite sons, followed by seconding speeches with more shouting and drumbeating. Lincoln's seconders from Indiana and Ohio rolled out a bandwagon, but Seward's obstinate delegates held firmly on the first ballot, giving the New Yorker 173½ votes to 102 for Lincoln. Cameron had 50½, Chase 49, and Bates 48; the "also-rans" took the rest. On the second ballot, Lincoln picked up 79 votes as Pennsylvania delegates gave up on McLean and swung their 48 votes to the Illinois nominee.

With 233 votes needed to win, Lincoln was close enough on the third ballot for Medill to make a deal. Lincoln had 231 1/2 when Medill offered a cabinet post to Chase if Ohio could put his man over the top. The chairman from Ohio shot to his feet, was recognized, and announced a switch of four votes from Chase to Lincoln. A cannon on top of the Wigwam blasted a signal that started a wild celebration as Chicago hailed the nomination of lawyer Lincoln. When the delegates finally calmed down, a former Democrat was chosen as Lincoln's running mate. Party chieftains thought Maine's Hannibal Hamlin, a U.S. senator, would balance the ticket—a former Whig for the top spot and a former Democrat for vice president. The appearance of unity was important.

Lincoln was swamped by well-wishers when the clattering telegraph key told the story of his nomination, made unanimous by a motion from a Seward man. Soon an official delegation arrived at the Springfield train station and proceeded to Lincoln's home to tender the nomination in highly formal terms. Lincoln shook hands, thanked them, and made some modest remarks as he joked about the week's proceedings.

Between May and November, sectional tension mounted as the Democrats split apart. The northern faction nominated Douglas while the southerners picked Vice President John C. Breckinridge after bitter meetings that ended in mid-June. By the last week in June, American voters faced a choice of four presidential candidates, but anyone with a pencil and paper could figure that these internal divisions would split the old Democratic vote three ways and thus make Lincoln's election likely. To stop such a possibility, southern states made it clear the Republican nominee's name would not be on their ballots. As Davis, Fell, Medill, and other managers of Lincoln's campaign realized, they would need solid electoral votes from every northern state to assure Lincoln's victory.

Greeley would help. Privately, Greeley thought Bates might have won more northern votes, but Lincoln was easier to take than Seward, so the *Tribune* masthead proclaimed the Lincoln-Hamlin ticket as best for the nation. Editorials praised the Republican platform, denounced the Democrats for their attachment to slavery in one form or another, and extolled Lincoln for his conservative approach to the nation's problems. Greeley claimed his various *Tribune* editions had over a million readers that fall, while a campaign manual written to help Republican speakers sold well enough to require seven printings.

Traditions of campaign dignity required that Lincoln stay home, be seen only infrequently, and speak not at all. At a time when whiskers were popular, well-wishers in New York sent Lincoln a request to add a beard to prop up his dignity. A little girl in upstate New York added her request, which seemed to carry more weight. Before the election, "Honest Abe" was sporting a fashionable beard. His office doors were open, he wrote many letters but made no speeches, and he reminded anxious voters that all four candidates were Union men. Secession talk was planted by his enemies, but Lincoln was convinced the threat of a southern exodus was "humbug." More than one editor pointed out that regardless of the fall election results, Democrats would still control the new Senate convening in 1861.

Strident threats from the fire-eaters that they would rush out of the Union if Lincoln was elected brought pleas to Springfield for some pacifying words. To all such entreaties, Lincoln's answer was the same, though couched in different words. "What is it I could say which would quiet alarm?" Lincoln asked. "Is it that no interference by the government, with slaves or slavery within the states, is intended? I have said this so often already, that a repetition of it is but mockery, bearing an appearance of weakness and cowardice, which perhaps should be avoided. Why do not uneasy men *read* what I have already said? and what our *platform* says?"

Lincoln had to depend on his position, moderate in tone and pitched to conservatives, that the Constitution secured slavery in the states where it already existed. That was what the Republican platform recognized, and Lincoln believed reasonable men in every section of the country could vote for him on that basis. Of course, no southern state carried the Republican ticket on its ballot. Thus Lincoln's chances depended on winning all of the North and a few of the border states.*

Lincoln still called the threats of secession "humbug" and sincerely believed the South was throwing out an egregious bluff. Greeley's correspondents in the South supported Lincoln's assessment of southern bluster. "There would be no secession, there would be no war," was the message sent to Greeley's office. As Jeter Isley noted, the *Tribune* correspondents reinforced the northern beliefs of southern hypocrisy. "None but the veriest fire-eaters contemplate disunion," an Alabama correspondent insisted. "They are but an insignificant clique. . . . The [southern] masses are heart and soul for the Union."

No wonder Lincoln felt the secession threat was empty. And it is likely that Republicans from Bangor, Maine, to Council Bluffs, Iowa, were similarly discounting all talk of disunion. The more they heard, the less they believed, and those who read the *Tribune* probably shared the same skepticism that pervaded the parlors of Seward, Chase, Colfax, George W. Julian, and others of influence in party councils. This amateurish effort to peer into the future was, as historian Allan Nevins wrote, "the cardinal error" of Republicans in 1860 when in fact the nation was on the edge of a precipice.

On the other hand, had Republicans campaigned on a war slogan, frankly saying a vote for Lincoln was a vote for war, they probably would have lost—and lost by a landslide. Their insistence that the South was not serious in its threats doubtless made the shocks ahead harder to understand. A war over slavery? Ridiculous!

Early in November, the last torchlight parades were held for the Republican ticket, Greeley wrote his editorials in a hysterical tone, and Raymond of the *New York Times* published more moderate appeals to the general voters. Then an election-day calm settled on the nation on November 6. A good sign for Lincoln had been the October returns from Pennsylvania and

---

*In Virginia, some of the western counties (which would soon be splitting off to form the new state of West Virginia) did allow voters to turn in a Lincoln ticket. Otherwise, the solid South would not permit canvassers to distribute tickets for the Lincoln-Hamlin slate.

Indiana, where Republicans won the governors' races handily. On election day, Lincoln cast his vote and went to the telegraph offices to see how the country was voting. By midnight the trickle of results revealed a fairly close race in the balloting, but by noon on November 7 the decision was beyond doubt. Lincoln had won most of the North plus California and Oregon; Douglas had taken New Jersey and Missouri, while Bell and Breckinridge split the border states and the South. Lincoln's three opponents had received nearly a million more votes than the Rail-Splitter, but in the electoral college he had won with an absolute majority— 180 votes to 72 for Breckinridge, 39 for Bell, and only 12 for Douglas.

Now there would be a time of terrible waiting, for Buchanan seemed powerless to stop the stampeding herd instincts of the fire-eaters. Until March 4, 1961, Buchanan exhibited none of the moral suasion that presidents before and since have used to calm an overwrought nation. Lincoln, for his part, thought a discreet silence was proper, since he had said many times that he would not try to interfere with slavery anywhere in the South.

But the fire-eaters had talked themselves into a frenzy. With the incumbent president almost a cipher and the president-elect loath to antagonize his late opposition, the secessionist leaders in South Carolina clamored for action. Calm voices in Virginia and Kentucky were shouted down as the Rhetts and Yanceys took center stage to declare, "Cotton is king!" Nobody stood up to them, and on December 20, 1860, they made good their threat and voted South Carolina out of the Union.

By their act of defiance the fire-eaters moved the Republican party, which had been standing on a political sandbar, onto firm ground. In trying to destroy the Republicans with their saber rattling, the fire-eaters instead gave the newcomers a permanent grip on the nation's loyalty. As Christmas of 1860 approached, the South Carolinian secessionists were in a double-holiday mood. They celebrated the birthday of the Prince of Peace while preparing for a war they welcomed.

The war would have to wait. Lincoln tried to choose a cabinet that would keep the country at peace. On Washington's birthday he made a speech at Independence Hall in Philadelphia that he hoped would pour oil on the troubled southern waters. Speaking at the shrine where the Declaration of Independence had emerged, "giving liberty, not alone to the people of this country, but hope to the world for all future time," Lincoln held out the olive branch to the South. "There is no need of bloodshed and war," Lincoln insisted. "There is no necessity for it . . . and I may say in advance, there will be no blood shed unless it be forced upon the Government."

Lincoln entrained for Washington, passed through a hostile Baltimore crowd, and reached the capital where an old friend was the sole reception committee. A few southern states had joined South Carolina in their exodus from the Union, but much of the southern leadership was hesitant.

So was Lincoln.

CHAPTER FOUR

The Republic Is Saved

The spotlight on Lincoln from mid-November onward created an opportunity for the Republicans in Congress to make the transition easier. Indeed, if the fire-eaters had not been hell-bent on picking a fight with the new administration, the war might have been averted.

The lame-duck Congress soon had a majority of northerners, but the conglomerate of anti-Nebraska Democrats, former Know-Nothings, and Republicans was badly split. One band of Republicans was ready to forget the high-blown rhetoric of the party platform and go for some compromise with the South that would preserve the Union. Senator Seward was thought to be leaning toward a settlement that would prevent bloodshed, and more than one New England senator began to backtrack on the boasts of June. Congressman Elihu Washburne, probably Lincoln's closest friend in the House, took back some of his bluster; but the moderates were offset by adamant midwestern senators who thought the time to temporize was past. Senator Sumner, partially recovered from his beating, made such wild-eyed statements that a witness to his conduct suggested the Massachusetts senator was nearing insanity.

Most alarming, to the Republicans who sided with Lincoln, was the suggestion that the thing to do was admit Kansas as a free state and place the slavery question in a capital cloakroom for a long rest. Seward and Representative Charles Francis Adams cooked up an alternative scheme that would admit Kansas as a free state and New Mexico (mostly a barren desert, with not a stick of cotton growing anywhere) as a slave state. A Thirteenth Amendment to the Constitution, guaranteeing the existence of slavery in the lower South, was proposed and passed by both the House and the Senate. Lincoln's closet cabinet advised him to accept all these concessions, and he did. Nothing could please the southern Democrats still in Washington, however, so the whole package was stillborn. Seward continued to wheel and deal as, he imagined himself, the assistant president. All the peace schemes came to nothing, for there was no discernible mood for compromise among the fire-eaters now hell-bent for secession.

Thus, Washington swarmed with rumors and newcomers on March 1, 1861. Lincoln was heartened by news that Texas had rejected secession, but every news report told of more forts and arsenals turned over to and occupied by soldiers from the Confederate States of America, as the secessionists had named their new nation. A friend from Illinois saw Lincoln and was shocked. Surrounded by office seekers and would-be advisers, Lincoln kept his doors open and his mouth closed. "He looks care worn and more haggard and stooped than I ever saw him," the friend noted. Lincoln had just turned fifty-two, but he looked ten years older.

No wonder Lincoln was worried. Not only were the saber rattlers dancing in South Carolina, but his friends also added to the misery of those first days in Washington. His campaign managers had made promises Lincoln was now bound to keep, and he planned to do his level best to assemble in his cabinet Republicans of all stripes—antislavery men, anti-Nebraska Democrats turned Republicans, and old-line Whigs such as Seward. Seward still had not figured Lincoln out, but he thought the Illinois lawyer was not up to the tasks ahead and began preparing a memorandum for the president. Seward was prepared to face the crisis and become acting president, if Lincoln showed the slightest inclination.

Seward's temperament was not fitted for an underling's post. Lincoln asked him to serve as secretary of state, and Seward accepted but then declined when he heard that Chase (whom he despised) had been named secretary of the treasury. Lincoln wanted no signs of early dissension. "I cannot afford to let Seward take the first trick," the president-elect jested, but he was serious. Seward relented and said he would serve after all. Lincoln also wanted a southerner in his cabinet, and he offered posts to several southern public men. All refused, so that ultimately Lincoln settled on Bates and Francis Blair, border-state men, in lieu of a genuine southerner. The cabinet finally in place was a mixture of old-line Whigs and former Democrats, with an emphasis on the latter. William Cullen Bryant advised Lincoln to pick his cabinet carefully so that it would not seem to be "only the old Whig party, under a new name."*

Washington resembled an armed camp as the day of inauguration dawned. A mixture of cavalry, infantry, and artillery troops guarded major intersections in Washington. Sharpshooters rested rifles atop public buildings on orders from their commanding officers, who had been warned that a plot to assassinate the president might be carried out. Lincoln took the presidential oath on the east front of the Capitol, with Douglas placed among the dignitaries. His inaugural address, now considered one of the great speeches in American history, was condemned by critics at the time as "cunning" or the pronouncements of the "Illinois Ape" (according to a Richmond paper); in fact, Lincoln was conciliatory as he tried to assure southerners that he was not out to end slavery in their region. He expressed his belief that "the Union of these States is perpetual," but not in a threatening tone. Lincoln did say that secession was "the essence of anarchy"; that because of geography, "we cannot separate" like a divorced husband and wife; and that the proposed amendment recognizing slavery in the South was given his stamp of approval. Lincoln said he had not actually seen the proposal, but he had "no objection to its being made express, and irrevocable." Lawyer Lincoln knew he was not violating the party platform, but he was stretching his hand pretty far in an act of conciliation.

Finally, Lincoln said the issue of war or peace was up to the South—"My dissatisfied countrymen." "We must not be enemies," the president pleaded. "The mystic chords of memory, stretching from every battle-field, and patriot grave . . . all over

---

*Quoted in Eric Foner, *Free Soil, Free Labor, Free Men: The Ideology of the Republican Party before the Civil War* (New York: Oxford, 1970), 183.

this broad land, will yet swell the chorus of the Union, when again touched, as surely they will be, by the better angels of our nature."

Lincoln's appeal for reason was wasted, however, and within six weeks the bombardment of Fort Sumter closed all avenues of peaceful discussion. Ironically, Lincoln listened to Senator Douglas during the days leading up to the war and was grieved when the Illinois lawmaker's health declined rapidly. Douglas was far more helpful in the crisis than were some members of Lincoln's cabinet, and when he came to the White House two days after the Sumter bombardment, it was to offer support from Democrats to preserve the Union. To back up his promise, Douglas began a speaking tour of northern cities to encourage support for Lincoln's program, but on June 3 Douglas died in Chicago. No other Democrat stepped forward with Douglas's prestige or commitment, and during the ensuing summer Lincoln must have wondered if any man in his own party could match Douglas's sense of patriotism.

No president in his first days in office had faced a crisis such as was handed to Lincoln in March 1861. An amateur executive whose only taste of public office was at the legislative level was thrust into a grave situation, and in those first weeks Lincoln proved to be more Republican than most of his party's supporters. Lincoln's only genuine asset when he entered the White House was his character. He had misjudged the South, he had no firm idea of how to organize a war effort, and he was totally dependent on some incompetent men (such as the army's senior general, Winfield Scott) who held the reins of government in their shaky hands.

The preservation of the Union was Lincoln's polestar, and he was so firm in pursuing that goal he soon made believers out of those who witnessed his steadfastness. Seward, who was perhaps as cynical as any member of the cabinet, soon realized that Lincoln had the determination and vision that a crisis demands of a great leader. Seward recognized his early error in judgment and began to support the president, whom he had once regarded as a political accident. Gideon Welles, the former Democrat who served Lincoln as secretary of the navy, wrote in his diary, "Seward has the inside track and means to keep it."

The war began in earnest when Lincoln reacted to the firing on Fort Sumter with a call for 75,000 volunteers to suppress the rebellion. The war dragged on through four bloody years, cost 620,000 lives, caused untold misery and disruption in the areas of the principal battles, and raised a crop of heroes and generals who would more than supply the political needs of the nation into the twentieth century. The conflict was not a short one, as nearly all participants believed likely in the spring of 1861, and the war plans of both sides miscarried more often than not. A host of mediocre generals lost their reputations, private soldiers with incredible courage marched to their graves in battles marked by furious carnage, and in the peace at Appomattox the futility of the whole exercise was a burden the nation acknowledged.

Before that peace, the Republicans suffered through four years of ups and downs that kept the party in a tentative state. Facing the uncertain 1862 congressional elections, and pressured by those anxious for a lift to northern morale, Lincoln issued the Emancipation Proclamation, although some of its conditions angered the very radicals in Congress he had tried to soothe. The restrictions on slavery were too limited, they shouted, and the edict would not become effective until January 1, 1863. Democrats pinned their hopes on a reaction to Lincoln's measures, which they deemed heavy-handed as they revived memories of more peaceful days. "The Union as it was, and the Constitution as it is," was trumpeted in their newspapers and on the hustings. State legislatures were returned to the Democratic fold in several northern states, and a Democrat won the governor's race in New York. Democrats also picked up thirty-three House seats, but enough Republican-Union candidates won for Lincoln's party to keep its majority.

Indeed, the exodus from Congress of Confederate sympathizers left the Republican majority in charge for the whole war, and Republicans were elected as officers in regiment after regiment in areas that had been Democratic strongholds a decade earlier. Increasingly, a man's loyalty to the nation was tested by his party affiliation, and Democrats in midwestern regiments found they had little chance of winning a field officer's or general's commission in the face of Republican hostility. Patronage, long denied to the old Whigs, was now a bonanza made available as new territories were created with Republican governors and judges, and the new states of Kansas, Nevada, and West Virginia were admitted with little fanfare to create additional safe Senate seats for Republicans to hold when peace came and every vote would count.

An overeager majority in Congress had moved in the summer of 1861 to confiscate all property of those persons who aided or abetted "the Rebellion." The purpose, obviously, was to provide for the confiscation and manumission of any slaves used "for insurrectionary purposes." Lincoln still preferred to leave to the states some kind of planned and gradual emancipation, but party leaders in Congress thought Lincoln acted too cautiously. A second confiscation bill, passed in July 1862, provided for the seizure of property held by rebels who resided in the South and paid taxes to the Confederate government.

Lincoln thought his party managers had gone too far. He refused to issue orders for enforcement of the second law, and when Greeley screamed at the president, Lincoln tried to clear the air. "If I could save the Union without freeing *any* slave I would do it," Lincoln wrote, "and if I could save it be freeing *all* the slaves I would do it; and if I could save it by freeing some and leaving others alone I would also do that."

Lincoln's first priority, and he never forgot it, was the preservation of the Union, but that was hardly the chief goal of many antislavery Republicans who had become almost irrational on the subject. Then, when Lincoln issued his Emancipation Proclamation, there was more criticism because the order provided for freedom only in places and states where the inhabitants "shall then be in rebellion against the United States." So slavery was left alone in Delaware, Maryland, Kentucky, Missouri, and any Confederate area then occupied by Union troops. Always ready to criticize Lincoln, the *New York World* complained that the president's order "proclaimed emancipation only where he has notoriously no powers to execute it." Many a Republican congressman made the same complaint, sotto voce.

Back stabbing and bickering aside, the Republican Thirty-seventh Congress probably passed more progressive legislation than any Republican-controlled session before or since. Honor-bound to redeem their campaign pledges (plank by plank of the platform, if necessary), the Republicans enacted the Homestead Act, a Pacific railroad bill, and the Morrill Land Grant Act. The latter created a system for financing higher education that in time benefited Michigan, Cornell, and over seventy other state universities. The Homestead Act was the jewel in the crown, however, for it allowed settlers to claim up to 160 acres of public land for $1.25 an acre or free if "proved up" for five years of tenancy.

With the war effort requiring all the men and metal the nation could muster, the Pacific Railroad Act was more symbolic than a call for immediate road building; meanwhile, surveys were made and routes planned to await peacetime construction. Lincoln signed all these bills and added to the laurels by setting aside a vast tract of scenic land in California that in time would become Yosemite National Park—a gesture on behalf of preserving the nation's natural beauty well in advance of the more publicized creation of Yellowstone Park in 1872.

Much of the beneficial legislation was barely publicized because it dealt with matters that mainly lay in the future. The war was ever present and wearisome. After the congressional elections of 1862, surly Republicans vented their wrath by criticizing various cabinet members and the conduct of the war on the battlefronts. After another disastrous Union defeat at Fredericksburg, angry Republican senators held a caucus and decided to confront Lincoln with their demands. Senator Sumner offered a resolution, which was approved, urging Lincoln to make "changes in conduct and in the Cabinet that will give the administration more vigor." In mid-December a senatorial committee went to the White House to confront the president, but Lincoln outsmarted them and drew from them the fact that one cabinet member—Chase—was fomenting dissension among his Republican brethren in and out of the president's council. Trapped, Chase offered his resignation; but Lincoln also had the resignation of a mortified Seward on his desk (Chase and

Seward had lost none of their personal animosity toward each other). Lincoln managed to talk his two chief cabinet members into withdrawing their resignations and at the same time sent a message to the Senate: Let me handle the war and my cabinet, too.

Despite losses of the Illinois, Indiana, and Pennsylvania statehouses, a solid base for the Republicans emerged in New England after the 1862 elections. New Hampshire, Maine, Vermont, Massachusetts, and Connecticut, once safely Democratic in a traditional pattern dating back to Jackson's administration, turned Democrats out of both statehouses and courthouses. They would stay that way until the advent of the New Deal some seventy years later.

Not typical of the process of conversion, but illustrative of the political earthquake that was taking place, was the congressional race in the river counties of Iowa in 1862. Dennis Mahoney, a Catholic Democrat who edited the local newspaper, ran for Congress and was summarily arrested during the campaign and taken to a jail in Washington, D.C., although never charged with any crime. After the election, in which his Republican rival triumphed, Mahoney was released and allowed to go home. The hapless Democrat complained, but Iowans were listening to newspaper editors and courthouse lawyers who told them that mysterious Copperheads were trying to weaken the war effort and were ready to turn traitors. "I do not say all Democrats are Copperheads," said one Republican candidate, "but I do say all Copperheads are Democrats." Thus pinned with the label of "traitor," Democrats deserted old allegiances by the thousands in the trans-Mississippi West and New England. Only in the large cities, particularly Boston and New York with their large immigrant populations, were Democrats able to hold on to their majorities. To city dwellers slavery was mostly an abstraction, but to farmers (and about 70 percent of the population was engaged in farming) slaves were a threat involving both morals and money, a combination Lincoln had grasped early on and held on to like a Holy Grail.

Lincoln had friends in Congress who shared his commitment for compensated emancipation of slaves in the border states. These Republicans introduced the president's bill, which appropriated $15 million to pay Missouri slaveholders for freeing their human property. Then old-line Democrats jumped on the bill with a filibuster that kept the measure from a final vote. The plan for compensation to slaveholders, once Lincoln's pet idea, was never revived. Meanwhile Thaddeus Stevens, a bitter opponent of slavery, became in effect the majority leader in the House, and his only solution was complete and unconditional abolition of slavery in every nook and cranny of the Union.

Lincoln's generals gave him almost as many headaches as did the Republican Congress. The Emancipation Proclamation was not popular with the ranking Union officers, and when Lincoln tried to encourage the enlistment of freed blacks into the army's ranks, the process involved many roadblocks. Pressure from Lincoln continued, however, and ultimately nearly 180,000 freedmen wore the Union blue uniform, including several who won the Congressional Medal of Honor for their valor.

The 1863 state elections saw more Democrats switching to the so-called Union party, as the Republicans raised that banner in Ohio and Pennsylvania to attract switchers who still did not like to be called Republicans. In New England, the Republicans kept their gains and solidified their base. Gideon Welles noted that the Connecticut Republicans had elected a governor "by three thousand majority," an event the former Democrat found "gratifying." The House of Representatives meeting in December 1863 easily decided on ex-Whig Colfax of Indiana as Speaker, and the president's message to the Thirty-eighth Congress urged the legislators to look ahead to the peace that would surely come. Once the Union was secure, Lincoln suggested, the backsliding South could reenter under fairly lenient terms. Both the House and the Senate reacted with disdain.

While Lincoln talked of the olive branch, Republicans in Congress wanted a rod of oak to mete out punishment for the recalcitrant South. Faced with turbulence in his party's ranks, Lincoln proceeded to implement his plan for a quick healing of war wounds. Arkansas and three other occupied southern states made moves toward readmission, but Lincoln's congressional critics—increasingly known as Radical Republicans—blocked the president's plan and came up with one of their own. The key provisions of the bill barred high-ranking Confederate officers from future government service and abolished slavery outright. Lincoln vetoed the bill, explaining his belief that the Constitution denied Congress any power to prohibit slavery. Thereafter, Lincoln and the Radicals were on a collision course.

The friction between the White House and Capitol Hill overshadowed changes taking place beyond the battlefields. The point of politics being power, the Republicans exerted their muscle in 28,000 postmasterships, some paying a nominal annual fee and some carrying stipends that exceeded a U.S. senator's. Customs duties were the chief means of paying the bills for the federal government, which meant that every seaport had an entourage of naval officers, collectors, and minor officials who could be appointed at the pleasure of the president. Indeed, the collectors of customs in New York and Philadelphia had salaries exceeding the $25,000 paid annually to the president.

Then there were the bureaucracies that expanded because of the war. Gone were the days when James Madison ran the State Department with a staff of less than a dozen clerks. When the war began some 50,000 held federal positions ranging from message runners to chief clerks; after four years of war their number had tripled. The war also required contracts for everything from salt pork to warships, and these lucrative government-guaranteed arrangements were often awarded to good Republicans with good party connections. This, of course, was nothing new. Had not the Jacksonian Democrats loudly and brazenly said thirty years earlier, "To the Victor belong the Spoils"? So, in the 1860s, Republicans reasoned (as did their counterparts a century later): "Payback time is here!"

As the chief executive, Lincoln found that his conduct of the war displeased many of his Republican colleagues in the Congress who were impatient for quick victories. After the jolt of the first battle at Manassas, the idea of a quick-and-easy war was dispelled, to the dismay of Senate Republicans such as Zachariah Chandler, Charles Sumner, and Benjamin Wade—all men of strong convictions with a thirst for vengeance. In the House, Thaddeus Stevens, George W. Julian, Schuyler Colfax, and John Sherman had well-defined views about the conduct of the war and the peace that would follow. Absurd resolutions, fatuous laws, and embarrassing speeches abounded as the lawmakers tried to run the war like a precinct ward and refused to admit their incompetence. Early in the war, Senator Trumbull of Illinois rammed a resolution through the Republican caucus calling for federal troops to occupy the Confederate capital no later than July 20, 1861! In retrospect, that proved to be one of the saner suggestions made by the congressmen debating in the unfinished Capitol while the statue of Freedom was still crated among the stones and pillars off Independence Avenue.

Lincoln tried to make sense of it all. He grieved when the casualty lists mounted, he urged generals to stop dawdling and attack the enemy, and he patiently allowed visitors to enter the White House in droves and listened to their problems. Meanwhile, the Republicans in Congress formed their own factions, one made up of old Democrats (now referred to in the press as "War Democrats") and moderate Republicans, the other of Radical Republican senators and congressmen who wanted to end slavery soon and punish the Confederacy for its political sins. A third group, the Peace Democrats, disliked Lincoln's policies, criticized the war effort, and in so doing left themselves open to criticism as near traitors.

Congress in time created a standing committee on the conduct of the war that was meant, so it seemed, to bedevil the president by second-guessing and interfering in White House business. In the official family, Secretary of War Cameron overstepped his bounds, and Lincoln was forced to squeeze the influential Pennsylvanian out; but it had to be done diplomatically, with a ministerial post at St. Petersburg for Cameron. Taking his cue from Seward, Lincoln appointed an anti-secessionist Democrat who had served in Buchanan's cabinet, Edwin Stanton. Stanton was pugnacious, efficient, and meddlesome, but Lincoln gave him plenty of rope in a community where popularity was scarce. The Washington community, as Secretary Welles noted, was pervaded with "a feeling of bitterness," and a "majority of the resident population, and particularly of those who formed the resident elite of society, were Secessionists, or in sympathy with Secessionists." Congressmen still stayed in boardinghouses on Capitol

Hill or kept rooms in the Willard and a few other hotels a stone's throw from the White House. A red-light district flourished, but Washington was hardly "a soldier's town" since most of the shopkeepers, livery stable owners, barkeeps, and camp followers were southern in their sympathies.

The first Union troops were volunteers, but as the war dragged on and casualties mounted, the army's demand for soldiers seemed insatiable. A conscription law was passed, allowing substitutes to be hired on the payment of a fee, but the basic unfairness of the act infuriated mobs in New York and led to a bloody riot that left 119 dead. All told, 118,000 Union substitutes were hired by drafted men, and almost 87,000 commutations were purchased for $300 each, gruesome facts that made Peace Democrats vow the struggle was "A rich man's war, and a poor man's fight."

Dissatisfaction over the war, bitterness because of the terrible casualties at Gettysburg, Antietam, and Cold Harbor, and plain sorrow in the homesteads of families where black crepe hung made politicians feel tentative about party loyalty as the presidential election of 1864 loomed. Some skittish congressmen believed that a wartime election was uncalled for, but no public man seriously suggested that the Lincoln administration stay in place without another election until the war ended. Meanwhile, Democrats found their hero in General George McClellan, the slow-moving but ambitious field commander Lincoln had twice removed in sheer exasperation. New York Democrats hailed "Little Mac" and appealed to voters who were tired of the fighting and businessmen who had lost their prewar trade with southern markets.

The 1863 elections had frightened more Republicans than most congressmen dared to admit. In the Ohio Valley the party lost ground, and spotty reports of Republican weakness scared the fainthearted. Lincoln took note of "the popular elections . . . just past, [which] indicated uneasiness among ourselves," in his State of the Union message late in 1863. Increasingly, timid officeholders spoke of running on a "Union" ticket that would appeal to voters who disliked the war and its conduct but still favored restoration of the undivided nation. The idea caught on, and while Lincoln took the time to write an eighty-four-year-old lady who had knit three hundred pairs of stockings for Union soldiers, the party strategists decided that their presidential candidate would not run as a Republican, but as the "Union" candidate for the presidency.

By the end of February 1864 the movement to hold a Union national convention was in place. The organization was Republican, but the name did not bother Lincoln and pleased a good many hangers-on who feared a backlash from voters who had lost loved ones or income because of the war. With Lincoln's approval, a Union convention was scheduled in Baltimore for June 1864, and the scramble began. Chase, convinced he was more capable than Lincoln, tried to torpedo his chieftain surreptitiously by issuing a pamphlet that claimed Lincoln was a total incompetent who could not be reelected. A pro-Lincoln congressman, convinced Chase was crooked, blasted the Ohioan with a series of accusations that left the cabinet member dangling on the ropes. The *coup de grâce* came when the Ohio legislature formally voted to support Lincoln's candidacy. Soon thereafter, Chase resigned.

"In nearly every Northern state," historian David Donald noted, "Lincoln's reelection was opposed by one or more factions within the Republican party." Meanwhile, Frémont was still chafing and eager to run again, but his credentials were so tarnished that his candidacy was not taken seriously and soon evaporated. That left Lincoln, standing alone. When the lukewarm delegates convened in Baltimore, they had little choice but to go with the president; and they did as Lincoln hoped they would when they included a platform plank calling for freedom for slaves through a constitutional amendment. On the first ballot, Lincoln had 506 votes and the only opposition came from the tipsy Missouri delegation. Anti-Lincoln to the last, they cast their 22 votes for General U. S. Grant.

Stuck with Lincoln as their candidate, the delegates threw up one feeble protest when they dumped Hannibal Hamlin from the ticket and made Andrew Johnson, an ex-Democrat and now the governor of occupied Tennessee, Lincoln's running mate. The point seemed to be that a truly Union slate needed a War

Democrat, and a Lincoln-Johnson ticket showed that, for the time at least, the Republican party was in hibernation. The Democrats, with lots of money from Wall Street at their beck, nominated McClellan. Radical Republicans, afraid of washing their dirty linen in public, thought about nominating another candidate, then retreated.

In retrospect, the Republicans (or Unionists) overreacted. Lincoln was more popular than the party strategists imagined; Johnson's name on the ticket added no luster whatever. Fearful of an upsurge for McClellan, furloughs were arranged so that soldiers could vote. Again, the main battleground for votes was in Indiana, Ohio, and Pennsylvania; there, the same strategy that had worked so well in Iowa and Illinois was used to tar Democrats with the "traitor" brush. The soldiers' vote proved critical, as the key states gave the Union ticket a comfortable majority and Lincoln won the electoral count with 212 votes to McClellan's 21. The popular vote was, of course, far closer, as Lincoln's majority was only 400,000 out of the 4 million votes cast.

Confident that he was in control, Lincoln pushed for lenient terms for the reentry into the Union of occupied Confederate states. In Grant, Lincoln had found a winning general, and the Confederacy was reeling. The national debt, Lincoln revealed in his State of the Union message, was hovering near $2 trillion at the end of 1864, but the bulk of it was owned by Americans, and the president suggested that some method of making interest payments "exempt from taxation" might be arranged, thus helping citizens plan "against a possible day of want." With Lee's army in retreat Lincoln delivered his inaugural address, "with malice toward none, with charity for all," and a plea for binding the nation's wounds. Lee surrendered on April 9, and five days later, Lincoln went to Ford's Theater to watch *Our American Cousin*.

The first presidential victim of an assassin's gunshot died at 7:22 A.M. the next day.

CHAPTER FIVE

~~~

The Party Predominant

Starting with Washington's inauguration in 1789, forty-one men have served as president of the United States, but only a handful have earned the title all have sought—"a *strong* occupant of the White House." After Washington, presidents earned their honors by working either with Congress or against it. Jefferson vetoed not one bill in eight years, but Jackson and Truman partly made their reputations with historic vetoes and fights with Congress. Polk earned his spurs because of his single-minded ambition to span the continent, and Lincoln ranks high because of his steadfast humanity and commitment to the Union. The two Roosevelts—Theodore and Franklin—were strong presidents who combined courage and conviction in their actions. Eisenhower seemed mild when in office, but his stature has grown since. The jury of history is still out on Reagan.

Andrew Johnson served almost four years and was hounded out of office. His credentials as a War Democrat did not hurt him, but he would have clashed with the Republicans in any event.

Lincoln's death allowed Congress a short breathing spell and prevented a showdown between the president and the Capitol Hill gang. We consider Lincoln "strong," but in 1865 scores of Republican congressmen and senators hated his guts. At issue was the matter of who was running the government, and Congress by its action in creating the meddlesome Committee on the Conduct of the War showed its pugnacious attitude toward the president. Lincoln had bypassed Congress in creating a plan to restore the Union to its old boundaries "with malice toward none." Congress, on the other hand, was full of malice. When Lincoln indicated he was eager to bring the South back into the Union quickly and with little federal interference in the process, Radical Republicans seethed with rage.

Andrew Johnson was placed on the ticket in 1864 out of expediency. Republican managers liked Johnson's tough talk, and as a War Democrat he helped the Union party appear to be something more than a Republican wolf in sheep's clothing. Congressmen read with glee Johnson's attacks on the slave-owning aristocracy and his implied promise of vengeance. "Treason must be made odious and traitors must be punished and impoverished," Johnson declared, to congressional applause.*

But the love feast between Johnson and Congress turned out to be temporary. Senator Chandler of Michigan, who had come to despise Lincoln, thought the new president an able man and told other Radicals that Johnson was a man after their hearts. This warmed-over Jacksonian Democrat wasn't interested in olive branches; Johnson was the real article and would cooperate with the Radicals in making traitors suffer for their sins. After about ninety days, however, Johnson's former admirers were ready to take up their slings and arrows. Like Lincoln, Johnson wanted the late Confederacy brought back into line with dispatch, and to that end he appointed provisional governors charged with creating state governments prior to readmission into the Union, with full representation in Congress based on a population count of black and white citizens. Nothing doing, Congress said. We will decide when to let southern senators and representatives back into these chambers.

Johnson declared his war with vetoes of a new freedmans' bureau bill and a civil rights measure passed by the Unionist Congress. The civil rights bill made blacks citizens qualified to vote and stirred a national debate that made Johnson look better in New York than he did in Washington. But the House voted to override the veto before the ink dried, and the Senate went along

*Quoted in Kenneth M. Stampp, *The Era of Reconstruction, 1865–1877* (New York: Vintage Press, 1965), 51.

after a tense weekend. Johnson was now a captive in the White House; all pretense of a Union party coalition disappeared, and the full-fledged Republicans were in control of Reconstruction pretty much on their own terms.

A proposed Fourteenth Amendment was soon in the congressional hopper, intended to make blacks full citizens, punish the southern rebels, and end debate on the limits of the national debt (including "pensions and bounties for services in suppressing insurrection or rebellion"). Chandler, Wade, Julian, Stevens, and other Radicals wanted a slow, torturous restoration of the Union that would punish the guilty and also make the South into a Republican stronghold. The eleven states in the Confederacy were, meanwhile, denied any representation in Congress. The trick would be to readmit the errant states without surrendering political power. To accomplish this goal, in the last days of Lincoln's tenure the Thirteenth Amendment had been ratified, banning slavery and creating millions of new black citizens who instantly became potential voters.

So far, so good. Were some 800,000 former slaves suddenly made into citizens eligible to vote? The Radicals had one idea; Johnson had another. The abolition of slavery had destroyed $3 billion in assets overnight, which Johnson thought proper; but Johnson wanted political power vested in the white yeomanry of the South, who would replace the planter aristocracy-oligarchy of antebellum days. Johnson also fretted because the issuance of government bonds to pay for the war had created a tremendous debt, held by northern financiers, and Johnson was as skeptical of northern "hard-money" men as he had been of the slave-owning planters.

The troubles grew when Johnson tried to imitate Lincoln and bring the rebel states back into the Union on lenient terms. He issued an amnesty proclamation, granted pardons right and left, called for land reforms, and seemed to have forgotten his implied promise of a harsh, punitive restoration process. Moreover, Johnson saw no need to give freed slaves anything approaching full citizenship. The provisional governments created by Johnson went too far in their efforts to restore antebellum political conditions, and their excessive zeal played into the Radicals' hands.

Once Congress was back in session, all hell broke loose. The military occupation of the South was high on the Radicals' list of measures, along with more legislation to punish the rebels and make life easier for the freed blacks. Southerners condemned "Black Republicans" who kept Negro troops in the South, but northerners saw the laws passed by white legislators—the "Black Codes"—as ill-disguised efforts to keep Negroes subjugated through local ordinances. The proposed Fourteenth Amendment was Congress's answer to Johnson's Reconstruction plan.

After Congress went back to work in December 1865 there was much shuffling around as moderate Republicans, a few War Democrats, and the Radical Republicans jockeyed for position. Eventually, the Radicals staked their claim: the federal government must grant blacks legal equality (including the right to vote) and crush any force that balked at this capstone of reform. Gideon Welles, who stayed on in Johnson's cabinet, was as shocked as the president by the Radicals' cry for blood. "Hate, revenge, and persecution" motivated the Radicals, Welles observed. "These fanatics want a God to punish, not to love, those who do not agree with them."

The Johnson-created state governments were replaced by a mélange of Republican officeholders. Backed by bayonets, southern legislatures soon had a good number of black members (around 600), while statehouses had black governors, and courtrooms had blacks sitting on the bench. Southerners reacted violently, but they were as powerless as Johnson to prevent the Radicals from dictating the terms for readmission or for withdrawal of the army of occupation. Carpetbag governments sprang up across the South, some terribly corrupt, some mildly corrupt, and some trying to be fairly honest. All were held in contempt by the dominant whites, many of whom were unable to vote themselves. In all the South, black voters outnumbered whites by a seven-to-six ratio, and in five states Negro voters constituted a clear majority.

Early on, the South tried to retaliate by rejecting the Fourteenth Amendment. At Johnson's urging, his designated southern lawmakers denounced the amendment and, when polled, resoundingly defeated ratification by lopsided votes (in three state legislatures the ratification measure was unanimously rejected). Radicals were not amused and sought to make good on their plans to make the South eventually become a pocket of solid Republicanism. Blacks, out of gratitude to the party that had freed them, would show their mettle by voting for Republicans. A solid Republican South? Why not?*

Meanwhile, fortunes were made in the North when greenback dollars were recalled and government interest payments resumed in gold. Higher tariffs were also on the congressional docket, along with vast subsidies for construction of the western railroads. The Gilded Age was just around the corner.

With the 1866 elections in the balance, the Radicals took over the Union party and renamed it the Union-Republican party with a call for support from anti-Johnson voters of any stripe. Johnson responded by scheduling a national speaking tour to rally support for his program, mainly to prevent black suffrage. A hostile press and unruly audiences turned the tour into an undignified shouting match. Johnson returned to Washington somewhat demoralized, and his low public standing was confirmed in the elections; Radicals added to their numbers as pro-Johnson candidates were swamped.

The Radicals rubbed it in. The Fourteenth Amendment could not be stopped by a presidential veto, but Johnson's presence in the White House offended too many of the senators and congressmen who wanted to move ahead at full throttle with their Reconstruction program. The issue came to a head when Johnson fired Stanton as his secretary of war and appointed Grant as his replacement. Radicals reacted by claiming the president had violated the law they had passed to prevent presidential removals; the situation was complicated because some Radicals had already talked about running Grant for president in 1868. The first House vote for impeachment failed. Meanwhile, Grant left the cabinet in a huff.

---

*The British were aware of the Republican effort to create a huge black voting bloc, as Arthur Conan Doyle's story "The Five Orange Pips" indicated. Sherlock Holmes learns of a murder victim who left the United States "about 1869 or 1870. . . . his reason for leaving them was his aversion to the negroes, and his dislike of the Republican policy in extending the franchise to them." Doyle, *The Complete Original Illustrated Sherlock Holmes* (Secaucus, N.J.: Castle Books, 1976), 70.

A tempest in a cabinet teapot soon turned into a national emergency, when Radicals in the House demanded Johnson's impeachment and the newly formed Grand Army of the Republic, made up of Union veterans, was called upon to send a force to Washington to "defend" Congress from a bomb threat. A hysterical House voted on February 24, 1868, to impeach Johnson for "high crimes and misdemeanors" and turned to the Senate for affirmation of the indictment.

With the Radicals in charge of the prosecution, for two months the press kept the nation informed of the trial meant to bring down Johnson. Nobody thought Johnson could survive, but as the trial dragged on some worried senators questioned the propriety of ousting a president who disagreed with Congress. Secretary Welles was one of the few who believed Johnson would not be convicted. "I cannot come to the conclusion that the Senate, feeble and timid as it is, will convict the President . . . yet I have no confidence whatever in the fairness or justice of that body," Welles wrote in his diary. "There is a party necessity to obtain possession of the executive, in order to put a Radical in the office of President next year."

Welles proved to be an able pundit. In the final test, only nineteen senators were bothered enough to vote against conviction, but that still left the Radicals one vote short. Old Thaddeus Stevens had been named chairman of the House managers in charge of the impeachment, but he became too ill to serve and died a disappointed man not long after Johnson's narrow escape. Congressman James G. Blaine said Stevens's death was "an emancipation for the Republican party." Now the House could conduct its business in an atmosphere lacking Stevens's hatred and rancor.

Fortunately, the nation could forget the embarrassment in Washington because the excitement of a presidential election took the spotlight. Seward had been busy on his own, and without fanfare he negotiated a treaty with Imperial Russia for the sale of Alaska to the United States for $7.5 million. The Senators thought the price for "Seward's Folly" too high but relented when the secretary of state whittled the price tag down to $7.2 million. Nobody can prove the rumor that prominent

Republicans in the House, where the first appropriation bill had been rejected, accepted bribes to approve the acquisition of an area twice the size of Texas; but the second vote went 37 to 2 in favor of the purchase. An effort to annex the Sandwich Islands (Hawaii) ran into trouble, but Seward did persuade Congress to annex the Midway Islands, and President Johnson was nodding in approval as the Republican party took credit for adding to the nation's Pacific holdings without firing a shot.

Speculation about Grant was more interesting to the party rank and file than were remote barren regions peopled by Eskimos and pearl divers. Grant had been sounded out by some senators, who were mindful that the old Whigs had won only when they nominated a military hero as their candidate. A scare had been thrown into party circles by reports from Oregon, where a Democrat had been elected to Congress to replace a Radical Republican. In New York Democratic newspapers mentioned Salmon Chase (now chief justice of the Supreme Court and a onetime Radical) as a possible Democratic presidential nominee. A pro-Johnson cabinet member thought politics had become topsy-turvy, for "Chase . . . is really the father of Radicalism, not of Republicanism."

Vindictive but outvoted, the Radicals promised to weed out the senators who had opposed Johnson's conviction, and they hurried to Chicago to nominate Grant as the Republican standard-bearer. The platform committee pushed through a watered-down plank on black suffrage, demanded full payment of the national debt, and avoided angering the low-tariff delegates from the Midwest by ignoring the tariff issue altogether. Grant's stand on the issues of the day was unknown, but his popularity in the North was unquestioned.

Democrats believed the Republican infighting gave them a chance to recapture the White House, and at their July 1868 convention they almost chose General Winfield Scott Hancock over Governor Seymour of New York. "Seymour, if nominated, will be defeated," an acute observer predicted. "Hancock, if the candidate, will be elected." Seymour's supporters finally won, confident that a divided Republican party would somehow manage to lose the election even with ten errant Democratic states still out of the electoral college.

So General Grant headed the Republican ticket and Speaker Colfax was his running mate. Grant, who had never voted for a Republican "until he was himself the candidate," as Wilfred Binkley noted, was now paired with a former Whig in the rush to create a winning ticket. Cartoonist Thomas Nast of *Harper's Weekly* lent his caustic pen to the Grant cause and came up with drawings that depicted Seymour as a friend of the New York draft dodgers, while Grant was by contrast the war hero of "unconditional surrender" fame. The Grand Army of the Republic issued thousands of copies of *The Soldier's Friend* newspaper and helped organize Boys in Blue clubs for the Grant-Colfax ticket. As a herald of the patriotic appeal that would dominate Republican strategy for the next forty years, the GAR offered a campaign song for every Union veteran's attention:

> We will vote as we battled in many a fight,
> For God and Union, for Freedom and Right,
> Let our ballots secure what our bullets have won,
> Grant and Colfax will see that the work is well done.

By raising the war cry as a rationale for supporting Grant, the GAR leadership skipped over such sensitive issues as Negro suffrage, which was not popular in the Ohio valley, where critical votes were needed.

Grant's views on hard money, Reconstruction, and other potent issues were never revealed during the campaign. Indeed, Grant returned to his home in Galena, Illinois, granted no interviews to the press, and wrote no letters explaining his views on political matters (or anything else). Seymour was branded as a "traitor" and "secession-lover," yet he ran a skillful campaign and managed to win eight states in the electoral college. Grant easily won the popular vote, with 3 million to Seymour's 2.7 million, and gained an overwhelming 214 to 80 electoral votes. The veterans' vote, plus support from newly enfranchised freedmen in border and readmitted states, was the key to Grant's victory.

Grant, Eisenhower, and Reagan are the only Republican presidents who were elected to, and served, two full terms in the

White House. Grant and Eisenhower were West Point graduates, and as professional soldiers they were more fitted to take orders than give them; hence, their administrations were marked by dominance from Capitol Hill and a conscious effort to keep the country on an even economic keel. More on Reagan later, but the Grant presidency is memorable for its remarkable progress in converting an agrarian republic into the industrial nation that emerged from the ashes of the Civil War. Indeed, whatever else he was, Grant as president was a friend to business interests, financiers, Union army veterans, and railroad builders. Those groups enjoyed boom times in the Grant years. Only the farmers who were the backbone of Republican support in both national and state elections made little progress from 1869 to 1877.

What was happening in American politics was the rise of a middle class that owed no particular allegiance to the farming majority but kept a close alliance with northern industrial and business sectors. From Grant's inauguration onward "the postwar era was the time of the Great Barbecue," wrote historian Kenneth Stampp, "when the federal government, under Republican control, generously turned the nation's natural resources over to individuals and corporations for private exploitation." Laissez-faire economics dominated in the marketplace, and in the America that emerged after 1868, success was measured more and more in terms of money. The Republicans were not to blame, and neither were the Democrats. Americans shook off the feudal trappings that still pervaded Europe but substituted new standards of wealth. No longer would either land or cotton be king, for the new monarch was accumulated wealth in the form of cash, stocks, bonds, real estate, and paper empires encompassing all assets.

The Republicans understood the change, and gloried in it. After the 1868 election, the Republican banner was unfurled without apology and a national party established that was no longer in need of fusion or coalition support. Wall Street shifted from a paternalistic center of finance to a thriving, dynamic vortex of the nation's wealth. The majority of Americans were farmers, and would be for another generation, but wheat and cotton no longer were dominant commodities. If the farm vote was weak, the veterans' vote was strong, as Republican congresses loosened the purse strings to give pensions to disabled veterans as well as the widows and orphans of soldiers who had worn Union blue during the war. Money was the new king. Favors for friends made sense.

Naturally, some bitter partisanship developed. As a lame-duck cabinet member, Welles believed Grant as president-elect was in deep water. "As regards policy and measures, he has none. . . . Yet he has shrewdness and a certain amount of common sense. . . . Of the structure of government, and a proper administration of its affairs, he is singularly and wonderfully ignorant." Welles was prejudiced, of course, for he sympathized with the pariah, Andrew Johnson. Grant informed the inauguration committee that he would not ride to the swearing-in ceremonies in the same carriage with Johnson, and Welles advised Johnson to avoid the whole embarrassing business. Johnson did so by staying at his White House desk until noon, then departing for his quarters as a private citizen.

Grant viewed his new role as similar to the part he had played as general of the army. He would preside over the executive office, appoint loyal men to key posts, and see that the law was enforced. That suited the Radicals, who had plenty of ideas on how to run the country; a complaisant president would fit nicely into their plans. Grant failed to consult them about the cabinet, however; and there was secret delight when the rumors that Charles Francis Adams would be secretary of state proved false. But Elihu Washburne was Grant's choice—and Lincoln's old friend lasted four days, to be succeeded by Hamilton Fish, an old-line Whig. The rest of Grant's nominees came under fire as well and withdrew or took office with little applause from the gallery.

Those who wanted inflationary policies found few friends in Grant's administration or the Congress. The Public Credit Act of 1869 provided for cashing government bonds in gold, a step Johnson had denounced but Grant embraced. Grant was not in Wall Street's pocket, however, for it was the president's order that broke the effort of Jay Gould and other speculators to corner the gold market. The price of gold shot up until Grant ordered the Treasury Department to sell gold bullion. In the ensuing debacle many speculators were ruined, and Grant's brother-in-law's meddling in the unsavory business discredited him and hurt the president's reputation.

The Senate Radicals had their own agenda. Reports of the intimidation and murder of freedmen in the South sparked inquiries that led to a series of "force bills" meant to authorize the use of federal troops in elections. With the readmission of Texas in July 1870, all of the old Confederacy was back in the Union, after ratifying the Fourteenth Amendment. But unless bluecoat soldiers watched the polls, Democrats captured most of the offices and turned out carpetbag regimes in droves.

Grudgingly, the Radicals gave ground to historic forces in the South that could not be overcome by passing any number of laws. The carpetbag regimes in some states saddled the people with oppressive debts, but they also created the first public school system in most of the South and moved the region into the Age of Railroads when further delays would have been an economic tragedy. Continued hostility between whites and blacks was a stumbling block nobody had counted on. Lower-class whites resented the political power of blacks and applauded the barriers to integrated life erected by resilient Democrats.

Grant's popularity saved the Republicans time after time. The Whiskey Ring scandals proved to be an embarrassment because corrupt officials with good Republican credentials were involved, and the Crédit Mobilier exposé showed that congressmen could be as corrupt and greedy as the railroad barons on Wall Street. The Crédit Mobilier scandal, when exposed by the *New York Sun*, showed that railroad builders made huge profits by giving congressmen stock that paid incredible dividends. Two Republican congressmen were censured, but nobody went to jail. Public opinion absolved the president. Grant was believed to be honest, and anyway, the Democrats had their own graft of great magnitude to face in the Tweed Ring scandals. Indeed, when the total cost of the Ring's corruption was revealed—in the neighborhood of $200 million—it proved to be far more than all of the carpetbagging boodle in the old Confederacy.

Not that Grant lacked critics both inside and outside his party. Horace Greeley applauded the higher tariffs but was disturbed by the spoils system and said so in stinging editorials. In the Midwest, Carl Schurz, the German-born Union general, was supporting an anti-administration candidate running for governor in Missouri, while in Ohio a reform ticket was boosted to counterbalance the pro-Grant forces. In the fall congressional elections of 1870, Republicans lost forty-one seats in the House and six more in the Senate but still held a majority. As a newly elected senator, Schurz spoke for a large number of Republicans who wanted to dump Grant in 1872 and nominate a reformer. Even old Senator Sumner was disenchanted with Grant and urged Republicans to replace the president or suffer a crushing defeat. Congressman James A. Garfield of Ohio, eager to push for reforms in the civil-service system, was covertly working for Grant's removal from the ticket.

Meanwhile, desperate whites in the South were terrorizing blacks in droves, intimidating potential Republican voters through beatings, lynchings, and house burnings. Congress looked into the campaign of terror and passed another bill that made it a federal crime to use force to prevent a citizen from voting. The recently ratified Fifteenth Amendment was supposed to have made blacks full-fledged voting citizens, but the Ku Klux Klan had other ideas. A third Force Act was passed in 1871 to punish any person conspiring to prevent men from voting, and Grant sent more federal troops into the South to give the laws some teeth.

The devastating Chicago fire in 1871 may not have been started by Mrs. O'Leary's kicking cow, but the city's destruction and quick resurrection proved that the business pulse of the Midwest was healthy. Insurance companies paid out millions to restore the city to its former grandeur, and within six months the building boom to replace destroyed buildings and homes promoted an economic boom that promised to last for a decade. Joseph Medill's *Chicago Tribune* boosted the city, while Medill kept his hand in Republican party affairs.

Charges of corruption, nepotism, and favoritism in the Grant administration caused the liberals in the Republican party to bestir themselves. Convinced that Grant was vulnerable, they hoped to nominate a reform-type Republican who would qualify as honest and loyal to Republican ideology. Two former members of Grant's cabinet joined in the call for a nominating convention; with all of the South back in the Union, southern Republicans who disliked Grant's presidential style would be fully represented.

Meeting in Cincinnati, the Liberal Republicans (as they chose to call themselves) gathered together a motley mixture of War Democrats, Lincoln Republicans, and many old Whigs. In short, the splinter movement was composed of the same political breed as the Republicans of 1856 and 1860; but there was a difference. In 1872 the Liberals lacked a charismatic leader and were mainly "agin" Grant, so that no presidential candidate emerged who was popular enough to win on the first or second ballot. To worsen matters, the front-runner—Charles Francis Adams, blessed with a genealogy that included being the grandson of one president and the son of another—proved to be a diffident candidate who seemed to be ready to run only if begged, flattered, and praised beyond reason.

The convention was floundering when a boomlet for Horace Greeley, the inveterate foe of Grantism, erupted and captured the delegates' imagination. He was one of the party's founders, in a sense, and Greeley controlled the newspaper that was accepted as gospel in over 200,000 American parlors. So the delegates swallowed Greeley's eccentricity, his variegated career as a onetime Prohibitionist, Abolitionist, vegetarian, and old-line Whig, and nominated Greeley for president on the sixth ballot. Many delegates could hardly believe their ears, but they went through the motions and also chose Governor Gratz Brown of Missouri as Greeley's running mate.

Grant's supporters did not panic, even when the desperate Democrats met in their convention and, to the amazement of the nation, also nominated Greeley as their presidential candidate. To make the confusion worse, a convention of the Liberal Colored Republicans met in Louisville and also nominated Greeley. The stage was set in the summer of 1872 for a political charade, as William Cullen Bryant, the former Democrat turned Republican, told readers of the *New York Evening Post* that the choice was between a crook and a clown, so there was little reason to support either.

Bryant's critique of the campaign was mild compared to the abuse heaped on Greeley. For nearly thirty years Greeley had attacked the Democrats tooth and nail, but now *he* was their candidate, and the shoe did not fit. Grant's friend Thomas Nast drew cartoons in *Harper's Weekly* depicting Greeley as a minstrel-show incompetent who had somehow blundered on the national political stage, to the embarrassment of all. Southern Democrats, ready to vote in the presidential election for a candidate who had a chance, could muster little enthusiasm for Greeley. To make amends, Greeley broke with tradition and traveled to Kentucky, Ohio, and Pennsylvania for speeches before large and curious crowds.

Grant's campaign coffers were substantial in an era when gifts to candidates were not a matter of public record. Railroad, mining, and banking executives contributed handsomely to Grant's campaign, and the Union League smoking rooms in New York were a kind of informal headquarters for the pro-Grant Republicans. Grant had angered some Republicans by an ill-advised effort to annex Santo Domingo that backfired when Senator Sumner denounced the whole business as a shameful landgrab. After the annexation treaty was blocked, the break between Sumner and Grant was complete.

Some concern was expressed in Greeley's *Tribune* when North Carolina voted early and gave Grant a slender victory. Democrats had hoped all states in the old Confederacy would come around for the bewhiskered Greeley. The outcome scared both sides, with the result that newspapers began a two-month orgy of mudslinging that was so rotten one wag said "he could smell the stench in Switzerland."* Grant kept quiet, but his newspaper supporters attacked Greeley as a "turncoat Black Republican" who had once offered bail for Jefferson Davis. Greeley's gesture won him no friends in the North, and southerners were more mystified than appreciative.

*Quoted in Mayer, *The Republican Party*, 184.

73

In one of the most predictable presidential elections in history, Grant won with 3.6 million votes to Greeley's 2.8 million. In the electoral college, Grant was far ahead, 286 to 66. A tragic ending to the farce was supplied by Greeley's breakdown and death on November 29. Grant led the parade of mourners, and in the electoral college Senator Thomas Hendricks of Indiana picked up most of the votes meant for Greeley.

The Grand Army of the Republic did well in the 1872 elections, too. A total of 274 colonels and generals in the Union army ran for and won seats in the next Congress, while 1,596 field officers and generals were elected to northern state legislatures. Nearly all ran as Republicans. This was perhaps the zenith of the GAR's power as a political force. At the time, no one seemed to notice that not a single private soldier had been elected—only men who wore the eagles and stars were found worthy.

A sidebar to the congressional elections that year was the news from Illinois that a young hayseed had won a Republican seat in the House. His coarse speech and rough manners reminded some of Lincoln, but the comparison was only superficial, for Joseph Cannon from Danville, Illinois, proved to be the quintessential hard-shelled conservative Republican of midwestern origins. When sworn in, Cannon started a forty-six-year career that would bring him into the national limelight as the unbeatable congressman who had opposed votes for women, tariff reform, and recognition for organized labor.

"Is the Democracy Dead?" asked an editorial writer who speculated that four straight election victories by Republican presidential candidates meant the Democratic party was ready for its last rites. The rush to judgment proved premature, however, as excessive speculation in railroad building and real estate promotion created a shaky economic picture early in 1873.

Loyalty is a cardinal virtue in politics, but tenacity in the face of evidence is not. Revelations of wrongdoing by Republicans at lower levels of the bureaucracy and in Congress only raised Grant's hackles. He coupled this with his anger at those who revealed rather than those who had concealed corruption. Digging into the Crédit Mobilier scandal, reporters exposed inside stock purchases by senators and congressmen at bargain prices. Except for two excessively greedy congressmen, nobody was reprimanded. In Congress, Grant's easygoing attitude was interpreted as "business as usual."

A far-reaching Supreme Court decision in 1873 hardly caused a ripple at the time but would have profound repercussions on the blacks struggling for justice in a white man's society. The high court, dominated by Republican appointees, decided in the *Slaughterhouse Cases* that the Fourteenth Amendment had not provided a national umbrella for citizens whose civil rights were violated. Taking a narrow view, the justices' decision prevented the nationalization of the Bill of Rights until the twentieth century and also made it harder for minorities to vote, use public facilities, travel on railroads, or find hotel rooms. In short, the Supreme Court, instead of trying to ease the movement of blacks into American society, helped throw up a wall of segregation. And the truth is that all the old steam was gone out of the idealistic Republicans who had been so alarmed in 1854 and 1860. Now they were either dead or disillusioned or inclined to keep quiet.

Supreme Court decisions made no headlines, but a series of bank failures in London and Paris caused a panic on Wall Street. Bankruptcies and foreclosures rocked the nation as the firm of Jay Cooke and Company, run by a close friend of the president's, closed its doors. Thousands of smaller houses either went into bankruptcy or retrenched as farm prices fell and real estate booms turned sour. Cooke's many contributions to the Republican campaign coffers came to light, and Grant's critics were quick to say that Cooke's Northern Pacific Railroad had received special favors during Grant's administration (which was true, for the railroad was granted a subsidy in public lands almost twice as large as that allowed to any other western rail enterprise).

Voters reacted to charges of cronyism and to the deepening effects of a depression in 1874 by proving that the rhetorical question about the death of the Democratic party was indeed premature. Grant vetoed a bill that would have increased the number of greenbacks in circulation but signed one calling for the resumption of specie payments, placing paper dollars and gold ones at par. The deflationary move delighted Wall Street, where *inflation* has always been a cussword.

The return to the gold standard worsened life for farmers with mortgages and for other debtors, and charges that railroads gouged the small shippers but favored the larger ones with rebates seemed more than idle speculation. Disgruntled farmers in Iowa stayed loyal to the Republicans, but unemployed Irish immigrants in Philadelphia and New York provided Democrats with hope that the next Congress would find Republicans back in the minority. Earlier panics, in 1819, 1837, and 1857, had been inconclusive insofar as national political parties were concerned. Monroe was not hurt by the first, although Van Buren suffered from the second, and Buchanan had larger problems than the short-lived recession. The 1873 panic, however, prodded voters into a vengeful mood. In the House of Representatives, Democrats won with a majority of sixty seats, but the Republicans held on to the Senate by sixteen votes. Missouri and several other midwestern states elected Democratic majorities in their state legislatures, thus making it likely that more Senate seats would be won by the Democrats later in the 1870s.

In truth there were two Republican parties, maybe three. Eastern Republicans favored protective tariffs, liked the Homestead Act (which provided a safety valve for the unemployed, who could seek out a free farm), and took pride in their party for its part in defeating the South. Midwestern Republicans wanted an easier money policy and lower tariffs to make farm equipment cheaper, but when the party did not seem sympathetic, few grumbled about switching parties. In the West and Midwest the orgy of railroad building benefited everybody who needed a market for produce, grain, or cattle, and Republicans knew how to build railroads (even though the cost was high). On the other hand, the Republican hangers-on in the South had little going for them except at convention time, when they could send delegations to nominating conventions and their votes were just as good as those from New England. As long as federal troops remained in some southern states, however, these "scalawags" (southerners who joined the Republican party and sought office) proved useful to the party and held a host of minor judicial and customs posts.

No former Confederate general did as well as the scalawag James Longstreet. An old friend of Grant's (his wife and Grant's wife were cousins), Longstreet was appointed collector of customs at New Orleans and later served as the American minister to Turkey. As a Republican, Longstreet was welcomed into the charmed circle of ex-Confederate officeholders, but the general was not greeted with open arms when veterans of the Lost Cause gathered, nor at assemblies of the growing and well-organized Grand Army of the Republic, which took on more significance after the 1874 elections showed how vulnerable the party could be in a time of economic downturn. One angry veteran wrote the GAR headquarters complaining that "as soon as the Elections are over they forget all about their promises and appoint some *Negro* or *Citizen* that Never was in the Army." Disgruntled members aside, ambitious politicians saw the GAR as more than a veterans organization, for its annual encampments, newspapers, and pamphlets created a following that would reach into thousands of northern homes. As the lure of pensions was dangled, the organization took on a lobbying role that was useful for public men such as John A. Logan of Illinois, a former congressman who began to have a presidential itch after he helped found the GAR and was elected to the Senate. He did not invent the "bloody shirt" campaign, meant to remind Union veterans of which party had "led the country to victory," but Logan sure knew how to wave the red symbol when it was time to vote.

Although the panic that began in 1873 deepened, Republicans looked beyond their losses in the off year of 1874 and thought their prospects were good. The transcontinental railroad system was working, the telegraph lines gave New York instant communication with San Francisco, the steel industry was beginning to show growing pains, and the discovery of petroleum in western Pennsylvania gave a hint of mineral wealth in the East to balance the silver and gold pouring from western mines. Wheat from midwestern farms was moving well in the European markets, as was cotton for the English mills that supplied the world with cheap cloth. So why would voters not continue to elect Republicans?

Grant's bosom friends thought he was so popular that voters would overlook precedents and give Grant what he probably wanted—a third term. Grant's enemies, and they were plentiful both inside and outside the party, were equally determined to pick a new face for the White House. Amid much speculation about Grant's plans, the Republican party gained a symbol that was enduring and affectionately embraced. *Harper's Weekly* in November 1874 carried Thomas Nast's cartoon "The Third-Term Panic," the first depiction of the elephant as a Republican behemoth capable of running roughshod over the opposition. The raging pachyderm is actually labeled "The Republican Vote," as he rampages near a dark pit bearing ominous tags: "Southern claims / Chaos / Rum." Nast also gave the Democrats their donkey image, and the two parties took the symbols good-naturedly as Nast's brainchildren fitted the nation's mood and love of animal symbols (including eagles, owls, and turtles).

Grant felt the pressure and, to his credit, made a public statement that he would not be a candidate in the year during which the nation was preparing to celebrate the hundredth anniversary of the Declaration of Independence. Much attention was focused on Philadelphia, the birthplace of independence, where a world's fair was scheduled to show off the nation's progress.

Once Grant was out of the running, a number of senators began to feel the presidential urge. One was Senator Roscoe Conkling of New York, and Logan of Illinois was surely available, as was Speaker of the House James G. Blaine from Maine. There were a few dark horses, chafing in the stables, if one of the front-runners stumbled. Foremost among these potential candidates was Rutherford B. Hayes, a former major general in the Union Army who had been elected governor of Ohio. Easterners liked Hayes because he had fought against the paper-money advocates in Ohio who wanted cheap dollars to pay off their debts. Wall Street heard that Hayes was a "Gold Republican," and, for some, that was all they needed to know.

Federal troops were still posted in a few southern states, although the war had ended in 1865. The Fifteenth Amendment was on the books, but there was uncertainty about the presidential election because the country was still feeling an economic pinch. Democrats needed a military hero to run, but they had none. The Republicans knew how popular a war hero could be, so they were looking for one as they headed for Cincinnati and a grand conclave. So it was back to the smoke-filled rooms, as party strategists ran down the list of possible candidates. Bitter rivalries (Conkling and Blaine despised each other) threatened to bring about chaos if they could not be controlled.

Could a goldbug who had worn stars on his epaulets be found? The safety of the Republic seemed to depend on it.

CHAPTER SIX

Popular Vote Lost, Electoral College Won

Blaine came into the Cincinnati nominating convention as the front-runner. His civilian background (he had not served in the Union army) was a negative factor, but the Maine senator (he had been recently selected by the Maine legislators) had friends galore. Perhaps the delegates were a bit cocky, buoyed by the fact that for sixteen years Republican or Union-Republican candidates had been elected president. Of course, the Democrats had repeatedly managed to shoot themselves in the foot by making improbable nominations. With all these factors in mind, and the Fifteenth Amendment in place, it appeared to most delegates at the Cincinnati convention that 1876 would be another banner year.

The format of the convention had changed but little since 1860. In 1876 the nominating speeches were full of excessive praise for favorite sons, the demonstrations were long and tedious, and the air inside was hot and humid. Few of the partying delegations were in a hurry to get down to the main business, selection of the man who would be the next president of the United States.

Despite his popularity, Blaine had a few drawbacks. For one thing, Blaine had been in his early thirties when the war broke out, and he had (like that other happy warrior, John D. Rockefeller) never traded civilian clothes for a Union uniform. Then there were rumors that as a congressman he had pulled strings for railroads, and enough evidence surfaced to force Blaine to denounce the slanders on the House floor. Nonetheless, the rumors persisted, and an exposé in the *New York Sun* added fuel to the flames of discord. What really knocked Blaine out of the race, however, was his health. On the eve of the convention, Blaine suffered a stroke while on his way to church. He lapsed into a coma, then quickly seemed to recover, and his supporters insisted their man was as fit as ever. Backers of Indiana's governor-turned-senator, Oliver Morton, thought Blaine's illness was a favorable sign; Conkling's men were not heartened, because Blaine's friends insisted their man was only temporarily hors de combat.

On the first ballot, Blaine had a comfortable lead but not enough votes to win outright, while a host of favorite sons persisted in staying in the race. Morton, no friend of Blaine's and running second, finally decided that the impasse could be broken only by a dramatic shift. Hayes had been far behind in the early balloting, holding his Ohio delegation and some old comrades-in-arms from other states; but Morton sent out the word: stop Blaine. In quick order the New York and Pennsylvania delegates swung to Hayes and the matter was settled. For balance, Representative William A. Wheeler of New York was placed on the ticket as Hayes's running mate.

There was more joy in the East than in the West when the telegraph tickers told the Cincinnati story. Two hard-money men were carrying the Republican banner in a time when an economic recession still persisted in parts of the country, particularly in the Midwest. In reaction to the Republicans' Coinage Act of 1873, which introduced a national currency based on gold alone, a Greenback party was formed, mainly to publicize the plight of in-debt farmers. The Greenbackers nominated their own ticket, headed by Peter Cooper, a political nonentity known chiefly for his large donations to charities.

A crafty Democrat, Governor Samuel J. Tilden of New York, played all his cards so close to his vest that few delegates to the Democratic nomination convention knew where he stood on anything. The issues of hard money, tariff, and an end to federal troops in the South were brushed aside as Tilden smiled and waved and won the nomination. For the financial community in

New York, long accustomed to backing the candidate of either party pledged to staying with the gold standard (that is, in favor of hard money), Tilden looked fairly safe; which meant that the Republicans had better prove that the hard-money credentials of their candidate were impeccable.

One plank in the Republican platform drew the attention of Democrats hungry for a peak inside the White House. Anxious to mollify the South and pick up electoral votes, the Republicans in Cincinnati adopted a plank that seemed to say the need for occupying troops was about over. Things were looking up. Then Indiana Democrats won the state elections in October, and Whitelaw Reid, Greeley's successor at the *New York Tribune*, began to worry. The GAR boomed for Hayes, while the candidate himself stayed close to his front porch and kept voters guessing. He had ripped into Congress in his acceptance speech back in July, blaming many of the House and Senate "gang" for holding back civil-service reforms, but that outburst could be written off as campaign oratory.

Determined Democrats in Mississippi had sent their own signal a year earlier as they chafed under the "Black Republican" Fifteenth Amendment and the presence of federal troops. They retaliated by forming private militia companies that shouldered rifles and paraded through sections heavily populated by blacks to intimidate possible Republican voters. The Republican governor of Mississippi reacted by ordering the irregular forces to disband, but they defied the order and continued to enroll "militiamen" who drilled and stood ready to work the polls. No whites would enlist in the state's National Guard, so a mobilization of that force would have ended in a confrontation of whites against blacks. Powerless to disperse the lily-white militia and fearing a race war in his state, the Mississippi governor backed down in the fall of 1875 and cleared the way for a Democratic victory in the next presidential election.

Although Hayes looked strong in the key northern states as the leaves in New England turned gold and yellow, Republicans were worried. The depression hung on like a bad cough that would not go away. Unemployment in the industrial East had its counterpart in the Midwest, where farmers banded into a

Granger movement to promote regulation of the railroads just as their friends in the Greenback party were championing a cheap dollar to pay off farm mortgages. In the far West, mining interests talked about a silver-purchase law that would feed the forces of inflation, which in 1876 were nearly at a standstill. The recent discovery of a major silver lode in Nevada, following short-lived gold rushes in the Dakotas, Arizona, and Montana, gave western mining interests political relevance. Colorado became a state in 1876, and Utah was knocking at the door of statehood. Republican strength in the West was considered safe enough to offset any defection that might appear in the farming areas of the Midwest.

Confidence in a Hayes victory melted when returns from New York and New Jersey were among the first counted. It appeared that Tilden was ahead of Hayes in crucial states. Further reports seemed to make Tilden the winner in both the popular vote and the electoral college. Then a sharp-eyed newspaperman saw that although the states of Florida, Louisiana, and South Carolina were Democratic, they were still "occupied" by federal troops and swayed by Republican-controlled election boards. If the electoral votes of those three states went to Hayes, he would be elected by one vote. If they stayed in the Democratic column, Tilden would win.

What happened in the next few months is still a matter of controversy among historians. None dispute that Tilden won the popular vote hands down, but Oregon was added to the list of states with disputed results. The House with its Democratic majority had one idea on how to settle the dispute; the Senate with a Republican majority had another. Tension was high when a legislative deadlock was broken with a compromise: an electoral commission would decide the winner. Along partisan lines, House and Senate conferees picked their commission members, creating a balance of seven from each party, with the final and fifteenth vote going to Supreme Court Justice Joseph P. Bradley, a Republican.

For weeks the commission looked at the poll records, interviewed officials, and pondered the evidence. Bradley was not naive, but he tried to put aside his party and vote based on the evidence. Nothing doing, said his Republican friends when they heard a rumor that Bradley was going to favor Tilden. Thus the final vote was strictly along party lines, eight for Hayes and seven for Tilden. Congress still had to approve the commission's decision, and southerners threatened a filibuster to keep the Republicans at bay. The threat evaporated, however, and by the end of February 1877 the headlines told the story. "Hayes Wins!" a jubilant Republican newspaper proclaimed on March 2, only two days away from the inauguration.

Did the Democrats scream bloody murder? No, they did not. And thereby hangs the tale of how the railroads and high finance made Hayes president even though Tilden had more votes. According to historian C. Vann Woodward, the leading southern politicians had cut a deal with the Republicans that allowed the commission's partisan vote to go unchallenged. "Republicans began to see the Southern problem . . . with new eyes, and the more they saw the more anachronistic seemed the Southern policy of the Republican party." Railroads and high finance were now at the top of the Republican agenda. "The party of abolitionist radicalism had now become the party of vested interests and big business; the old Whig element was on top, its program had been enacted, and its leader was Rutherford B. Hayes, an ex-Whig and staunch conservative." Hayes's advisers pleaded with him to abandon efforts to Republicanize the South. Instead, a deal could be struck to "place the Negro under political fealty to his former master," the federal troops would be withdrawn, and a Congress long deaf to pleas for southern internal improvements would be ready to act.* The South would also get its Texas and Pacific Railroad built.

This so-called Wormley Hotel deal, named for the hostelry where the two parties buried the political hatchet long enough to see Hayes inaugurated, is disputed by a few historians, but the facts are there for all to see. The deal was struck after an alarming "bloody shirt" editorial appeared in a Columbus, Ohio, newspaper that hinted Hayes was not going to cut any deals

*Quoted in C. Vann Woodward, *Origins of the New South, 1877–1913* (Baton Rouge: Louisiana State University Press, 1971), 28–29.

whatever. Threats of a filibuster brought Republicans in Congress to the hotel, where assurances were made.

And promises were kept. Hayes mentioned internal improvements for the South in his inaugural address, a southerner was appointed to Hayes's cabinet, and after a decent lapse of time an executive order from the White House removed federal troops from the remaining occupied states of the old Confederacy. "The last Carpetbag regimes immediately collapsed," Woodward noted. The president also told reporters he favored "such government aid as may be appropriate to secure the completion of the Texas and Pacific Railway." The "done deal" was done.

No election had ever been so close as that of 1876, nor the outcome so far-reaching. As Reconstruction ended, President Hayes toured the South to assure civic and business leaders they had nothing to fear from a Republican administration. But southern blacks thought they had much to fear, and they migrated in droves, mainly to Texas or Kansas. A group of Lexington, Kentucky, Negroes sought out public lands in the Solomon River valley in Kansas and promised "All Colored People" who had five dollars to spare that they could become colonizers. Some 40,000 blacks moved to Kansas, and probably as many shifted across the Sabine River into Texas. A loyal black corps remained behind, disfranchised and, in one sense, abandoned by their Republican friends in the North.

The year 1877 also saw another minority on the run. The Nez Percé Indians, a small tribe of about 800, rebelled at their treatment by federal officials and tried to escape from their reservation. They headed for the Canadian border and were thirty miles from their destination when federal troops overtook them; after a five-day siege, Chief Joseph surrendered on October 5, 1877. A year earlier, at the Battle of the Little Big Horn, General George Custer's small force had been annihilated by Chief Sitting Bull's warriors, but a strong cavalry force soon subdued the Sioux. The Republicans had ended the policy of recognizing Indian tribes as sovereign powers in 1871 and pursued an 1867 plan to centralize all tribes on western reservations. The Sioux and Nez Percé uprisings dramatized the tribes' resistance, but in Congress the main reaction was more appropriations for the army.

There were several public reactions. In the South and Midwest, the drive to clear Indians off the public domain and open more land for settlement was popular. In New England, the same impulse that had pushed the antislavery movement took a similar twist with the plight of the Indians. Helen Hunt Jackson's book *A Century of Dishonor* attacked the nation's handling of the Indians as repressive and cruel, but in general the public applauded the Republican administrations as they approved plans to make the reservation system work, whatever the cost. And to make the policy more popular, heroes of "the late war" were made field commanders of the armies that enforced the policy, Generals William T. Sherman and Philip Sheridan being the most prominent.

With the withdrawal of federal troops from the South and the passage of the Amnesty Act, which restored full citizenship to most former Confederate officers and officials, the way seemed clear for binding the nation's wounds. Only one Republican taboo remained. Pensions for Union veterans were enthusiastically hurried through Congress, but no effort to give Confederate servicemen a cash payment would be considered. "Are we to give away public funds to traitors who tried to destroy this Union?" was all a northern congressman had to say to put the question on the back burner indefinitely.

The increasing stocks of silver, fed by more discoveries in the West, placed pressure on Congress to consider a "bimetallism" program that would either permit the unlimited coinage of silver dollars or establish a ratio of gold to silver on a sixteen-to-one basis. The schemes were popular in the same areas where the Greenback party had its greatest support. After the 1876 election the House passed a bill sponsored by Representative Richard P. Bland of Missouri calling for everything the bimetallists desired, but the Senate allowed the bill to die. Late in 1877, the bill was revived by Senator William B. Allison of Iowa, whose farmer constituents were in a rebellious mood. The Bland-Allison Act, requiring the government to buy from $2 to $4 million in silver bullion each month and coin dollars with dispatch, was vetoed by Hayes—much to the relief of the eastern hard-money interests.

Midwestern and western senators had a rebellion of their own and pushed and shoved enough colleagues to override Hayes's veto. Economic discontent still lingered, however, and in 1878 the Greenbackers joined with a labor movement to hold a convention in Toledo, which attracted delegates from twenty-eight states. The fusion group condemned the resumption of gold payments, demanded unlimited coinage of silver, and insisted on a limit to work hours in industrial plants. The western delegates also sought, and obtained, a resolution calling for severe restrictions on Chinese immigration. Republicans in the wheat states were quick to note the trends, and their fears were realized in the congressional elections of 1878 when the Greenback-Labor party won fourteen seats in Congress and formally endorsed voting rights for women, a long-smoldering issue the new party brought into the open.

President Hayes had his problems in civil-service reform, too. One of the choice plums of the spoils system was the customhouse, where port collectors shared in the receipts of their stations and could earn salaries rivaling the president's (who received $50,000 a year after the "salary grab act" of 1874). Senator Roscoe Conkling of New York believed he had a right to control federal appointments in his state; when Hayes asked for the resignation of Conkling's pal Chester A. Arthur as customs collector for the New York harbor, a battle ensued. Arthur refused to resign; Hayes suspended him and appointed his own man. Then Conkling blew up and with the help of Senate friends blocked Hayes's nominee from confirmation. Southern senators came to Hayes's aid, and in time his man got the job, but recriminations were sure to follow. Hayes's pledge that he would not seek a second term seemed only to confirm the enmity boiling under the surface of the Republican party.

The internecine fighting in Republican ranks gave Democrats their chance in the 1878 fall elections for Congress. For the first time since 1862, greenbacks were back on a par with gold (during the war, greenbacks sank as low as thirty-two cents against a gold dollar), but the deflationary trend continued to hurt commodity prices. Wheat, corn, and cotton prices were far below their highs, falling in 1878 to the unheard-of price of seventy cents a bushel for wheat and eight cents a pound for cotton. Democrats took advantage of the economic slowdown and regained control of the House and narrowly held on to a Senate majority.

Hayes was in no mood to make deals. The Democrats wanted to repeal laws that permitted the use of federal troops in congressional elections when intimidation or threats were involved. But Hayes vetoed their bill and four other attempts to repeal similar "force acts" still on the books from Reconstruction days. Hayes's confrontation with the Congress raised his stock in Republican circles, although Senator Conkling vented his spleen by trying to create a boomlet for U. S. Grant. Republicans who sided with Hayes on civil-service reform would not stomach the aging former president and looked for a candidate who had none of the corruption of Grantism attached to his coattails. Conkling, as leader of the "Stalwart" faction in the Senate, was notorious for his devotion to the spoils system. His rival, Blaine, led a band of "Half-Breeds" who favored reforms of the civil-service system and other mild changes in the federal structure.

The strength of the boom for Grant revealed a pattern of Republican forgiveness that seems to be a permanent party fixture. After he left the White House, Grant took a world tour that left him out of the spotlight for the first time in fifteen years. When the Conkling crowd began to boost Grant in 1879, the public had only a vague memory of Whiskey Ring scandals but was ready to remember the general who whipped Lee. (The same kind of public forgiveness would reappear to disconnect Harding from the Teapot Dome scandal, allow Richard Nixon to become an elder statesman, and make Reagan beloved beyond the reach of the Iran-Contra mess.) Grant was ready to take advantage of this party myopia when the delegates gathered in Chicago for the 1880 nominating convention.

On the first ballot at Chicago, Grant was ahead. John Logan and his GAR followers whooped it up for Grant when the results showed their hero was less than seventy votes short of victory. Senator Blaine of Maine, still the darling of a faction, had a smattering of votes, as did John Sherman of Ohio, Hayes's secretary of the treasury, who was favored by the hard-money interests for being "safe as gold" on the money question.

Sherman might have forged into the lead, but Sherman had one enormous problem. As historian George Mayer noted, Sherman was from Ohio, and "every active Ohio [Republican] politician thought he was Presidential timber." Chief among the field of aspirants, after Sherman, was Ohio Congressman James Garfield, who had a reputation as a strong backer of civil-service reform. Senator George Edmunds of Vermont was more outspoken in his demands for federal civil-service laws, but he was not aggressively seeking the presidency and left that chore to friends. Conkling, making no bones that he was for the spoils system hook, line, and sinker, kept the lid on Edmunds's pretensions until the Vermont senator's friends finally switched to Sherman.

Instead of boosting Sherman into the catbird seat, Edmunds's delegates actually hurt the Ohioan's chances because their switch caused no sudden groundswell among other delegations. Ballot after ballot saw no dramatic shift, until the thirty-fourth round, when the governor of Wisconsin switched his state's sixteen votes to Garfield. Soon Sherman released his loyal Ohio delegates, allowing them to give another Ohioan their ballots. Blaine sensed the inevitable and released his backers, and on the thirty-sixth ballot the convention made Garfield the Republican party nominee. To say that Garfield was a dark horse is about as true as saying that Grant did not want the presidency. Garfield knew how to keep his mouth shut and be ready, and that was the strategy that worked best in the end.

On one count, Garfield's credentials were nearly perfect. He had won a reputation during the war as a self-made officer with plenty of concern for his men, and after the bloody Battle of Chickamauga, Garfield was recognized for his valor and promoted to major general. Reformers hailed his selection because Garfield had, since early in his tenure as a Republican congressman, promoted civil-service reform in the federal government. To them, his "Half-Breed" connections were nearly perfect.

Conkling's supporters were not pleased and let their anger be known. To keep them quiet and thus angle for the New York electoral votes, the convention took Conkling's pal Arthur (now chairman of the New York State committee) as the vice presidential choice.

Democrats, sick of losing votes when Republicans waved "the bloody shirt," decided to nominate a general with good Union credentials: Winfield Scott Hancock. The Greenback Labor convention chose Iowan James B. Weaver for that party's nominee. Both Hancock and Weaver must have known their candidacies would split the votes of anti-Garfield men, and once again the main battlegrounds would be in Indiana, Pennsylvania, and New York.

The GAR managed to wave the bloody shirt at every likely occasion, and by offering another Union Army hero the Republicans probably tilted the election in their favor. Out of more than 9 million ballots cast, Garfield's plurality was a mere 7,000; but in the electoral college he looked better with 214 votes to Hancock's 155. The Greenback Labor party proved to have more sound than fury but might have tipped the balance anyway as its ticket attracted 325,000 votes. In the congressional races, Republican candidates rode to a House majority, but the election of two independent senators made every vote critical, particularly with the "Half-Breeds" and "Stalwarts" at each other's throats on nearly every issue.

At a testimonial dinner held at fashionable Delmonico's restaurant in New York to celebrate Garfield's triumph, Grant presided and Chester A. Arthur was on the podium. A celebrant, probably drunk and certainly indiscreet, claimed he had carried Indiana for Garfield and hinted that plenty of cash was spent buying enough votes to ensure victory. The speech was reported in Democratic newspapers with charges that reformer Garfield had won with tainted ballots. Senator Chandler was outraged and wrote the president-elect that the New York celebration was a plot "to degrade and injure the party and the new administration by public proclamation that they hold power through the corrupt acts of corrupt men."*

Once the election was over, Garfield tried to stay away from being labeled a "goody-goody" reformer or a conservative stand-

---

*Quoted in Robert D. Marcus, *Grand Old Party* (New York: Oxford, 1971), 43.

patter. He corresponded with Blaine, who was all too eager to advise the newly elected president on any number of matters. Eventually Garfield's friendship with Blaine drove the Conkling wing of the party into a rebellion of sorts. When newspaper stories hinted that Blaine would be Garfield's secretary of state, that news forced Conkling into a corner, and he came out fighting. The rupture was complete when Garfield rejected Conkling's choice for the New York collector of customs. Conkling made the fuss into a party cause célèbre by telling his Senate colleagues that the time-honored senatorial prerogative of approving high appointments in one's own state had been smashed to smithereens by the Garfield choice.

Soon the nation beheld the spectacle of a senator vowing to fight to the end rather than approve the president's appointment in his own backyard. Then the Democrats provided some relief for Garfield by supporting the president's nominee; the upshot was that Conkling resigned from the Senate and pressured his friend and New York colleague, Senator Thomas Platt, to follow suit. Instead of calming troubled waters, however, the confirmations brought on salvos from Conkling as the rotund former senator tried to maneuver the state legislature into reelecting him. That ploy failed, even though Vice President Arthur did all he could to pressure old friends in Albany. The Republican machine in New York State subsequently fell into disrepair, Conkling sulked and pouted, and party regulars realized the party had been damaged far more than either the president or the senator had intended, since all the dirty linen was washed (and washed, and washed) in public.

There matters stood when Garfield went to the Washington railroad station on July 2, after barely four months in office. An unstable Republican who thought Garfield had slighted him was waiting in the depot, and as Garfield headed for his railroad car the man shot the president in the back. One bullet struck Garfield in the spine, and he lingered until September 19, when his death sent the nation into mourning. His assassin, despite a plea of temporary insanity, was tried, convicted, and executed after lengthy proceedings. A statement the assassin allegedly made, that he hoped to make Arthur president by his act, vaguely identified the crime with the "Stalwart" wing of the party. Thus Arthur, a "Stalwart" to the core, was somewhat discredited as he was sworn in as president.

A tall (six feet, two inches "in his stockings"), handsome man with a splendid set of muttonchop whiskers, Arthur fooled many of his Republican friends who thought the civil-service reformers would be stopped in their tracks. Blaine and his "Half-Breed" friends were soon out of the cabinet, but Arthur moved slowly and surprised nearly everybody by appointing as his attorney general Benjamin Brewster, a reformer who had prosecuted a friend of the president's for mail fraud. The president also saw the force of public opinion at work, for the voters were sick of the wrangling over patronage that Garfield's death precipitated, and Arthur endorsed a law that provided for competitive examinations for federal jobs. A large surplus in the treasury proved to be a siren song, enticing Congress into a bill-passing spree for pork-barrel projects and more pensions for Union veterans. Veterans were sacrosanct, but a rivers-and-harbors gouge was derailed by Arthur's veto. Rumblings from the farming Midwest also forced the Republican congress to cut tariff rates, legislation that Arthur signed without a tinge of conscience.

During the Arthur administration the Gilded Age hit its stride. Carriages and livery, champagne and oysters, velvet curtains and horsehair sofas were all the rage in Washington and New York. If all that glittered was not gold, it was certainly high-quality brass, shone and polished. The president himself personified the Gilded Age. President Arthur liked to wear fashionable clothes, enjoyed dinner parties, and restored some of the easygoing atmosphere that had been missing from the White House since Grant's days there. In Hayes's administration the use of liquor at White House functions had been banned, but widower Arthur brought back the custom of serving good bourbon and delectable wines. There were also whispers in Washington's drawing rooms that the president liked to play poker into the wee hours. For a man who came to the capital as the supposed lackey of a bullying senator, Arthur showed himself to be remarkably independent, cautious in his judgment and appointments, and willing to listen to both sides. There were even some Democrats who liked Arthur.

The trouble was that Arthur probably had more Democratic friends than he had Republican supporters. The New York machine that Conkling had built into a dreadnought was in shambles, and Blaine's friends had never forgiven the "Stalwarts" for what they did to Blaine's hopes at the 1880 nominating convention. Before long, Blaine was openly contemptuous of Arthur, and most of the "Half-Breeds" acted as though Arthur was a temporary aberration. In party councils, support for Arthur dissolved early on; when Arthur asked for $15,000 from Congress to revive the Civil Service Commission, only five Republicans supported him.

Then, another recession hit the country, and Democrats took advantage of the rise in unemployment and drop in farm prices by blaming the Republicans. The voters responded (and in the 1880s about 75 percent of the eligible males voted) by electing a Democratic majority in the House in the fall of 1882. This trend of blaming the party in power for economic ills was becoming more pronounced; from 1877 until 1893 neither Democrats nor Republicans managed to hold on to power in both houses for more than two years, with Democrats able to win the House as the Republicans controlled the Senate. The result was a legislative stalemate.

Meanwhile, the country changed rapidly, both intellectually and technologically. Western Republicans demanded, and received, a law that excluded Chinese from the normal immigration process, while state laws were prepared to deny Chinese the right to own real estate. While the Chinese had trouble in California and Nevada, blacks continued to face discrimination in the South. Life for white citizens was a bit easier, however, as the invention of the incandescent electric lightbulb and of the telephone brought rapid changes in home and street lighting and a crisscrossing of telephone lines in downtown areas. Railroads were improving in speed and comfort, too. Indeed, by the middle of Arthur's term it was probably easier to send a letter from Chicago to New York, and certainly cheaper and faster, than it was a century later.

Late in 1883 General William T. Sherman retired and was boomed for the prize his brother had long sought: the party's presidential nomination. Republican bosses on the Atlantic sea-board used newspapers to whip up sentiment for a "Draft Sherman" movement. The general found it embarrassing, and when the party insiders talked about Sherman's "duty" to run (and place another war hero on the ticket), the old soldier let loose with both barrels. "If nominated, I will not run," Sherman said, "and if elected, I will not serve." That ended the Sherman boom, to the discomfort of more than one postmaster who feared a Democratic victory.

Without Sherman, but not without hope, Republicans returned for the 1884 convention to Chicago, where the convention hall filled with favorite sons, would-be standard-bearers, and a noisy band of GAR members. Arthur was washed up. He concealed a serious illness (he suffered from Bright's disease) and at one point pretended to be interested in another White House term. Few Republicans in high office were eager to help the president, however, and blame for the acquittal of the infamous "star route" mail fraud defendants (whose enormous graft tainted the Post Office) was laid at Arthur's doorstep. Within Republican ranks, the contributions expected from officeholders—postmasters and others on the federal payroll—also backfired. A disgruntled postmaster reacted bitterly when the Republican National Committee sent out his "assessment" for the forthcoming campaign. Informed that he was expected to give $150 to the party, he protested: "*My whole time* is devoted to the labors of the canvass . . . and at an outlay, so far, from my own pocket of over $600."*

By the spring of 1884, Arthur had no chance of being nominated, so he accepted the inevitable with good grace. A supporter in New York sent $100,000 in cash to help gain the nomination, and must have been shocked when the president had the money returned. The president became the lightning rod for discontent from both rank-and-file Republicans and those on Capitol Hill. An informed New York politician tallied votes and thought 21 counties favored Blaine, with only 8 favoring Arthur. The *Erie*

---

*Quoted in Thomas C. Reeves, *Gentleman Boss: The Life of Chester Alan Arthur* (New York: Knopf, 1975), 103.

Dispatch claimed that its five-state poll gave Blaine 151 counties, Arthur 20. Meanwhile, reporters told readers that at least eighteen potential candidates had set up convention headquarters or allowed their friends to establish message centers. Senator Sherman was back, along with the GAR-supported Logan and old Senator Edmunds. More notable than the old faces were the new ones. From Ohio came Representative William McKinley and his friend Mark Hanna; New York had a youngster in its delegation, Theodore Roosevelt, while his bosom Harvard buddy Henry Cabot Lodge represented Massachusetts. One other fresh face was supplied by Stephen Benton Elkins, who came from West Virginia with a reputation for making money and having a rich father-in-law. These newcomers came to Chicago to listen and learn.

Blaine came to Chicago to win. Ever since 1876 he had been mentioned as a presidential nominee, but always the cup passed from his lips at inopportune moments. Loyal Blaine supporters believed that their time had come. James Clarkson, editor of Des Moines's influential *Iowa State Register,* told his eastern friends that Blaine ought to have a "wigwam" in Chicago to imitate the Lincoln strategy that paid off so handsomely in 1860. The times had not changed. Blaine's managers made deals and promises almost as fast as had Lincoln's in 1860, and again the backstage dealings paid off. Arthur was second to Blaine on the first ballot, then faded fast as a disastrous split in the New York delegation caused defections right and left.

Blaine's managers moved for continuous balloting and kept the delegates on the convention floor for three ballots, until Ohio switched from Sherman to Blaine. Then the shouting was all over. By his persistence, Blaine may have deserved the nomination, but many delegates left the hall in a bad frame of mind. A last-minute deal to place Logan on the ticket made few friends and some enemies.

To satisfy the growing voter strength in the West, the Republican platform in 1884 included a plan calling for a further crackdown on Chinese immigration, and the festering crisis in Utah created by the polygamy practiced by Mormons also drew a rebuke from the platform planners. There were some platitudes on civil-service reform and a protective tariff and, almost by accident, a generous allusion to the need for legislation creating an eight-hour workday. If you were not a Chinaman or a Mormon, there was nothing in the platform to offend, and Blaine gladly accepted the honor that had escaped him since 1876.

Reform-minded Democrats chose Governor Grover Cleveland of New York for their presidential aspirant, to be balanced with an Indiana lawmaker of tested party loyalty for vice president. What helped Cleveland, Democrats hoped, was his financial conservatism and his known hostility to the discredited Tammany Democratic machine in Manhattan. Anybody who hated Tammany, particularly a Democrat, couldn't be all bad. Nobody imagined that what began as a scurrilous campaign would become the knock-down-drag-out affair it turned into long before November.

For openers, Cleveland was attacked as a draft dodger who admitted he had fathered a bastard child. Cleveland admitted he had hired a substitute during the Civil War but claimed the act was necessary because he supported a widowed mother. As for the bastard child, Cleveland candidly admitted to a youthful indiscretion. His honesty made Cleveland the butt of many jokes but probably helped him win over voters who thought Blaine was too slick for their tastes.

Another drawback for Blaine was the purchase of the *New York World* by Joseph Pulitzer. Pulitzer came to Manhattan after a successful venture in journalism out West, and he quickly converted the *World* into a strong rival of the Republican-inclined *Times* and *Tribune*. Pulitzer launched a circulation war that he won, and when Cleveland was nominated the *World* found its political hero. After another Delmonico's dinner staged by Republicans, the *World* reported: "Beaten by the people, hopeless of an honest election, Blaine's appeal at the banquet of the millionaires was for a corruption fund large enough to buy up New Jersey, Connecticut, and Indiana, and to defraud the people of their free choice for President." Labor also leaped into the fray when the typesetters' union, surmising that the *Tribune* was still the leading Republican journal in the nation, struck over a wage dispute and ordered a boycott of "the *Tribune* and James G. Blaine."

Republicans struck back. The *New York Independent* cited Cleveland's confession in the bastardy incident and predicted that his election "would argue a low state of morals among the people" and "a disgrace to the nation." More than one Republican newspaper gave the Cleveland "bastard baby" story prominence, and several reprinted the ditty "Ma, Ma, Where is my Pa? / Gone to the White House, Ha! Ha! Ha!" From pulpits dominated by Republican ministers, Cleveland was condemned as a "moral lecher" unfit for high office.

Blaine's men felt comfortable as the campaign swung into the final lap, when a sudden miscue threw everything into confusion. The Republican nominee attended a rally where a starched-collar preacher lauded Blaine and used a sentence that would soon haunt all concerned. "We are Republicans," the minister shouted, "and don't propose to leave our party and identify ourselves with the party whose antecedents have been rum, Romanism, and rebellion." That did it. In a single sentence the Republicans, probably with Blaine's implicit approval, had insulted the drinking classes, the Catholics, and the entire South.

When the blunder rocked their campaign boat, the Blaine men tried to mend the damage and whistled in the dark until election day. But the remark somehow changed the course of history. Blaine won all of New England except Connecticut, but he needed New York. The typesetters' union had 3,500 members in New York, and perhaps it is fair to say most of them took an occasional swig; whether they did or not is moot. But the fact is Blaine lost New York by 1,500 ballots, and that was the election. For the first time since 1856, a Democrat had been elected president.

As it turned out, Grover Cleveland was about as conservative a president as any Republican who might have been elected. Some postmasters were replaced, but in general Cleveland was devoted to the principle behind civil-service reforms. Moreover, Cleveland despised the clamoring office seekers who besieged the White House. After his cabinet was in place, with some *very* savvy conservatives holding key positions, the business community and Wall Street in particular breathed a collective sigh of relief. The Haymarket bombing in Chicago took the lives of sixteen policemen and parade marchers and caused a wave of resentment against Socialists and labor organizers. Cleveland was asked to pardon the men convicted of the crime, but he refused, and four were executed late in November 1887.

Bombings and strikes aside, Cleveland's big problem was handling the $165 million surplus of paper, gold, and silver dollars in the federal treasury. Pensions to Union veterans could not be passed out fast enough, even though within a few years 30 percent of the total federal budget was earmarked for the former "boys in blue" and their widows.

The only difference between Cleveland and his Republican adversaries was the tariff: Cleveland wanted it reduced as the platform had promised, and Republicans wanted it left alone or even raised. The Democratic House passed the bill Cleveland wanted, but Senate Republicans managed to kill it.

Democrats who were upset by Cleveland's slight bow to the spoils system were angry. The tariff issue was not their cup of bourbon. When Cleveland tried to arouse the party, he gained halfhearted support from the Midwest but alienated the machine politicians in the large eastern cities. Republicans accused Cleveland of secretly admiring the British with their ideas on free trade, and that angered Irish immigrants who did not understand what free trade was, but knew they hated the British. Cleveland also vetoed a number of private bills granting pensions to Union veterans with doubtful credentials. In short, in his four years Cleveland managed to make a large number of voters "sore as hell."

Cleveland was nominated at the 1888 Democratic convention in St. Louis, and his party platform was an endorsement of the president's call for tariff overhauling. The Democrats were not to be outdone and also called for the exclusion of Chinese labor.

The national Republican campaign committee had plenty of contributions in its bank account when the nominating convention met again in Chicago on June 21, 1888, to pick a president. The party had changed dramatically since the 1884 debacle. Grant, Logan, and Arthur were in their graves, and some of the vigorous men of 1868 were now either dead or politically defunct. The off-year elections in 1886 had ended in a virtual draw, but Republican chieftains thought Cleveland had committed a major error in staking an exclusive claim to tariff reform. At the Chicago convention it seemed at times that there were more candidates than delegates. Senator Allison of Iowa was making noises, John Sherman was still around and buttonholing delegates, and right behind them stood two more Ohioans brimming with hope, Governor Joseph Foraker and Congressman William McKinley, while ambitious Mark Hanna waited in the wings. New Yorkers backed Chauncey Depew, the rich, heavyset boss of the powerful New York Central Railroad who could have bought and sold most of the delegates without batting an eye. Indianans had their eyes on former Senator Benjamin Harrison, who was sound on the tariff, hard as granite on the money issue, and above all else a former Union general. Finally, there was old Blaine, defeated but not humbled by the 1884 experience and ready for one more try.

To dramatize his availability from a distance, Blaine went to Europe and let it be known he would not return until the convention made a choice. The existence of a trans-Atlantic cable made the gesture appear to be more dramatic than it was politically clever.

But in any American nominating convention, before the era of early presidential primaries, polls, and television, anything could still happen.

CHAPTER SEVEN

Wheeling and Dealing

Virginia early on claimed to be "the mother of presidents," after five of the first ten presidents were natives of the Old Dominion. Then Republicans took center stage and Ohio yearned for the title, as five presidents came from the Buckeye state between 1841 and 1921. What the two claims really showed was the shifting political focus of the nation from the seaboard to the grain-growing midwestern states.

Actually, Ohio-born Benjamin Harrison was from Indiana, but the Hoosier State was straddling both midwestern camps and had become the new "keystone" state insofar as its off-year elections portended victory or defeat for either party in a close contest. Delegates at the 1888 Republican convention were well aware of this fact as they pondered the choice between Senator Sherman, who led on the first ballot, and General Harrison, who was trailing far behind. The changing sands of fortune shifted on the fourth ballot, when most of Depew's New York support eroded into Harrison's camp. Still, Harrison was gaining, but not spectacularly, when delegates adjourned on Saturday night. Sunday would be a day of rest, perhaps worship, and definitely some wheeling and dealing.

Not in a smoke-filled room, but in a sunny carriage, Senator Elkins of West Virginia invited Senator Platt to ride and talk. Rumors that Platt would be offered a cabinet post in a Harrison administration flew through hotel lobbies. On Monday morning, two more ballots proved inconclusive. Then a Maine delegate, supposedly a Blaine man with a pipeline to the veteran Republican, announced a switch to Harrison. On the eighth ballot, Harrison was nominated to a clash of cymbals and much shouting. When the yelling was over, Levi Morton, a New York financier, was added as the vice presidential candidate, and everybody went home relatively happy.

Harrison proved to be an able campaigner, even though he never left his front porch. He spoke far more than any other Republican candidate had ever dared; sometimes speaking "off the cuff," Harrison actually talked about some of the vital issues of the day, including Negro suffrage, the tariff, and the high cost of pensions for Union veterans (eight dollars per annum for each month served).

This was probably the last campaign in which the "bloody shirt" was waved to excess by Republicans ready to exploit prejudice against Democrats and the Democratic South in particular. In the Midwest a poster was circulated showing the two presidential candidates under the heading, "1789–1889— George Washington, first president inaugurated / Who should be his successor at the Centennial?" Over Harrison's likeness the caption was, "The man who risked his life to preserve it." Over Cleveland's picture it said, "The man who sent a substitute." Another tactic was offered in this widely printed ditty:

> Let Grover talk against the tariff,
> tariff, tariff, and pensions too
> We'll give the working man his due
> And pension the boys who wore the blue.

In New York about 45,000 veterans were drawing pensions in 1888. Another key state, Indiana, had 38,000 pensioners.

There was a "dirty tricks" aspect of the campaign that Harrison did not know about and that did the Republicans no honor. Anxious to make it appear that the British favored Cleveland because of his low-tariff pitch, a Republican wrote to the British minister in Washington and (pretending he was a British subject) asked who a good Englishman should support: Harrison or Cleveland? The naive British envoy replied, advising the pseudo-Englishman to vote for Cleveland. The letter was gleefully printed in the *Los Angeles Times,* which was fast becoming the voice of Republicanism on the West Coast; reprintings in the East helped reinforce the gossip about Cleveland being pro-British. The blushing British minister could not undo the damage, and Cleveland's Irish American supporters either stayed home or switched sides for the November balloting.

Harrison carried his home state and Cleveland lost his—and that was the election, for (as in 1876) the Democrat actually received more popular votes than the Republican. Indiana, for example, went for Harrison by only 6,000 votes. In the electoral college, however, Harrison was way ahead—233 to 168. In Congress, the Republicans came back with a slight majority in the House, and a 39 to 37 advantage in the Senate. Democrats were quick to point to their two losses when supporters of a Democratic candidate actually had more popular votes, and they talked about the need to abolish the electoral college "and let the people speak directly and to the point." Nothing came of such talk, as Harrison was inaugurated with all the fanfare and bunting Union veterans could scrape together in Washington.

The plain truth was that except on tariff issues, the two parties were becoming more alike than different. The Republicans lacked confidence in 1860, 1864, and 1868; but from 1872 onward the party had a solid, loyal group of supporters. Blaine, the only loser in the presidential race, did not lose because he had not been a Civil War hero; he lost because his organization let him down. The Midwest was upset over hard-money policies, but still firmly Republican. Most of those states had been consistently Democratic before 1860. In addition, the Republican congressional leaders found it easy to work with the southern Democrats. As historian Kenneth Stampp noted, the coalition of southern Democrats and northern Republicans working together in Congress in the 1980s and 1990s had its antecedents in the identical coalition working on Capitol Hill from 1877 into Theodore Roosevelt's second term.

Harrison kept his distance in the White House. Like John Quincy Adams, Harrison also had presidential antecedents, since William Henry Harrison was his grandfather. Fiscally sound, Harrison was reserved; once he was in office, his natural demeanor (one observer thought Harrison had the personality of an iceberg) made him few close friends. His administration inherited the Dawes Act of 1887, which was supposed to end the troublesome freeze of tribal lands in the Indian Territories. The idea was to divide the tribes' lands into 160-acre parcels to be given to individual Indians as headrights, making them into farmers and merchants who would renounce the cumbersome tribal holdings "in severalty." One outcome was the Oklahoma Land Run of 1889 in Harrison's first year in office.

The embarrassing treasury surplus was dispensed through a generous pensions bill for Union veterans. The tariff revenues were another matter, for it was necessary to hold the line on tariffs, even if the treasury was overflowing with dollars. Representative McKinley introduced a tariff bill that raised customs duties to an all-time high but also placed duties on some imported farm products in a bow to the Midwest. Overall, the McKinley tariff was supposed to reduce customs revenues and thus help ease the problem of a treasury too full of money!

A cutback on the treasury surplus was only part of McKinley's excuse for a new tariff that would protect some of the industries known to send large checks to the national Republican committee. Three western Republican senators complained that the bill would make American buyers pay as much as 60 percent more than consumers in foreign markets. Concessions were made, but the Ohioan's bill generally pleased the protectionist element in the party and only mildly upset farmers and ranchers. Nonetheless, voter discontent over monetary policy, the McKinley tariff, spotty recessions, and high railroad rates was apparent in the 1890 off-year elections in thirty-nine states, where Republicans lost control of the House (both Cannon and McKinley lost their seats) but kept a comfortable majority in the Senate. The possibility of drastic congressional action was unlikely, even with a 147-seat (235 to 88) Democratic majority in the House; but a public statement from former president Cleveland blasting the plan for the unlimited coinage of silver left thousands of westerners dismayed by the posture of both parties.

To keep the midwestern and western Republicans fairly quiet, a silver-purchase act was also approved. The law provided for the purchase of 4.5 million ounces of silver each month, with the treasury then authorized to issue "silver certificates" backed by the purchases. Conservative Republicans convinced Harrison the policy was basically unsound, and he agreed. The Treasury Department was ordered to redeem the new bills in *gold,* which defeated the whole purpose of the law.

Republican congressmen saw that European nations were going into Africa and the Pacific at a fast clip, annexing territories and creating colonies that would become sources of raw materials and markets for manufactured goods. Mercantilism was still alive and goading England, France, Germany, and Italy into a race for new lands to conquer. The Monroe Doctrine left South America off-limits to the European marauders, but "darkest Africa" was fair game and black tribesmen were no match for rifles and Gatling guns. Not a few congressmen saw an opportunity for the United States to strengthen its hold on the Pacific, but a treaty of annexation with Hawaii was postponed in the Senate, and Harrison's only colonizing success in the vast ocean was the protectorate status offered to Samoa.

Ultimately, Harrison saw the new tariff laws as potentially punitive. The McKinley law had a loophole, which provided that certain nations that lowered their tariff barriers to the United States would be treated with reciprocity. Eight treaties reducing the excessive duties were negotiated by the Harrison administration, not always with applause from the makers of steel and iron in Pittsburgh or the farm-machinery moguls in Illinois.

Publicity for the sugar, oil, and other trusts forced the Republicans to pass the Sherman Antitrust Act, which made it illegal for big corporations to fix prices or receive discriminatory rail rates or rebates. Corporations were urged to adopt a new economic philosophy of serving "the public good," which seemed counter to the laissez-faire approach extant from Alexander Hamilton's tenure in the Treasury Department down to 1890. Unfortunately, court decisions hamstrung the law's provisions so that its enforcement was lax during the next decade.

Further entrenchment of northern states to offset the returned southern bloc came about in 1889 when Congress passed an omnibus bill that provided for admitting the new states of North Dakota, South Dakota, Washington, and Montana. Idaho and

Wyoming were not far behind in the race for statehood. The practical effect was the addition of twelve more Republican senators and the defeat of a Democratic attempt to repeal the old force bill that was designed to protect black voters in the South.

At this fifty-first session of Congress a significant step was made in the House, where Representative Thomas Reed of Maine was elected Speaker by his fellow Republicans. Under Reed, who served several terms, the House rules were changed to increase the Speaker's powers, and a bill designed to speed up the legislative process was approved.

As chairman of the House Rules Committee, Reed had heavy-handed powers. He pushed a bill that lowered to ninety days the time a veteran must have served in the Union army in order to receive a pension; the bill also allowed children, widows, and even dependent parents to receive a federal stipend. In short order, the number of pensioners on federal rolls increased from 676,000 to 970,000. Harrison's commissioner of pensions, a past commander of the GAR, heard the good news and is said to have exclaimed: "God help the surplus!" In Harrison's four years in office, the pension budget leaped from $81 million to $135 million. Southern states generally were too hard-pressed to pension any Confederate veterans, but retirement homes for those soldiers who once wore gray uniforms sprang up, supported by private donors and a pittance from local governments.

In the East, the GAR and its entourage of veterans thought the Harrison administration was doing splendidly. But western Republicans were upset. Midwestern Republican farmers were frustrated. In such circumstances, the opportunity for another third party seemed at hand. Farmer and labor groups had been trying to merge their common interests for years, and Granger, Greenback, and Labor leaders had held preliminary meetings in 1889 and 1890. In May 1891, delegates from thirty-two states met at Cincinnati, and early in 1892 the People's party held a convention in Omaha to nominate James B. Weaver for president. Newspapers soon rechristened the group the Populist party and helped publicize its July 4 platform, calling for unlimited coinage of silver at a ratio to gold of sixteen to one and for government ownership of all railroads and telegraph and telephone lines, plus a graduated income tax (the Civil War income tax law had been declared unconstitutional by the Supreme Court).

The seriousness and noise generated by the Populists caused Republicans in the Midwest to fret that their voting base would be eroded by the new party. Some disaffection was soon evident; the organized eastern Republicans kept matters under control, however, when they called all the schemes for silver and greenbacks inflationary. The point was, if you were a clerk or drayman living in Manhattan with a fixed salary, *inflation* sounded ominous. The farmers, for all their bluster, would not vote Democratic, and the city dwellers just might swing to the Republican column.

Early in 1892 Harrison had let it be known that he had no stomach for another presidential race; but then Blaine, his secretary of state, managed to bungle everything in a halfhearted attempt to keep his own hat out of the ring. Blaine's seeming duplicity and ill health caused Harrison to become his own secretary of state, and when a band of anti-Harrison men gathered to discuss alternatives, they found few. Most prominent was McKinley, now governor of Ohio, who had found a firm friend in Mark Hanna. Hanna, one of the most clever men ever involved in American politics, kept a small fire lit for the McKinley candidacy just in case Harrison stumbled badly. In that case, McKinley could wait until the lightning struck.

No lightning struck, however, and McKinley, John Sherman, and the other hopefuls allowed the nomination to become a matter of inertia rather than enthusiasm. Meeting in Minneapolis as a bow to the discontented farmers in the Midwest, the convention was somewhat like a movie filmed in slow motion. The nominating speeches were made, the banners were waved, and decorum prevailed almost to the point of boredom. Harrison was nominated on the first ballot. The eastern branch of the party was allowed to nominate the newspaper editor Whitelaw Reid, Greeley's successor at the *Tribune,* as vice president.

Tariff was the talk of the day, particularly after the protectionists won their fight in the platform committee for endorsement of a still higher tariff wall. Cleveland was picked by the Democrats, who fought long and hard over their tariff plank before deciding (as Calhoun had said fifty years earlier) that the Constitution did not permit the federal government to collect duties "except for purposes of revenue only." In addition to the Populists' nomination of the irrepressible James Weaver, the Socialist Labor party and the rising Prohibition party, insisting that liquor consumption was the nation's number-one problem, also nominated presidential candidates.

Harrison, the consummate front-porch campaigner, was in for a tough fight and knew it. By-elections in 1891 left little room for optimism, since the Democrats continued to make inroads— not as spectacularly as in 1890, but enough to make Harrison a possible liability in 1892. Disturbing reports came from the Midwest, where the loyalties of immigrant farmers appeared to be on the wane. The civil-service investigations of the upstart New Yorker, Theodore Roosevelt, had angered Republicans over patronage problems; Roosevelt thought that asking for donations from petty officeholders was a kind of "shakedown." Big donors were better than tiny ones, the national committee ultimately agreed. More than $2 million was raised, much of it coming from corporations and wealthy individuals and little from postmasters and mailmen.

Harrison had planned to leave his front porch and make a campaign swing into crucial New York, but his wife's illness and death caused the president to cancel the trip. He stayed in Ohio, while Cleveland remained in Buffalo and let the other three candidates blow off steam. The whole campaign lacked the joyful fervor evident in 1868 or 1872. Pamphlets and newspaper editorials replaced torchlight parades and brass bands. Farmers were too busy, and city dwellers also had other things to do.

Harrison lost New York and the East, and that was the election story in a nutshell. Farmers' discontent was most evident in Illinois, which Cleveland carried as the Democrats won the state for the first time since 1856. Moreover, Democrats captured majorities in both the House and the Senate for the first time in a generation. So hard hit were the House Republicans (winning only 126 seats) that their numbers would not be so low again for almost two generations. Cleveland's final tally was 5.5 million votes to Harrison's 5.2 million, with 1.2 million votes scattered among the runners-up. In the electoral college, Cleveland was ahead 277 to 145.

In his parting shot, late in 1892, Harrison defended his policies and made this assessment of the burning tariff question:

> I believe that the protective [tariff] system . . . has been a mighty instrument for the development of our national wealth and a most powerful agency in protecting the homes of our working men from the invasion of want . . . [and preserved for] our working people rates of wages that would not only give daily bread, but supply a comfortable margin for those home attractions and family comforts . . . without which life is neither hopeful nor sweet.*

There is evidence that thousands of mill workers and factory hands saw the tariff as a kind of job insurance to protect their paychecks. Distant echoes of Harrison's ideas were heard in Hoover's time with the phrase *full dinner pail,* which explained, in part, why eastern workers and western farmers stayed loyal to the Republican party until 1932.

From 1892 onward, the Republicans dropped the "bloody shirt" and emphasized fiscal conservatism as the key to continued prosperity. Since both Cleveland and Harrison were conservative on money matters, no huge swing to the left was anticipated. Indeed, Cleveland's embrace of the gold standard made him more popular on Wall Street than his Republican opponent, while in the South the newly inaugurated president found himself at odds with party leaders. Storm clouds gathering in the West blew eastward as European grain markets stabilized after several disastrous years and exports of wheat and corn fell drastically. That triggered renewed protests over rail rates; and the fall in real estate prices that started in the late 1880s began to accelerate. The bankruptcy of a major British bank also had repercussions in banking circles. Cautious investors began to convert their assets into gold, which in turn caused a drain on the federal treasury's gold reserve.

If one straw broke the camel's back, it was the announced drop in the nation's gold reserve to less than $100 million, the

---

*Quoted in Carl Degler, "American Political Parties and the Rise of the City," *Journal of American History* 51 (1964): 46.

"floor" set when specie payments were renewed in 1879. The run on gold weakened every segment of the nation's economy, causing the price of everything from corn to railroads to drop dramatically. In short, a panic soon hit the country right between the eyes and would affect American politics for at least the next thirty years.

The panic of 1893 struck in full force a few months after Cleveland took office for the second time, as the nation was making a huge conversion from an agrarian society to an industrial one. Real wages for workers fell almost 18 percent over the next two years, with similar losses for farmers, and price drops in manufactured goods affected profits in industry and business. As historian Frederick Jackson Turner noted in 1893, the free-land policy of the past two hundred years came to a halt as the frontier closed. By 1893 the population shift had changed a nation that once consisted almost totally of farmers into 60 percent farmers and 40 percent city (or town) dwellers. The flight from farms to towns and cities would continue; meanwhile, industrialism was the new king, not cotton or corn or wheat. The new monarch was held aloft by millions of low-paid laborers, unskilled immigrants often forming huge workforces for employment in coal mines, steel mills, railroad gangs, and similar endeavors that quickly reflected economic trends. Lower wages by late 1893 made for tension everywhere.

Strikes, lockouts, and pitched battles between police and labor union members were to become more common after 1893 and be a part of the industrial scene after the 1894 boycott by workers of Chicago's Pullman Company. Violence in the Illinois strike prompted Cleveland to send federal troops into the troubled area, a move ratified by a court decision granting an injunction against strikes that interfered with the mails or interstate commerce.

Cleveland's philosophy of government prevented him from becoming an activist, ready to use governmental resources to combat the agonizing depression that threw thousands out of work each week. Farmers, even in hard times, have shelter and food available; city-dwelling workers feel the effects of a recession quickly if forced out of their jobs. In short order, the city's jobless blamed the work stoppages on Democrats and Cleveland.

The unrest spread to the Midwest, and in March 1894 a manifesto from Populist Jacob Coxey led to the formation of "Coxey's Army" of unemployed men who vowed to march from Ohio to Washington, D.C., and demand relief from Congress. Newspaper coverage of the so-called march exaggerated the strident claims for a work-relief program and the issuance of $500 million in legal tender notes, but only about four hundred unshaved, hungry men straggled onto Capitol Hill in late April to voice their demands. Coxey and several others were arrested for trespassing, and the incident blew over, although it was symptomatic of the public's distress and shock.

In a nation of belt tighteners, the Republicans watched the Democrats make mistake after mistake, or even helped them blunder. A stock market crash in June 1893 was the starter's gun for a panic. A major railroad defaulted on its bonds, the bankruptcy court dockets were crowded, and before the year ended 491 banks had failed. Cleveland called a special session of Congress, hoping to halt the drain on the treasury's gold reserves. The Sherman Silver Purchase Act was repealed with Republican support, but midwestern Democrats felt betrayed. Organized labor blamed Cleveland for breaking the Pullman strike, the gold reserves fell to $41 million, and the federal government was forced to borrow money at high rates to keep public confidence from eroding.

The panic had scarcely abated when Republicans began to think about recapturing Congress. Cleveland was on the defensive, blamed by the public for the unemployment that was causing misery in every section of the country. Intractable when cornered, Cleveland proposed to ride out the storm without drastic action, and Congress's lowered tariff bill became law without presidential approval because the new act had something in it that made nearly everybody angry. Commodity prices fell to new lows, the number of business failures skyrocketed, and dole lines in the big cities reached pitiful lengths. In the off-year elections of 1894, a high turnout of angry voters sent a blistering message to the Democrats, who lost control of both houses— from 218 seats in the House to 105, with similar losses in the Senate. Republicans almost doubled their number in the House, going from 126 to 244, with some gain in the Senate, too. In Kansas, where a Republican governor had been turned out by a Populist in 1891, agrarian resentment was at a high pitch. In 1892, Kansas Populists elected four congressmen, but they lost three of those seats in 1894. A young editorial writer in Emporia would become famous for his question: "What's the Matter with Kansas?" What was wrong, William Allen White wrote, was that Kansas had flirted with some wool-hat philosophers and turned its back on the Republican party. The Populist-Democratic nominee for governor, White insisted, was "another shabby, wild-eyed, rattle-brained fanatic." Even so, John W. Leedy was elected governor in 1896.

Cleveland was caught in the same kind of philosophical bind that would affect Herbert Hoover in 1930. He had no solution except for local relief and pronouncements of hope. Voters, even the most conservative, resent inaction in a crisis. Leadership is a simple matter of standing aside during good times and allowing the ship of state to sail itself; but in wars and depressions, the voters want action. Cleveland misjudged the temperament of voters and was excessively stubborn when his judgment was questioned.

Off the presidential stage, events with long-reaching effects took place almost unnoticed. Without fanfare a Supreme Court decision in the election year of 1896 whittled away more of the protection afforded to blacks by federal law. In 1894 the Republican-dominated Congress had repealed the force laws, opening the door for widespread coercion of Negro voters in the South. That was child's play, however, to the high court's ruling in *Plessy v. Ferguson,* the 1896 decision involving a Louisiana law that created segregated seating for black and white rail passengers. The court's decision gave a backhanded stamp of approval to the southern laws erecting barriers of legal separation between blacks and whites. A court dominated by Republican justices held that southern "separate-but-equal" facilities in schools, public conveyances, hotels, theaters, and other commercial ventures were not in violation of the Fourteenth Amendment. Thereafter, Jim Crow sections on railroad cars, in train stations, and in nearly all public places in the South became commonplace and would stay that way until after a dramatic reversal by the Supreme Court fifty-eight years later.

A major shift in the American political spectrum was just around the corner. In their calculations the Democrats ignored the rise of cities and let the farm-bloc philosophy take hold after William Jennings Bryan made his emotional "Cross of Gold" speech. Tons of silver and plenty of paper money were offered as the Democrats' solution to the nation's economic woes. McKinley was talked about as the chief Republican challenger, and his manager, Mark Hanna, perceived the flaw in Bryan's plea for the unlimited coinage of silver. "He's talking silver all the time," Hanna remarked, "and that's where we've got him."

"And they did have him," historian Carl Degler noted. "Free silver was at best uninteresting to the urban population and, at worst, anathema to them." Guided by Hanna, McKinley made no foolish statements about bimetallism or anything else. His critics claimed McKinley lacked intellectual depth, but if he was no great brain, neither was McKinley shorn of assets by his long association with Republicans in Congress and the Ohio statehouse. His chief asset was Hanna's loyalty. Hanna worked steadily for two years lining up convention delegates in all sections of the country. By Christmas of 1895, with the nominating convention still many months away, the Hanna-McKinley team had produced enough votes to make McKinley's nomination a foregone conclusion.

The main excitement at the 1896 St. Louis convention was a floor fight over a platform plank endorsing the gold standard. A silver-state senator almost wrecked the whole business with an impassioned speech that left him crying like a baby. All for naught, it turned out, as the convention rejected all efforts to imitate the Democrats with talk of sixteen-to-one ratios as a panacea for the depression.

McKinley won on the first ballot; his running mate, from the weather-vane state of New Jersey, was Governor Garret Hobart. The race against the thirty-seven-year-old Bryan, a former congressman with a silver tongue to match his monetary policy, was a mismatch from the start. The Populists also nominated Bryan, but that futile gesture only emphasized the nature of the race—Bryan was labeled a radical with little experience and a single solution to the nation's ills. The campaign was hard fought and appeared close in the summer but not so close in the late fall.

What McKinley and his supporters tried to emphasize was the need to rely on Republicans to uphold the American tradition of sanity in the face of threats from wild-eyed liberals. The Republican party was more responsive to changing circumstances, its campaign literature insisted, and the main issues in 1896 were fiscal soundness in the face of simplistic solutions such as the unlimited coinage of silver. Strange as it may sound, Hanna went for the rank-and-file voter by making Bryan and the Democrats into Humpty-Dumpties ready for a gigantic fall. Hanna also patched up old intraparty quarrels, such as the one that had kept Harrison at odds with Platt in New York. Platt became McKinley's New York campaign manager and helped swell the party coffers; eventually, over $3 million was raised to combat Bryan and his inflationary pleas. Among the big contributors were John D. Rockefeller's Standard Oil ($250,000) and John McCall of the New York Life Insurance Company ($50,000). Such alliances between the Republicans and big business were not one-time ventures in expediency, but rather became the bedrock of party finance on a permanent basis.

The *New York Tribune* was no longer the dominant weekly in the Midwest, but it was still the most powerful journalistic voice that Republicans could count on during a crisis. The *Tribune* attacked the silverites head-on by claiming that "the triumph of free silver would mean the payment of every pension at the rate of fifty-three cents on the dollar." Not to be outdone, the *Chicago Tribune* echoed this charge and told Union veterans that if Bryan won their pensions would be slashed in half.

Finally, the campaign ended and the hard-fought battle— the most strident since 1860—was over. The Democrats' "Boy Orator from the Platte" had broken all tradition and traveled over 18,000 miles to make six hundred speeches in twenty-nine states. All unprecedented, and all in vain, for McKinley sat on his front porch in Canton, Ohio, and let Bryan exhaust himself. The rocking-chair candidate had 7 million votes to 6.4 million for

Bryan, with a smattering for the four other nominees. A school-room map showed an odd pattern, with all of the West except Oregon, North Dakota, and California going to Bryan, and all of the North from Wisconsin eastward voting for McKinley. Wall Street and Main Street heaved a collective sigh of relief. "Upon Bryan's defeat," historian Samuel Hays noted, "the eastern critics were convinced that civilization had barely been saved." In the electoral college it was 271 for McKinley and 176 for Bryan. Bryan was not crucified, but this was the high point of his political life. Thereafter he waxed and waned, but he was never a serious political threat again, although the Democrats refused to face that fact, time and again.

Happy Republicans had cause to pop the champagne by the caseload, for this 1896 victory was not just another election won, but was a watershed for the Republican party. A long struggle was over, the electorate had given the party a resounding vote of confidence, and as more voters became city dwellers every year, the Republicans proved that, with a few exceptions, *they* could benefit from big-city machines and forge an alliance with midwestern farmers and western ranchers that would keep the White House in the family for the next generation and beyond. New York, Boston, and San Francisco stood out as the major cities with Democratic majorities, but after 1896 it became routine for the Republicans to carry handily most of the large cities. Carl Degler's research showed that Chicago, Cleveland, Philadelphia, Cincinnati, Buffalo, Milwaukee, Newark, Minneapolis, Des Moines, and Syracuse all went Republican and would stay safely Republican for more than a generation. These cities easily offset the heavy Democratic majorities in Atlanta, Richmond, Nashville, and New Orleans; outside the South, twenty-six of the largest forty-four cities became Republican strongholds from 1896 onward.

The fundamental shift that took place in 1896 showed voters' change of heart. The old Democratic loyalties were in disarray; the periodic shifts from party to party, usually noticed more in off-year congressional elections, were abandoned. A Republican majority brought together middle-class voters, city dwellers, veterans, farmers, miners, factory workers, bankers, small merchants, and professional men in a way that the Democratic party had never been able to accomplish. The rejuvenated Republican party had become "the party of respectability, wealth, and the Union," Carl Degler observed. "It was also the party of progress, prosperity, and national authority . . . [appealing as much to] the poor and the immigrants of the cities . . . as they did in the silk-stocking wards."

From 1896 onward, one could safely assume that the town banker, the leading lawyer, and the owner of the town's largest mercantile establishment were all Republicans. In New England, the Republican majority became so overwhelming the joke was that the only Democrat left was the town drunk. *Respectable* and *Republican* became synonyms in the vocabularies of millions of citizens. The two-party system survived, in part, because the South still nursed its wounds and sent a phalanx of Democrats into Washington every fall to offer what was often only token opposition to Republican programs. Only when the Republicans scrapped among themselves would the Democrats have a chance in a national election. And something new had been added— Republican boosters campaigning for McKinley began referring to the "Grand Old Party." Soon the nickname stuck, abbreviated to the GOP.

The devastated Democrats also had to face some unpleasant facts from the border states. Maryland, West Virginia, and Kentucky voted for McKinley. On the other hand, Bryan's evangelical style helped carry most of the western states where silver was the chief factor in payrolls. But that alliance was tenuous, as subsequent votes proved. "Nobody knows precisely why voters behave as they do," George Mayer noted, "but the prevalence of one-party domination [after 1896] suggests that they stay with their party except in times of unusual stress." Hundreds of thousands of voters who cast ballots for the first time in 1896 became lifelong Republicans, giving the party a loyal base that Democrats could not crack until 1932.

Debts had to be paid. McKinley maneuvered his pal Hanna into the Senate by offering John Sherman a cabinet post, thus creating a vacancy to be filled by appointment. The Ohio governor bowed, but then spilled the beans to the press that he had appointed Hanna under pressure from the White House. Hanna went to the Senate, but the incident left a bad taste in the mouths of many Ohio Republicans.

Petty squabbles always bedevil incoming presidents. McKinley had his share, but a cooperative Congress was called into special session to pass the Dingley Tariff Act, which boosted rates from the already high level set by the act that bore the president's name. Business revived, wheat prices rose, and it seemed that the party's boast of good times "around the corner" had been amazingly prophetic.

One critic of the GOP left the scene in 1897, and his death was not lamented in party circles. Henry George, the noisy advocate of a single tax on land only, was buried, and his ideas almost died with him. Republicans had paid little attention to George's theories as expressed in his book *Progress and Poverty*, which had far more impact in Europe than in America. Republicans were "pragmatic" men of business or action, not thoreticians who talked and dreamed and accomplished little. Or so the stereotype ran as the nineteenth century wound down.

Mineral wealth was also on the American agenda during McKinley's White House tenure. Huge strikes of copper and silver ore in the West fueled a new wave of investment and railroad building; then the huge Klondike gold rush lured thousands to the Alaskan border with Canada. New millionaires appeared at Delmonico's restaurant to celebrate these rich mineral stakes, and the off-year elections in 1898 were a celebration of the return to prosperity, with more seats added to the Republican majorities in the House and in the Senate.

Americans began to smell the roses, and the scent of empire was also pretty strong. The Democrats under Cleveland had no desire to make Hawaii an American outpost, and the rebellion in Cuba had been ignored despite Republican pressure to recognize the rebel government. McKinley had other ideas, after the fighting in Cuba heated up. A diplomatic mission to Madrid caused a scaling back of the war against the Cuba revolutionaries, but the cooling-off period ended with the explosion of the USS *Maine* in Havana early in 1898. Spanish authorities protested that they had no part in the disaster, in which 258 died, but

New York newspapers competed in their efforts to fan the flames of war.

Onto the stage strutted Undersecretary of the Navy Theodore Roosevelt, who moved ships into the trouble zone and issued other orders in the absence of his boss, who happened to be out of town. Roosevelt also sent a message to Commodore George Dewey in the Manila harbor, ordering him to be ready to attack the Spanish fleet if war broke out. To his credit, McKinley saw that he was being badgered and began to back off. Instead of bending to the warhawks' demands, the president used diplomatic channels to seek Spanish concessions for the embattled Cubans. Lest it be forgotten, Spain in 1898 was still considered a major European power, with a stable monarchy, a far-reaching colonial empire, and what appeared to be a crack army as well as a respectable navy. No wonder McKinley was moving slowly toward a fight.

Spain tried to ward off a full-scale war by agreeing to some humiliating concessions, but McKinley fell into a diplomatic trap and was embarrassed by the obsequious Spaniards. Harassed and unsure of himself, McKinley threw the whole mess into the lap of Congress with a war message on April 11. The senator from Colorado who had cried at the 1896 convention, Henry Teller, tossed a wrench into the declaration of war by offering an amendment that pledged the United States to recognize Cuban independence, thus forswearing annexation of "the pearl of the Caribbean."

The New York newspapers got their war, McKinley stopped wringing his hands, and Theodore Roosevelt got all the glory he needed. The war with Spain lasted a merciful three months, created a new supply of veterans for the pension bureau to handle, and made the United States a colonial power—of sorts. The Philippines became an American protectorate, a naval base on Cuba was set in permanent place, Puerto Rico was annexed, and Hawaii became an American territory through the backdoor of Congress. In less than four months, the United States became an imperial power.

The Democrats, of course, objected. Bryan raised as much hell as a defeated presidential candidate can by denouncing the new course of empire that McKinley had charted, or at least approved.

Bryan was not alone in worrying about the direction the country was taking, however, and in 1899 Speaker Reed resigned to dramatize his belief that McKinley's imperialism was taking the country in the wrong direction. Most Republicans approved of McKinley's leadership, however, and Reed's sacrificial gesture had no impact whatever.

The war had been so short that Theodore Roosevelt was left with nothing to do. He had resigned his naval job to lead a band of "Rough Riders" at San Juan Hill, where he captured as much glory as newspaper banner headlines could confer on a nearsighted cavalry officer. Roosevelt talked to McKinley about a cabinet position but got nowhere with the president; he soon found a job, however, when he ran for governor of New York and won in a landslide.

Except for a brief fling at ranching, ever since Roosevelt had graduated from Harvard in the class of 1880 he had been a public servant as he served successively in the state legislature, as a federal civil-service commissioner, and as the New York police commissioner, before becoming undersecretary of the navy. He was, it seemed, always in a hurry and extremely proud of his brief western experience as a cattleman. The governor's office in Albany came alive when the forty-year-old Rough Rider took charge and soon offended some important Republicans on Wall Street by pushing for a tax on corporations. At the same time, Roosevelt harangued the state legislature into civil-service reforms he had favored while in federal service. When corruption was discovered in the office of the insurance superintendent, Roosevelt fired him despite the man's good Republican credentials. All these stirrings turned the downstate political chieftains against the young governor, and they figured out a way to get rid of him. Fate suddenly took a hand in the business when Vice President Hobart died. The bosses looked on Hobart's death as a providential sign. They would make Roosevelt the next vice president, and he would never be heard from again.

Lincoln's portrait, made after he became war weary, shows the strain of office on the fifty-five-year-old president.

Theodore Roosevelt was the youngest man ever to take the presidential office, for he was forty-two when an assassin's bullet killed President McKinley. Roosevelt's pince-nez and heavy gold watch chain were the trademarks
of respectability during his first term, 1901–1905.

An uncomfortable Calvin Coolidge posed with visiting Indian chiefs on the White House lawn around 1925.

Following his landslide victory, President Herbert Hoover rode a wave of popularity as he observed the time-honored spring ritual of tossing out the first baseball to open the 1929 season at Washington's Griffith Stadium.

Everybody liked Ike, or seemed to, when he ran far ahead of the rest of the Republicans in both 1952 and 1956. He was more comfortable in a golfing outfit, but for formal pictures he chose a businesslike dark suit.

Even in his seventies, President Ronald Reagan retained some of the handsome features of his Hollywood days, and the flag backdrop was almost obligatory in the Reagan White House.

Cartoonist Thomas Nast gave the Grand Old Party a lasting symbol when he first created an elephant labeled "The Republican Vote" for the November 7, 1874, issue of *Harper's Weekly Magazine.* The Democratic donkey, labeled here as the *New York Herald,* failed to frighten the indomitable pachyderm. The caption read: "The Third Term Panic. 'An Ass, having put on the Lion's skin, roamed about in the Forest, and amused himself by frightening all the foolish Animals he met with in his wanderings.'—Shakespeare or Bacon."

CHAPTER EIGHT

~

Bully Pulpit for a President

Theodore Roosevelt stares at us from Mount Rushmore alongside Jefferson, Washington, and Lincoln. He deserves to be among the great presidents, yet he came onto the political scene in 1900 with tattered credentials. Business leaders in his home state feared Roosevelt because he was a silver-spoon politician—the kind who inherits great wealth and then turns on his rich friends. Roosevelt was no demagogue, but some of New York's leading bankers distrusted him. New York Senator Thomas Platt wanted Roosevelt out of the way because the upstart governor was all for merit in the appointments for public jobs, and a meritocracy would spell the death-knell of an effective patronage system.

McKinley was immensely popular as the time to elect a president rolled around in 1900. The only question for the nominating convention was the selection of McKinley's running mate, a replacement for the late Garret Hobart. Massachusetts Senator Henry Cabot Lodge, a good friend of Roosevelt's, talked to the governor about accepting the post but was reminded by the ambitious Roosevelt that the vice presidency was a political graveyard. When word leaked out that Platt also wanted him on the ticket, Roosevelt became obstinate and made a deal with the senator. Platt promised he would hold off and not push the nomination without Roosevelt's consent.

To emphasize his distaste for second place, Roosevelt took the train to Washington and had an interview with McKinley. The topic of conversation was the vice presidency, and Roosevelt told

McKinley he did not want the job. No record of the conversation was kept, but it leaked out that McKinley said, in effect, "Glad to hear it, because I have somebody else in mind."

Suddenly, Roosevelt was interested. He must have secretly wanted the post, and he may have gone to Washington hoping McKinley would try to talk him into accepting it. But when Roosevelt found the president disinterested in his political future, he changed his course 180 degrees. He wanted to be vice president, after all! Still pretending he was not a candidate, Roosevelt went to the Philadelphia convention and had a wonderful time telling people he was happy where he was. Platt and his friends had other plans, and by some clever maneuvering in the smoky hotel suites they created a boomlet by playing on old enmities within the party. Hanna got wind of the deals and panicked, but McKinley would not involve himself, and within forty-eight hours it was a done deal. Hoarse delegates hoisted banners for the McKinley-Roosevelt ticket as they trooped out onto the streets where Ben Franklin had once trod.

Perhaps McKinley accepted Roosevelt's place on the ticket because Hanna was against it; and Hanna opposed Roosevelt in part because the word *trust* was becoming troublesome in the politician's vocabulary. A big-business man himself, Hanna was energized by the talk of laws to curb the giant corporations that were fixing prices, controlling railroad rates, and squeezing out competitors. Not that McKinley wanted to make a fuss about trusts, but he saw dangers in Hanna's truculent defense of trusts as beneficial to the American consumer. Convoluted logic to the contrary, Hanna insisted that trusts helped ensure American prosperity. What was good for the trusts was good for America, seemed to be Hanna's message. And it gave McKinley pause.

The 1900 campaign was a cut-and-dried affair before it moved into autumn. Bryan was chosen by the Democrats again, and his campaign attacked the imperial bent of the Republican administration and the gold standard that it sustained. Roosevelt had a great time traveling around the country, shaking thousands of outstretched hands from the rear end of an observation car and reminding voters that they had a "full dinner pail" because a Republican was in the White House. Unlike any other vice presidential candidate up to that time, Roosevelt logged 21,000 miles on his eight-week tour preaching "the four-square gospel" that ignored the issues and pleaded for "duty, responsibility, Republicanism and Americanism." As a feisty Republican gad-fly, Roosevelt was something new on the political scene. The popular newspaper columnist "Mr. Dooley" noted that McKinley stayed at home and turned Roosevelt loose. " 'Tis Teddy alone that's runnin'," Mr. Dooley said, "and he ain't runnin' he's gallopin'."

Although the "bloody shirt" was stored away, Union veterans were still active, and the GAR kept them alerted to the dangers of a Democratic victory. During the 1900 campaign a GAR commander notified members that the civil-service reform movement (which favored merit over wartime service as a qualification) was "a plan of foreign origin, imported into this country by pedants" and "antagonistic to [Union] soldiers' interests." Mark Twain, master of poking fun at the pompous, wrote that America was the most patriotic nation on the face of the earth. The patriotism, moreover, "is all lodged in the Republican party. The party will tell you so. All others are traitors."

Twain's tongue-in-cheek remarks did not hurt the Grand Old Party one bit. The Republican ticket won by almost a million-vote plurality, which seemed to show that the nation wanted to be in the race for colonies, favored a larger navy (part of the imperialistic program), and wanted no monkeying around with the currency. In the electoral college, Bryan was swamped, 292 to 155; Congress stayed Republican in both houses, but the margins of control were slightly lowered. Utah, which came into the Union in 1896 and voted for Bryan, changed its direction when Hanna persuaded leaders of the Mormon church that Bryan was unsound. The disaffection in Kansas in 1896 (when six Populists or "fusion" candidates won congressional seats) was similarly reversed.

Both parties paid little attention to the suffragettes, but the movement for a woman's right to vote was picking up support. The impetus came from the West, where Wyoming had granted women votes in territorial days and continued the practice when statehood came in 1890. By that time, Utah's territorial government was permitting women to vote, and in 1893 Colorado passed laws giving women full voting rights. Idaho moved in the same direction in 1896, but then the momentum faltered, in part because the eastern leadership saw no need to involve ladies in the messy business of politics. Partial suffrage was granted in the middle seaboard states and the South, but when McKinley was inaugurated for the second time no woman could vote for the presidential ticket in any state east of the Mississippi.

A second movement that was gaining support was the Prohibitionist party, encouraged by votes in a number of states that forbade the sale of distilled spirits or denied saloons permits to operate. The driving force for the Prohibitionists was the Anti-Saloon League, founded in 1895 as a means of pressuring state legislators and congressmen to pass laws cutting off all supplies of beer, wine, whiskey, and other "poisonous" libations. This temperance drive had zealous supporters, including the ax-wielding Carrie Nation, whose activities landed them sometimes in jail and always in the headlines. But the issues that aroused suffragettes and temperance groups were foreign to the Republican party conferences, where the chief topics included—always—tariffs, as well as some discussions of controls on immigration.

Another voting bloc going nowhere was that of the southern Negroes. In state after state, laws were enacted to impose poll taxes, "grandfather" clauses, literacy tests, and other ruses to prevent blacks from voting in the old Confederacy. The Democrats did not want their votes, and the Republicans, for the most part, decided the black-vote cause was hopeless. Wealthy southerners had called for what amounted to a Republican national policy at their Southern Industrial League convention in Atlanta. At their July 1900 meeting the SIL members called for protective tariffs, adherence to the gold standard, and government subsidies for shipyards. This plea came from what historian Woodward called "the lily-white Republicans," strong in Virginia and North Carolina but also with a following throughout the South. McKinley took several tours through the South, but the purpose was not to rejuvenate Republican support so much as to keep the fences mended for those who served as delegates to the national conventions.

Huge crowds awaited President McKinley when his entourage visited the Pan American Exposition in Buffalo six months after his second inaugural. On his second day in Buffalo, the president set up a receiving line of admirers and was shaking hands when a demented young anarchist stepped forward and shot McKinley at close range. Roosevelt was on vacation but soon hurried to the president's bedside. McKinley improved, and Roosevelt went back to a resort, convinced the president would soon recover. Three days later, McKinley died.

Three men—deranged, disappointed, or supporting some cause—had managed to evade presidential guards and kill three Republicans over the span of forty years. No other civilized western power experienced such a bloodletting over four decades, yet the American system of presidential succession and the public's acceptance of a constitutional solution were remarkable in themselves. The nation mourned, the flag-draped casket went along a muffled pathway, and the new president took charge.

At forty-two Roosevelt was the youngest man ever to take over as president. He must have known, as the funeral train moved to Canton, Ohio, that McKinley's friends were still in a state of shock. Senator Hanna was crushed but still able to talk enough to tell a friend how he felt about "that damned cowboy" who was now president. Hanna's distrust of Roosevelt was shared by half the Senate, in all likelihood, yet there is always a tendency to give a new president the benefit of the doubt. Maybe Roosevelt would calm down; maybe he would stop pushing for needless reforms. Maybe.

Roosevelt could not slow down. Gregarious, energetic, and possessed of a sense of humor, Roosevelt would enjoy the office of president more than any other man who had ever held it. Talk? The man loved to chat, converse, tell a joke, harangue a crowd, or make a speech to thousands. As a Harvard graduate he could rub elbows at a board of directors meeting, then drive a few miles and visit with policemen returning from their beats. His love for people was returned. People loved him, and it is fair to say that no president elected after Washington ever enjoyed the popularity and respect that Theodore Roosevelt attained between 1901 and 1909, when he turned the office over to his handpicked successor.

Not that Roosevelt was a sissy or pollyanna. For one thing, he never liked Democrats. As historian George Mowry noted, Roosevelt was born in a place and time "when to be a gentleman in the North was to be a Republican." Individually, Roosevelt might stomach a Democrat who came to a White House dinner; but for most of his political life, Roosevelt looked on Democrats "with a feeling akin to contempt." Was he snobbish? Yes, but the American people have never held a grudge against a rich man simply because he was rich; and Roosevelt was a blue blood who could easily convince a streetcar conductor that he was simply a good old boy who happened to be a temporary resident of the White House.

So Roosevelt was a Republican, but not the kind of Republican that Wall Street was going to embrace. For one thing, Roosevelt was interested in conservation of natural resources and parklands. He had a valuable ally in Senator Lodge, but Senators Platt, Nelson Aldrich of Rhode Island, and Matthew Quay of Pennsylvania could shut down the Capitol if they chose, so Roosevelt had to tread lightly on the key issues or risk an open fight.

One program that was noncontroversial involved beautifying the Mall in Washington. Major L'Enfant's 1791 plan for the Mall had long since been scrapped, and the Pennsylvania Railroad had a track going smack-dab across the Mall beside its passenger station. Civic-minded Washingtonians appealed for a restoration of the Mall as the center of a beautiful national capital; Roosevelt was sympathetic, especially when Republicans began talking about a memorial for Lincoln at the west end to complement the Capitol on the eastern hillside. With Roosevelt's blessing, and the agreement of the Pennsylvania Railroad president, legislation moved forward to return the Mall to L'Enfant's plan, with an awesome Union Station to be built close to Capitol Hill but not on it; agreement was sought as well on an appropriate memorial to Lincoln. Meanwhile, a Lincoln Centennial commission would make plans for a 1909 celebration. Democrats were not interested.

No Republican president ever marshaled support for a strong army and navy as did Roosevelt, not even the cold-war occupants of the White House. For one thing, Roosevelt was far better informed. In an era when Admiral Alfred T. Mahan's strictures on naval power were taken as gospel truth, Roosevelt believed in military preparedness even if Congress did not. The Philippine insurrection dragged on during Roosevelt's first years as president, but once that was settled the army returned to its peacetime role. Roosevelt was ever ready to rattle the saber, but he knew when to keep it sheathed, too.

Roosevelt was also the first president to invite a black man to come and have dinner at the White House. What could have been more innocent than to break bread with Booker T. Washington, when the Negro educator was advising the president on Alabama appointments? Yet the news that Roosevelt had dined with Washington in October 1901, only weeks after becoming president, caused a storm of abuse in the South. A Memphis newspaper given to overstatement blasted the president in an editorial, claiming the occasion was "the most damnable outrage that has ever been perpetrated by any citizen of the United States." That was one of the calmer assessments of Roosevelt's gesture toward Washington, but although shocked by the reaction, Roosevelt passed off the incident as a trivial matter. On the other hand, he never invited another black to dine at the White House.

The status of blacks in the South was a puzzlement to Roosevelt. While Hanna was alive, Roosevelt feared the Ohioan's influence with blacks might be a factor at the 1904 nominating convention, but after Hanna died the president still was perplexed. In time, both Roosevelt and his successor decided to stay out of the local fights and let the lily-white Republicans have their way. The result was that federal appointments in the South went to whites, no federal agencies were told to help the blacks denied suffrage by local laws or coercion, and blacks were excluded from convention delegations. As Roosevelt ended his second term a muckraking journalist concluded: "The fact is, the Republican party, as now constituted in the South, is even a more restricted white oligarchy than the Democratic party. In nearly all parts of the South, indeed, it is a closed corporation which controls or seeks to control all the federal offices."* Roosevelt's conduct

---

*Ray Stannard Baker, quoted in Woodward, *Origins of the New South*, 462.

after a tumult involving black troops on the Texas border seemed to confirm the president's tendency to stick with the whites' viewpoint in settling racial issues. Roosevelt ordered three companies of the blacks dishonorably discharged, including some veteran soldiers with long service records.

If 10 million southern blacks were appalled by Roosevelt's tough stance, whites in the South and elsewhere probably approved the 1906 orders. Voters like a president who exhibits courage in the face of danger. The blacks were not a political force to reckon with, but big business was. The power of big business had been recognized in the legislation aimed at curbing the various trusts, but Roosevelt was not content to let the matter rest. In his first State of the Union message to Congress, Roosevelt had warned that trusts needed to be monitored and new legislation might be required to hold them in line. The mythical saloon keeper, Mr. Dooley, was quick to see Roosevelt's attempt to play on both sides of the trust issue:

> [Trusts can be, sayeth the president] heijous monsthers built up by the inlightened intheprise ov th' men that have done so much to advance the progress of our beloved country. On wan hand I wud stamp thim undher fut; on th' other hand, not so fast. What I want more thin th' bustin' iv th' thrusts is to see me fellow countrymen happy an' continted. I wudden't have thim hate th' thrusts. . . . Lave us laugh an' sing th' octopus out iv existence.

Mr. Dooley's creator joked, but Roosevelt was serious. What Roosevelt sought were legal curbs on abuses of laissez-faire policies. Early in 1902 he sought Congress's aid, and when his party's leaders backed off, Roosevelt ordered the attorney general to file suit against a gigantic railroad combination. The creation of the United States Steel Corporation, the largest merger in the history of American business enterprise, was pulled off without a hitch; but the watchful eye of the executive branch was noted by Andrew Carnegie and his cohort Judge Elbert Gary.

Eager to whip up public support for his curbs on business behemoths, Roosevelt toured the Midwest that summer and asked audiences to help him achieve "a square deal" for all. "We do not wish to destroy corporations," Roosevelt told the crowds, "but we do wish to make them subserve the public good." Senator Hanna and his friends in the "Millionaires' Club" (as one wag called the Senate) were skeptical. Lodge could assure them that Roosevelt meant well, but they were not so sure.

As John Morton Blum and other historians have noted, Roosevelt was haunted by the specter of a bloody revolution touched off by the excesses of big business. The Socialist Eugene Debs was to the president a reincarnation of the French revolutionary Robespierre. But on the other side were the "malefactors of great wealth" who had the mind-set of King Louis XVI and were blind to the social injustices created by untrammeled industrialism. Roosevelt's effort to involve the federal government in beneficial programs was, in part, based on his belief that unless government played a positive role in solving social problems, a blowup of monumental proportions would occur.

Thus Republicans of a conservative bent instinctively distrusted their trustbuster president. Like many presidents, Roosevelt thought he could go over the heads of his critics and appeal to the people directly. He soon was chummy with newspaper reporters, established rapport with editors and publishers, and became an expert at leaking his views to cooperative newsmen to send up "trial balloons" for a public reaction.

To assist his press secretary, Roosevelt added clerks, secretaries, and messengers until the White House had a staff of thirty coming and going. "This White House is never closed," one reporter observed, "and the staff processed the average daily flow of one thousand letters, hundred of telegrams, and numerous official documents." The building itself was overflowing, and Roosevelt's solution was to extend a corridor to provide room for the executive offices while leaving the main house as a kind of museum and grand reception hall. Whether or not some of Roosevelt's children ever rode ponies in the East Room is still a moot matter. Roosevelt did make one thing official: his residence was not to be called the Executive Mansion but henceforth was officially the White House.

Details could bore Roosevelt, but he appointed his share of postmasters and undersecretaries, with the key factor being the person's party affiliation. Certain placemen, the real party hacks, were approved with a tinge of conscience. "In politics, we have to do a great many things we ought not do," Roosevelt once confessed, but for the major offices he took pains to pick men of proved ability. The biographer William Harbaugh wrote that Roosevelt drew the admiration of Lord Bryce, the perceptive British ambassador, for his selection of "eager, high-minded, and efficient" public servants. Overall, Harbaugh rated Roosevelt's choices the best of any president since James K. Polk. And Polk's appointments were the best since Thomas Jefferson's!

When necessary, Roosevelt liked to aid the Republicans and do the right thing at the same time. When the Democrats made a desperate effort to wean the substantial bloc of Jewish voters in New York away from the Republicans, Roosevelt countered with the appointment of Oscar Straus, a wealthy Jewish merchant, to the newly created post of secretary of commerce and labor. This placed Straus in charge of the bureau that handled immigration, at a time when many congressmen were considering drastic downward revisions of quotas for persons coming from eastern Europe. One measure meant to cut the flow would have forced newcomers to take a literacy test on Ellis Island. In this fight, Speaker "Uncle Joe" Cannon kept the Republicans in line, despite heavy pressure from conservative and patriotic groups that bemoaned the "mongrelization of America" in their speeches and literature.

In spite of Roosevelt's personal popularity, the Republicans made few gains in the 1902 off-year elections. Democrats gained 27 House seats, but Republicans still held a majority with 208 there and picked up 2 Senate seats. A tug-of-war was in the offing when the building of a canal across the isthmus of Panama began to be publicly debated. A French company had abandoned its work in the fever-infested jungles and sought $109 million for its claims. A second part of the arrangement called for a ninety-nine-year lease to the United States from Colombia before work on a canal could begin. The U.S. Senate ratified the proposal, but a hitch occurred when the Colombian senate rejected it and held out for more money. Roosevelt was ready to step in, when the Panamanians revolted late in 1903. In a matter of days, Roosevelt recognized the new government, and a fresh treaty allowing the United States to proceed with canal construction was ratified early in 1904. Critics said the whole deal sounded like gunboat diplomacy, but Roosevelt let them denounce the exploit as he ordered the steam shovels to their tasks.

To the majority of Americans, this swaggering president who could use his "bully pulpit" to denounce a tinhorn dictator or cuddle up to the crowned heads of Europe was about the ideal of what a president ought to be. Moreover, Roosevelt had a flair for the dramatic, as he proved in 1904 when a North African bandit kidnapped an American citizen and held him prisoner in Morocco. Roosevelt ordered naval vessels to steam to North Africa, just as the Republican convention was meeting in Chicago. Cheering delegates heard the president's message to the American consul read: "We want either Perdicaris [the American citizen] alive or Raisuli [the bandit] dead." The American was released.

Nor could Roosevelt be a passive spectator to a slugging match. The open-door policy in China, a joint United States–British venture, was jeopardized by the Russo-Japanese war in 1904. The Japanese surprised the Russians, and the world, by their rapid destruction of the imperial fleet. Roosevelt intervened and negotiated a peace settlement for which he received the Nobel Peace Prize in 1906.

If that wasn't enough, Roosevelt stepped into a scuffle between the Germans and the French over the status of Morocco and mediated the Algeciras conference in the spring of 1906. Roosevelt managed to defuse the crisis by placating the kaiser with a Franco-British entente. An amiable Senate even endorsed the president's actions with an ambiguously worded ratification.

By that time, the elections of 1904 were history. And not much history at that, for the Democrats had become the walking wounded after Roosevelt's succession of triumphs. Bryan was around, but to avoid the taint of his "free-silver" ideas the Democratic party platform specifically endorsed the gold standard. After that slap in the face, Bryan headed for the exit, and Judge Alton B. Parker, a colorless New Yorker of no particular distinction, won the presidential nomination. A host of minor party candidates also emerged, and Roosevelt beat them all without working up a sweat. He polled 7.6 million votes to 5 million for Parker. In the electoral college it was Roosevelt 336 and Parker 140. In the House, Democrats lost 42 seats, giving Republicans an edge of 250 to 136. Senate control remained safely in Republican hands for the Sixtieth Congress, 61 to 31. During the 1904 campaign Roosevelt had to take some good-natured kidding from the press. Partly in humor and partly in sarcasm, Mark Twain chided Roosevelt in *Harper's Weekly* for his election-year pitch for the veterans' vote: an executive order extending to widows the pensions of deceased Union soldiers. In his jocular biography of the president, Twain said that Roosevelt

> took San Juan Hill, without concealment, but in the most public manner. . . . Next he accepted the Vice Presidency of the Republican party, which is in the United States. Presently he became President and Government by the visitation of God. By and by, he took fourteen million dollars out of the public till and gave it away, dividing it among all elderly voters who had had relatives in the Civil War.

Roosevelt was able to laugh at his critics, as long as their remarks were made tongue in cheek.

As another Roosevelt would learn, a lot of things can go wrong for a popular president right after he wins reelection by a handsome plurality. Theodore Roosevelt learned his lessons when gruesome statistics from the Panama Canal site told of a yellow-fever epidemic that brought construction of the locks to a halt. On Wall Street, well-heeled Republicans were questioning Roosevelt's intentions, for he had pushed Secretary of State Elihu Root into making a statement on the responsibilities of big business that had not sat well with some large donors to the party coffers. Still concerned about a shoot-out between labor and business, Roosevelt prompted Root to say publicly that the best way to protect capital from labor was by giving working men a square deal. Instead of buying legislators, Root said, a better way was "that capital shall be fair . . . fair to the consumer, fair to the laborer, fair to the investor. . . . Never forget that the men who labor cast the votes, set up and pull down governments," and wealth could only be enjoyed if workingmen had faith "in American liberty and American laws." This sounded like poppy-cock to some capitalists, and downright revolutionary to others. Was this Roosevelt a Republican, or not?

Firing from the right was followed by firing from the left, or what Roosevelt regarded as the left. The newspapers and magazines, the chief sources of information for most Americans, had become enthralled with exposés of corruption in the big cities, in factories, and in the Senate. The journalistic cult was led by Upton Sinclair's shocking disclosures in his novel *The Jungle,* which told of an immigrant family's disintegration and also revealed unsanitary conditions in the Chicago meatpacking plants, describing rodents being ground into bologna and similar atrocities. David Graham Phillips's *The Treason of the Senate* portrayed the upper house of Congress as a plutocracy and named some prominent Republicans as the worst of the corrupt body. Other revealed scandals in the Standard Oil Company, as well as the role of the California railroads in corrupting legislators and newspaper editors, aroused the public until the clamor invaded the White House corridors.

Roosevelt reacted like a wounded animal. "Muckrakers!" the president shouted, and thus coined a word or at least gave an old word a new meaning as he denounced reporters who "raked muck" (a line from Bunyan's *Pilgrim's Progress*) while overlooking the better side of life. Angered by the attack on his friends in the Senate, Roosevelt savagely accused the reporters of gross distortions and implied that the public should join him in condemning their brand of "yellow journalism."

This was one fight Roosevelt was bound to lose. For the truth was that big-city machines, whether dominated by Democrats or by Republicans, were making corrupt deals with businessmen for franchises and monopolies and red-light district shenanigans. In the meatpacking business, and in the manufacture of many patent medicines, a poisonous pill or a contaminated piece of bologna was sold across the counter to an unsuspecting consumer. This was laissez-faire capitalism run riot, the muckraking journalists insisted, and they made their point. The ubiquitous Mr. Dooley had fun with his account of how the president took the news across the White House breakfast table:

> Tiddy was toying with a light breakfast an' idly turnin' over th' pages iv th' new book. . . . Suddenly he rose fr'm th' table, an' cryin': "I'm pizended," begun thrown' sausages out iv th' window. Th' ninth

wan sthruck Sinitor Biv'ridge on th' head, an' made him a blond. . . .
Sinitor Biv'ridge rushed in thinkin' that th' Prisidint was bein' assas-
synated by his devoted followers in the Sinit, an' discovered Tiddy
engaged in a hand-to-hand conflict with a potted ham.

Perhaps Roosevelt was amused, but the country was not. Sensing
the country's disgust with the errant industries, Roosevelt jumped
into the debate and had the stockyards investigated. With the
facts in hand, and aided by Senator Albert Beveridge of Indiana,
he threatened to make the findings public unless Congress enacted laws to protect consumers. Within months instead of the
usual year or two, the Pure Food and Drug Act and the Meat
Inspection Act were on the president's desk for his signature.

On other legislative matters, Roosevelt had less success during his second term. Always impatient, Roosevelt increasingly
regarded the slow processes of Congress with disdain, while
the lawmakers often took presidential energy to be excessive
zeal. Roosevelt peppered Congress with more than four hundred
special messages, and as the flow increased the reaction became
more negative. First-term cooperation faded, historian Lewis
Gould wrote, and Roosevelt's mannerisms increasingly "became
an irritant on the Hill during his second term."

A pesky Congress was bad enough, but Roosevelt had other
problems. In his 1906 State of the Union message, Roosevelt
called for laws barring corporate contributions to political campaigns and regulating the use of children in factories. Neither
proposal had much support in Congress, where a $29 million fine
against Standard Oil raised eyebrows in the Senate. Wall Street
took a distinct dislike to Roosevelt after prices tumbled in March
1907, and a recession hit after prices fell further in the autumn.
Depositors started a run on New York banks, threatening a panic
of 1893 proportions. To meet the crisis, Roosevelt tried to calm
big business by approving the pending merger of U.S. Steel with
Tennessee Coal and Iron as being no violation of antitrust laws.
To shore up New York banks, the Treasury Department sold
bonds at huge discounts to keep the banks supplied with cash.
Fears of a panic faded.

Politicians who occasionally mixed with their constituents
were amazed at the president's hold on the public imagination.

On one long trip from Washington to his home base in Idaho, Senator William Borah was struck by Roosevelt's popularity. Borah told the president that as he went up and down the train, once the passengers knew he was close to happenings in the capital, they regaled him with affectionate questions: "Well, how is Roosevelt? How is Teddy?" "I never expected to see . . . such a universal feeling of devotion to a man as the good common people of this country exhibit towards you," the baffled senator wrote "Teddy."

No doubt, the American people loved Roosevelt. Their affection was returned, but in all probability, Roosevelt's first love was the navy. He pushed Congress for more money to build battleships, a gesture applauded by the steel and shipbuilding industries. Convinced it was time to show other nations that the United States had plenty of muscle, he sent the U.S. fleet on a round-the-world goodwill mission. Westerners were not so enthusiastic about a boon for the Atlantic Coast, so they were handed relief for their water problems with laws providing for huge subsidies for irrigation projects.

For all his energy and confidence, Roosevelt also harbored a grudge against those who fought him. To aides he sometimes referred to a particular senator as a scoundrel, or to a cranky congressman as a rascal; but his real venom was directed at those who were not Republicans. When the Democratic publisher Joseph Pulitzer attacked the Panama Canal contracts as fraudulent, Roosevelt tried to bring a seditious libel charge against the *New York World* for its exposé. That move was one of Roosevelt's rare failures, as was his hope to indict the Socialist Eugene Debs for a newspaper article that blistered the Roosevelt administration. In one of his frequent messages to Congress, Roosevelt showed his animosity by asking for a curb on newspapers that "promoted anarchy." Congress ignored the message.

None of Roosevelt's pettiness was ever made public, for the reporters covering the White House felt genuine affection for the president of a kind not seen in Washington again until another Roosevelt was in the White House. Popular with the people, Roosevelt was not so beloved by big business. With the approach of 1908 some industrial leaders were concerned that a third-term boomlet might saddle them with Roosevelt for another four years. To calm such fears, Roosevelt made public his vow that he would step down in March 1909, and he groomed William Howard Taft as his handpicked successor. Roosevelt's most faithful supporters, who would become Progressive Republicans a few years thence, still kept rumors floating in the press to the effect that Roosevelt could be drafted by an enthusiastic convention.

Early in 1908 Roosevelt talked like a man who was not quitting. In his last State of the Union message he blasted "corrupt men of wealth" who used money to buy votes and newspapers, and he took a parting shot at the Supreme Court for its rulings restricting the rights of unions. It was sheer hypocrisy, Roosevelt wrote, to say "a young girl working in a factory under hazardous conditions had a 'right' freely to contract to expose herself to dangers to life and limb." After the message was read, Senator Foraker of Ohio reported that Wall Street took the president's remarks with bitter resentment. Speaker Cannon was of a similar mind. Roosevelt, Cannon said, "wants everything, from the birth of Christ to the death of the devil."

No Republican was more upset with Roosevelt in 1908 than Senator Aldrich. His resentment went back a few years to the fight in the Senate for Roosevelt's bill to regulate railroad freight rates. Aldrich deserted Roosevelt and turned management of the bill over to Senator Ben Tillman, a southern Democrat. The strange bedfellows, Roosevelt and Tillman, applied all the pressure the White House could, but the Georgian came up two votes short. In desperation, Roosevelt persuaded Senator Allison of Iowa to rescue the bill. In May 1906 the bill passed, but the scars remained. From that time forward, Aldrich tried to thwart Roosevelt's programs, and more than one newspaperman called Aldrich "J. P. Morgan's floor broker in the Senate." (Aldrich was also the father-in-law of John D. Rockefeller Jr.) After the death of Mark Hanna early in 1904, Aldrich moved forward as the power broker in the Senate, and he wanted Roosevelt out of the White House in March 1909, or else.

"Roosevelt had crossed the Rubicon," historian Edward Cadenhead observed, and was trying to carry the Republicans with him. The president hoped to convince reluctant Republicans that a strong federal government could be a positive force in society, by helping people achieve a fair share of the rewards created by a freewheeling, laissez-faire economy. Senator Lodge listened to him sympathetically, but Senators Quay, Platt, and Aldrich thought Roosevelt had turned into a radical and had to go. So Roosevelt told convention leaders that he wanted his secretary of war, Taft, to get the nod. A behind-the-scenes effort to give Governor Charles Evans Hughes of New York the nomination was a Wall Street concoction, but Roosevelt outfoxed Hughes's supporters by making him the head of the state's convention delegation. That cooked Hughes's goose, because convention etiquette forbade the nomination of a seated delegate. Roosevelt gloated a bit. "If Hughes is going to play the game, he must learn the tricks," the president said.

Democrats, still in shock from Roosevelt's popularity, turned again to Bryan in a lackluster effort based chiefly on an antitariff platform that generated little cash for the bruising campaign ahead. Ordinary citizens were not asked to give money to the party, but business leaders and corporations usually worked both sides of the fence, giving a token amount one year to the Democrats and a large sum to the Republicans. Then, four years later, the amounts might be reversed, depending on the way political winds blew. Judges and higher officials appointed by the president were also expected to make their gratitude known in tangible form. The money thus raised was poured into campaign literature, headquarters staff, telephone and telegram bills, railroad fares for "the right people," and sign painters. In a perfect year, contributions and expenses would nearly be in balance. In bad years, "fat-cat" contributions in the postelection months were sought to erase campaign debts. Losing candidates also had more than political debts to pay.

Republicans had plenty of cash in 1908. Money was not the problem. Taft was reluctant to go on the road. Whistle-stop campaigning had no appeal for the heavyset Ohioan. Bryan made so much noise the party leadership decided Taft ought to be out shaking hands, so he took a western tour in September and learned to smile and lean over the rear end of an observation car for the handshakes sought by eager spectators. Debs, running as the Socialist candidate, was popular in the German American communities but had little following elsewhere.

Oklahoma had been granted statehood in 1907 and had elected a headstrong Democratic governor in Charles Haskell, who was smoked out by the muckrakers as being on the Standard Oil payroll. So was Senator Foraker, but as a "lame duck" Roosevelt knew who was untouchable and who wasn't. In September as the campaign heated up the president called on Haskell to resign as governor or get off the Standard "boodle list." Bryan defended Haskell, who happened to be treasurer of the Democratic campaign committee, and Roosevelt replied with more pressure on Haskell, who eventually quit his party post. This was about the last battle Roosevelt fought while in the White House.

Bryan fought his good fight and gave up, having struck out for the third time. Taft beat him in the popular vote, 7.6 million to 6.4 million, and Bryan was swamped in the electoral college, with 162 votes to Taft's 321. Republicans slipped slightly in the House but held the Senate firmly.

The report that President Taft could not fit into the White House bathtubs was slightly exaggerated. He could get in, but getting out was not easy, since he weighed 350 pounds. Not long after March 1909, a new tub was installed. If Taft was going to fight for his mentor's program, that would involve taking on Aldrich and his cohorts, so he needed to be as clean as a hound's tooth. In the new administration, the bathtubs would be larger, and so would the antitrust division of the Justice Department.

CHAPTER NINE

Trouble in High Places

Whether Theodore Roosevelt spoke softly but carried a big stick, or preferred instead to use strong-arm tactics in a pinch, the ex-Rough Rider had kept a group of insurgent Republicans in check during his two presidential terms. With Roosevelt out of the White House, these senators and congressmen were soon labeled the "progressive wing" of the Republican party, and they chafed under Taft's leadership. For Senators Robert La Follette of Wisconsin and Beveridge of Indiana, in the vanguard of the Progressive movement, there was a need for reforms at all levels. Taft was not sympathetic to their pleas for election reforms, and demands for an income tax, woman suffrage, and direct election of senators were all on the Progressive agenda.

The income tax problem arose because the Supreme Court had repeatedly held that taxes on personal incomes were unconstitutional. As revenues from tariffs were falling, the cost of running the federal government rose with the increased expenses of a huge navy and a growing federal bureaucracy. A modest 2 percent tax on incomes over $4,000 had been overturned by the Supreme Court, and the Progressives wanted an amendment that would clarify the matter for all time. Western states had allowed women to vote, but the suffragettes were jailed and harassed in the East, and Progressives listened to them with great empathy. Twenty-nine states had direct election of senators by 1910, but the Old Guard in the Senate did not want to talk about the proposition, which would require all senators to scramble for popular votes every six years.

The younger Republicans itched for a fight and found it when Cannon sought reelection as Speaker. Taft called for some downward revision of the tariff, and Cannon, sensing a battle, said he would do the president's bidding. Aldrich, as head of the Senate Finance Committee, had other ideas; he packed his committee so that he could block any bill from the House that cut tariffs beyond a nominal amount. Meanwhile, the Progressives in the House came within a whisker of defeating Cannon in his bid for the speakership. Only timely intervention, with aid from Tammany Democrats, saved Cannon—temporarily. The House tariff bill gave no great alarm to protectionists, but Aldrich's committee found 847 items that needed revision.

Aldrich almost met his match in Senator Jonathan Dolliver of Iowa. For his entire career, Dolliver had apologized to his constituents about the party's devotion to a protective tariff. His head crammed with facts and statistics, Dolliver tore into the Aldrich revisions. The attack by Dolliver was dumbfounding, for here was a Republican whose criticism of the Aldrich faction made a lot of sense. Standpatters in the Senate were not moved, however, and a toned-down version of the Payne-Aldrich tariff bill passed. Taft, who had asked for lower duties, found he would have to take half a loaf or none. The president took the half-loaf, which made the Progressives howl and delighted the Old Guard.

Taft might have left well enough alone, but he couldn't pass up the chance to make his first year in office look good. He went out West and made speeches, ate rich food, and made the mistake of bragging in public about how good the Payne-Aldrich bill was for America. Progressives read the newspaper accounts of Taft's speech and were stunned. Then "Uncle Joe" Cannon told his constituents the young whippersnappers in the House who had tried to oust him were nothing but a bunch of "traitors." The Republican party was about to experience the biggest and most explosive split in its history.

Taft probably was not aware of the groundswell of Progressive resentment until he stepped into a controversy between the secretary of the interior and an old friend of Roosevelt's, Gifford Pinchot. Pinchot, the head of the forestry service, made public his accusations of wrongdoing against his superior, Secretary Richard Ballinger. Taft, loyal to his cabinet member, fired Pinchot. Within weeks, the Progressives decided to make the Ballinger-Pinchot fight into a public scandal, and the upshot was that Ballinger resigned.

The Progressives, feeling they were on a roll, then went after Speaker Cannon. After months of sapping and mining Cannon's territory, the young Republicans forced a showdown vote in March 1910. Cannon was stripped of his powers in the Rules Committee, which was made into a regular body with twelve members and a powerful chairman. Humiliated, Cannon retreated but did not surrender.

Then, with great fanfare, Theodore Roosevelt came home from his African hunting trip and a triumphant European tour. The latchstring was always out for old friends, particularly old Republican friends, who called at Roosevelt's Long Island mansion. When Governor Hughes asked for help in pushing a direct-primary bill through the New York legislature, Roosevelt signed on but soon found himself involved in an unpleasant petty party squabble. Taft appointed Hughes to the Supreme Court, leaving Roosevelt isolated and mired in a local squabble that he did not relish.

Typically, when the going got rough, Roosevelt decided to get out of town. Indeed, Roosevelt probably had intended to be a good former president and keep quiet, but that was not possible, given his temperament and energy. Taft was doing his best to break up the trusts, but for Roosevelt that was not enough. After seeing that his friend Henry Stimson was nominated for governor, Roosevelt took a sixteen-state tour of the West and made a remarkable speech at the John Brown "battlefield" dedication in Kansas, where he adopted the Progressive agenda and struck a blow against the "mossback" Republicans. Roosevelt added to his list of reforms by pushing for workers' compensation laws, a vigorous conservation program, and government intervention when private property was misused or wealthy groups ignored "the interests of the whole nation." Roosevelt's plea for social justice and a "square deal" for workers, farmers, and capitalists was fully reported in the eastern newspapers. Not long thereafter, Roosevelt and Taft met in New Haven; instead of being a happy meeting between the new president and his old boss, the conference broke up on a sour note.

The off-year elections in 1910 revealed a widening split in the Republican ranks but no deep chasm. Supporters of the tariff bill had to apologize to some constituents, but most Progressive Republicans were reelected while dozens of standpatters lost their seats. In California, Hiram Johnson, a rising reformer, took control of the Republican organization from the conservatives by divorcing himself from the Southern Pacific Railroad's stranglehold. Final returns showed the House was Democratic by a margin of 228 to 161. The Senate was no longer a Republican playground, with the GOP margin falling to ten seats: 51 to 41. Aldrich retired, and Beveridge lost his bid for reelection.

The end of Republican party unity came early in 1911, when the party rebels announced the formation of the National Progressive Republican League, with Senators La Follette and Jonathan Bourne of Oregon heading the list of founding members. All together, the statistics were not impressive, for only eight senators, six governors, and a dozen or so congressmen made the declaration of insurgency. Roosevelt was asked to join the new group but begged off.

Taft added to his own woes by calling a special session of Congress to ratify a trade agreement with Canada. Instead of finding smooth sailing, the treaty exposed all kinds of gaps in party unity, and the debate grew rowdy when a prominent Democrat praised the accord because it would eventually lead to the Stars and Stripes floating over Canada. Canadians were hardly amused. Even though Taft won his congressional approval, north of the border the debate had caused great resentment. Finally, Canada rejected the treaty, leaving Taft empty-handed after a three-month-long futile demonstration on Capitol Hill.

Taft was nobody's fool, and when the law books were consulted, he had accomplished a great deal more than his predecessor in the field of trust-busting. But Taft's way was the quiet, steady manner of a trained, careful lawyer; he could not be the reporters' pal or hold a reunion for his former comrades-in-arms. With dogged determination, Taft took the antitrust law and said it "ought to be enforced, and I propose to enforce it." Standing behind his attorney general, Taft was as good as his word. The Supreme Court returned the favor and stood behind Taft as it ordered the breakup of the Standard Oil and American Tobacco corporations. In his four years as president, Taft brought more antitrust actions than Roosevelt had in seven years. Yet in popular history Taft has become the friend of big business and Roosevelt is alluded to as the foremost trustbuster.

"Progressivism" appealed to many voters in 1911 because it was new, and the name itself connoted a change in direction for the country that was on the verge of becoming a major industrial nation. One vital statistic told the story—the number of weekly newspapers in America would peak at around 12,000 in the days ahead. Soon daily newspapers entered most households as thousands of farmers and farmworkers abandoned their toilsome life for wages in factories or salaries in the rising skyscrapers appearing in New York, Chicago, Cleveland, and other northern metropolitan areas. Streetcar lines made suburbs attractive, home building surged, and the rise of the motion picture theater made town-city entertainment cheap and attractive to citizens who once headed for bed when the sun went down. Perhaps most significant of all the changes was the increasing number of automobiles moving along the nation's inadequate highways. A Model T Ford sold for $850, and clever salesmen could arrange for a purchase on the installment plan.

So change was in the air, even literally, as the Wright brothers had proved with their Kitty Hawk flight. Airplanes from the Wright factory were demonstrated during Roosevelt's second term, and competing companies in England and France made plans to invade the American market.

Indeed, change was everywhere, except in the inner sanctum of the Republican party. Aldrich and Hanna were gone, but Lodge was very much alive, and so were Elkins, Platt, Quay, and a conservative phalanx that viewed change with a jaundiced eye. After the Canadian treaty fiasco, the stock market sold off and many of the leading industrial leaders voiced their lack of confidence in Taft. They thought his ardor for trust-busting grew out of his frustration in other endeavors. Not that they would rush to embrace Roosevelt, if he came out of retirement, but the idea persisted even after the former president wrote an open letter in which he made his 1912 plans explicit. "I am not a candidate," Roosevelt wrote an admirer, but in newspaper offices, stockbrokers' ticker stalls, and corporation boardrooms there were plenty of skeptics.

Several events moved Roosevelt from the sidelines into the main arena. Senator La Follette, apparently believing he could count on Roosevelt's support, announced in June 1911 that he was a candidate for the presidential nomination. Now the Progressives had a public man they could rally behind, provided Roosevelt had been serious in his letter disavowing another presidential campaign. Roosevelt had been upset by the firing of Pinchot, for he thought Taft had sold out to the lumber and mining interests that had long opposed Pinchot's conservationist policies. Fuel was added to Roosevelt's burning resentment when Taft ordered the attorney general to sue the U.S. Steel Corporation to force divestment of the Tennessee Coal and Iron business. Roosevelt had told the steel companies there was no need to worry about an antitrust suit; the order from Taft to his legal adviser called Roosevelt's judgment into question. Roosevelt was enraged; Wall Street was greatly annoyed. Taft was sure he had done the right thing.

La Follette's summertime announcement had stoked the embers but had not set off a prairie wildfire of support for the Progressive movement. Roosevelt perceived the lack of fire in La Follette's demeanor and must have been pleased when the powerful president of the Baltimore and Ohio Railroad made a public endorsement of Roosevelt as the best candidate the Progressives could choose.

The railroad magnate's backhanded slap and other sniping from the wings angered La Follette. Early in December 1911 he asked for a meeting with Roosevelt to clear the air, as Progressive Senator Borah of Idaho began sounding out other lawmakers about their intentions in 1912. Roosevelt apparently told La Follette that, as far as he was concerned, the nomination was

La Follette's; *but* he did not rule out a draft movement if his supporters could muster one.

Apart from presidential skirmishing, 1911 proved to be a good year for the Progressives. A Nebraska Republican, George Norris, was pushing constitutional amendments through the House, which was controlled by Democrats amenable to reforms. Two significant proposed constitutional amendments, one introduced in 1909, slowly made their way through the legislative maze. One called for a tax on incomes; the other dropped the inner-sanctum method of selecting senators and opened the Senate to citizens elected directly by their constituents. If Cannon had still been Speaker and Aldrich still in the Senate, these reforms would probably have died in committee. Within eighteen months they would become the Sixteenth and Seventeenth Amendments to the Constitution.

The Progressives were shoving the Republican party into the twentieth century, whether the Old Guard in the Senate liked it or not (and they didn't). Before 1912 the states having presidential preference primaries had not been in the limelight. The national party conventions were controlled by the highest level of officialdom—governors, senators, congressmen, state legislators, bosses of local machines, and wealthy party supporters—with spots on nominating delegations awarded to safe, loyal party regulars. The Progressives saw state presidential primaries as a way to give the process over to the voters at the grassroots level. La Follette's supporters were keen for such a reform, which was exactly what the Old Guard Republicans did not want, and when Progressives began calling for state primaries to create "a weapon in the hands of the people," the standpatters cringed.

Fate stepped in to make Roosevelt's decision easier. La Follette, already distraught over personal problems, lost control at a meeting of publishers and spoke for two hours in a wandering diatribe that indicated he was on the verge of a nervous breakdown. La Follette's closest friends realized that the Progressives must switch to Roosevelt or see the movement collapse. Before the month was over, Roosevelt made up his mind, and on February 24 he sent out the word: my hat is in the ring.

Taft was furious, Lodge was bewildered, and the Democrats were scared. Roosevelt was so popular that the chances of beating the former president in November seemed remote. The only hope would be that the Old Guard could block Roosevelt's nomination and keep Taft as the Republican standard-bearer. Speaker Champ Clark was eager to win the Democratic nomination and appeared to be the Democratic front-runner.

To sugarcoat the pill so his fellow Republicans could swallow it, Roosevelt explained his reentry into politics as an attempt to promote Progressive programs. Taft, he implied, had failed; Roosevelt said he had trusted a man who could not be trusted. Waving a sheaf of endorsements from the governors of seven states, Roosevelt announced he would enter the presidential primaries and fight to seat Progressive delegates at the June nominating convention. From California, Maine, Ohio, and Kansas reports came of support from regular Republicans who were eager to join Roosevelt in his crusade to revitalize Progressivism. Less enthusiasm was evident in New York, Pennsylvania, and the South, where the Republicans had few officeholders but plenty of clout at the national conventions.

Roosevelt, fifty-four and full of beans, welcomed the primary battles and entered all of the thirteen state presidential contests. The campaign was not pretty. Roosevelt tried to make Taft look like a traitor to the Progressive cause, while Taft (in great discomfort) accused Roosevelt of betraying him personally and trying to stir up class hatred. Meanwhile, La Follette recovered from his winter setback and ran in several of the primaries as an alternative to Roosevelt. In the North Dakota primary, the first one held, La Follette won in the three-man race; most embarrassing of all, Taft received only 1,659 votes, an abysmal number considering there were nearly 1,700 federal employees in the state!

Newspapers played up the North Dakota win for La Follette, but the results were deceptive. As more states voted it was clear that Roosevelt had greater appeal than any other Republican candidate. When the state primaries ended, Roosevelt had won 278 delegates, Taft 46, and La Follette 36.

During the rest of the century, a fast start out of the gate in the state primaries often created a bandwagon sentiment that carried the early victor into an easy win at the convention. The 1912 primary wins worked in the opposite way, since they only increased the determination of the Old Guard Republican leadership that Roosevelt must be rejected at the Chicago convention. During the campaign, Roosevelt did nothing to pacify the Old Guard. Instead, he talked at length about such reforms as an initiative and referendum that would recall judges and overturn judicial decisions. Declaring himself a "true conservative," Roosevelt defined conservatism as the philosophy of "he who insists that property shall be the servant and not the master of the commonwealth." His call for federal aid to the unemployed was another strike against Roosevelt in the boardrooms where campaign contributions were discussed. The captains of industry had long regarded Roosevelt as an unpredictable maverick, but now he was a dangerous radical. The Old Guard had made certain that the convention credentials committee would be safely favorable to Taft.

Roosevelt was not naive. He knew that the inner workings of the convention would probably be fixed to hurt his chances, so he took the precaution of going to Chicago before the convention began. There were rumors that "frauds would be attempted," Progressive supporters were told. Roosevelt welcomed delegates to a meeting on the day before the convention started and boasted to newspapermen (who asked how he was feeling) that he was "strong as a bull moose." Henceforth, to reporters the Progressive campaign was a call to action from the "Bull Moose" candidate. Skeptics observed that physical strength plus vigilance would be needed to keep the convention from becoming a farce controlled by Taft's men.

Warnings did not help, for Taft's men took charge from the opening day, and from that point on Roosevelt's chances of winning the regular Republican nomination were doomed. Breaking precedent, for no other candidate had ever appeared on a convention floor before the balloting, Roosevelt strode into the convention to an ovation the chairman could not control. But that was about all the regulars failed to keep in line. The solid South was for Taft, and with that base the credentials committee awarded Taft men 238 of the 252 contested seats. Furious at the heavy-handed methods displayed by the Old Guard, the Progressive floor managers despaired and instructed their delegations to stage a walkout before the balloting began. Rebellious to the last, 107 hardy Republicans remained in the hall and voted for Roosevelt. Taft had 561 votes on the first ballot, and La Follette had 41. So that battle was over. Outside the convention hall, the 343 nonvoting delegates who supported Roosevelt made noises, shouting "Highway Robbery!" and vowing the results would be overturned. Indoors, jubilant regular Republicans tooted their horns in derision and triumph.

"The Old Guard dies," a veteran reporter noted, "but it doesn't surrender." Former Senator Beveridge, not without some prejudice, recalled the events and denounced "the incredible high-handedness of the reactionaries" who were running the show. They were ready to do anything, Beveridge insisted, "short of murder . . . it was anything to beat Roosevelt."

Undaunted, the Roosevelt forces moved swiftly, convening in a hired hall, where their candidate reminded them that they had witnessed a blatant theft. "Thou Shalt Not Steal" was to be their watchword as Roosevelt urged the disappointed delegates to form a national Progressive party and go forth to battle in November under the Progressive banner. The riotous delegates vowed to return early in August and start a third party on the election trail to victory.

Democrats, sensing their chance of winning after so many decades of frustration, chose the reformer Governor Woodrow Wilson of New Jersey, who was about as Progressive as Roosevelt in many respects and far ahead of Taft in his desire for change. The Democratic strategy was simple: let the Republicans kill each other off and hold on to the traditional party base.

The halcyon mood of February faded in August as the Roosevelt bandwagon slowed down, allowing many of the early-bird governors who had pleaded for his candidacy to head for the sidelines. The number of senators dwindled, too; Hiram Johnson was faithful, but a handful of would-be Bull Moosers also declined to endorse a separate candidacy. Where the regular Republican convention was dominated by austere conservatives, the Progressive meeting had a lunatic-fringe element that was far more interested in extolling issues than winning the campaign. This was evident in the platform, which included a plank calling for legalized "social and industrial justice," whatever that meant. The entire platform was labeled "A Contract with the People," which gave it a Populist ring that made some of the delegates suspect they were also tilting at windmills. But confidence exuded from the platform as Roosevelt was duly nominated and Hiram Johnson of California chosen as his vice presidential candidate.

Although all the candidates tried to reach out to the two major voting blocks—farmers and workers—the real creative energy in all three party campaigns was supplied by the growing middle class, which was by nature conservative in outlook and voting patterns. Senator Francis Newland of Nevada, a powerful Democrat, perceived the changes taking place around him and lamented the disaffection of men-on-the-make as their incomes rose. "For years past," Newland confided to a friend, "it has been the case that whenever a Democrat makes fifty thousand dollars, he became a Republican." The ante went up in the years ahead, but the exodus Newland saw in 1912 would accelerate throughout the remainder of the century.

With the ardor of crusaders, the Progressives went back home and arranged for their candidate to be on the ballot in every state. Providence seemed to take a hand in the matter when a deranged gunman in Milwaukee tried to kill Roosevelt, but the bullet was slowed by a thick sheaf of papers protecting the candidate's heart and barely grazed him. Dramatically, Roosevelt wiped off the wound with his handkerchief and made the scheduled speech to enormous cheering. Wilson talked like the Princeton professor he had once been but made it clear that the Democrats deserved a chance to show what their brand of Progressivism could accomplish with White House leadership.

In one sense, 1912 was 1896 all over again. "The main issue is the tariff," a *New York Times* editorial proclaimed on the eve of election day as the paper gave Wilson a backhanded endorsement: "He has had advantage over Mr. Roosevelt in appealing much more directly and cogently to the good sense and sound judgment of the 'people.'" On that same day, the *Times* noted that on Wall Street the betting favored Wilson.

"The Wilson odds have been 4 to 1 for some time," the *Times* reported, while "most of the Roosevelt betting has been that he would run second." Two days before the voting, the once solidly Republican newspaper took notice of the assassination attempt, which had aroused "of late, intense sympathy." Having said that, the *Times* noted that as the campaign wound down, Roosevelt had changed his tactics. "To his native self-confidence there has been added a fierce fanatical impulse," the editorial observed, capped by Roosevelt's "unbridled criticism" of the courts for their conservative stands on business regulation. The net effect of this kind of attack, the *Times* predicted, would be an undermining of both the Roosevelt and the Taft candidacies, causing voters to side with the staid Wilson and shy away from appeals "to the passions and prejudices and appetites of the unthinking."

Roosevelt, cocky and confident, went back to Oyster Bay to await the results. Republicans soon learned that splitting the vote was just as disastrous as running for office during a depression. Nearly everywhere in the North and West, the combined Republican vote totaled more than that for Wilson, but the split vote gave the Democratic candidate states that had not gone Democratic in a generation. The popular vote gave Wilson 6.2 million, Roosevelt 4.1 million, and Taft 3.4 million. The real shock was in the electoral college, where Wilson had 435, Roosevelt 88, and Taft only 8 (Vermont and Utah). For the first time since 1852, Iowa gave its electoral votes to a Democrat. Thus Wilson, like Lincoln, wound up with 42 percent of the vote but won the election, which turned out to be the worst electoral college whipping ever administered to the Republicans. True, no third party had ever done so well (or would), but Roosevelt's candidacy had been an exercise in futility.

In the Congress, Democrats took over the Senate for the first time in decades, with a margin of 51 to 44, while in the House their margin was 291 to 127. A Progressive was elected to the Senate from Washington, leaving the Old Guard with a shrinking band led by Lodge of Massachusetts. Among the Republican casualties was Joe Cannon from Illinois, his second loss in over forty years of campaigning.

Happy with Wilson's victory, the *New York Times* had some consolation for Republicans. "It is to the interest of the Nation that the Republican Party should be preserved as an organized, coherent opposition," the *Times* suggested. "The public welfare is not served by the collapse of a great party, by the rise of discordant factions in place of a compact organization." Let the Republicans rebuild on their historic foundations and shove aside discordant "influences that have diminished [their] estate." Rarely was such good sportsmanship evident in the nation's newspapers. As bad as the wreckage appeared on the day after the 1912 election, the Republicans took solace in totaling the votes for the two Republican rivals. The nation was still ready to acknowledge the Republicans as the majority party, at least at the executive level; if Wilson could be limited to a one-term presidency, little harm would be done.

And what of Taft? He was far from finished. A judgment from the heartland of America reflected more than local sentiment. Taft, the *Tulsa Daily Democrat* noted, "the worst beaten man in American political history, is still an admirable and worthy national figure." The opposition newspaper praised Taft as "an amiable and high-minded and able man, [who] was made to answer for the sins of two or three perverse generations of stand-patters, treasurer-looters, and bunco steerers. . . . He is discredited, but not disgraced."

The legacy of nearly fifty years of Republican leadership, either from presidents or from strong congressmen, was that American policy had become expansionist, with a protective tariff almost a given, along with an enlarged naval force and a strong commitment to veterans of the Civil and Spanish-American Wars. Abroad, the Franco-British entente and the growing naval rivalry between England and Germany seemed remote and, to introverted Americans, mainly irrelevant.

If Cleveland had been a conservative in disguise, maybe the prissy Princetonian might prove to be far easier to deal with than the rambunctious Roosevelt had been. Wall Street took Wilson's election in stride as the calendar leaf was flipped to March 4, 1913.

William Jennings Bryan had helped ensure Wilson's nomination by giving his support to the New Jersey governor, and his payoff was a prime cabinet post as secretary of state. Bryan, who has been depicted late in the century as something of a buffoon, was in 1913 an able and experienced politician. He was by nature a peacemaker, but his abilities were tested early on by the growing problems along the Rio Grande border, where Mexican guerrillas camped and sometimes moved for safety or loot. Republicans looked on Wilson's Mexican policy with disdain, particularly after the president tried to ease tensions following the rebellion that ousted longtime strongman Porforio Díaz, who had run Mexico most of the time since 1877. Wilson proved to be inept in his efforts to democratize the Mexicans, and when he proposed giving $25 million in "hush money" to Colombia (whose politicians were still smarting from the Panamanian revolt), Republicans reacted with sarcastic condemnation of the scheme. Then Roosevelt returned from one of his foreign jaunts, saw the Colombian payment as a slap in the face for his Panamanian policy, and howled to high heaven with criticism of the president.

The Republican focus on Wilson's miscues in foreign policy was partly owing to the success of Wilson's domestic program. (It is axiomatic in American politics to raise hell on the foreign front if the opposition's domestic agenda is hale and hearty, and vice versa.) The two constitutional amendments were ratified during Wilson's first term, and late in 1913 the Federal Reserve Act creating a federally controlled but decentralized banking system was enacted. Pushed by Senator Carter Glass of Virginia, the law was intended to control discount rates and prevent the credit supply from going out of control when panics or depressions loomed. Essentially a conservative measure, the law also required reserve banks to keep a large gold deposit to back up banknotes issued from regional centers. The Clayton Anti-Trust and Federal Trade Commission Acts of 1914 gave teeth to older, less effective legislation. Organized labor was particularly heartened by the Federal Trade Commission's provision that exempted unions from antitrust laws and another that stopped the practice of issuing injunctions to break strikes or prevent peaceful picketing.

Wilson's domestic programs were humming along when the world fell into the chasm of a horrendous European war that began in August 1914 and soon involved all the major powers. Prodded by Bryan, who wanted the United States to adopt a strict code of neutrality, Wilson affirmed a national determination to stay out of the war. Republicans could not quarrel with this stance, but they thought the army and navy needed more attention and launched a preparedness movement as the fall by-elections grew heated. Roosevelt and Henry Stimson spearheaded a plan for training camps for volunteers as Wilson issued a proclamation of neutrality. Roosevelt tried to keep the tattered remains of the Progressives together, but the sledding was rough. Most of the enthusiasts of 1912 had wandered back into the regular fold, or were headed that way. In the fall elections, Republicans picked up 69 House seats, while the Progressives lost 8 of the 17 seats they had won in 1912. But the Progressives kept their spoiler role in the Senate. Their candidates cut into Republicans' votes and thus increased the Democrats' margin to 56 out of 96 votes in the upper house.

Then the war in Europe heated up. America's Anglophilic literati decided Germany was about to destroy western civilization and reacted with fund drives for the Allies and numerous pro-Allied magazine articles; along the Atlantic seaboard, citizens seemed to swallow the Allies' propaganda like pabulum. The Germans didn't help their cause with clumsy efforts to bid for American neutrality, although sentiment for the kaiser and his armies was manifest in river towns such as Cincinnati and St. Louis and among the enclaves of German immigration in Wisconsin, the Dakotas, Kansas, and Texas. As these second-generation Americans perceived the direction in which Wilson was taking the country, many of them would switch their political loyalties away from the Democrats and vote Republican for the first time in the 1916 presidential elections.

Peace was on the president's tongue, but the nation was moving toward a fight in 1915 after the *Lusitania* was sunk by a German submarine. Republicans sensed that Wilson was weak in the hinterlands and believed that a strong candidate could wrest the White House away from the pince-nez president. Party insiders liked former Governor Charles Evans Hughes of New York, who had a reputation for breaking up trusts but was generally acknowledged to be brilliant, absolutely honest, and highly electable. Taft had appointed him to the Supreme Court in 1910, so to make the race Hughes had to resign from his safe seat and slide into a hot one.

In many respects Hughes was similar to Roosevelt—a loving family man with Ivy League schooling and impeccable family credentials. The real difference between them was that Roosevelt laughed a good deal and loved to shake hands with the crowds. Perhaps because of his years on the bench, Hughes was staid, reserved, and, as one admirer admitted, "something of a cold fish."

There was no great effort to draft Roosevelt to run again in 1916, although he would have loved one more good scrap. He stayed out of the presidential primaries but let it be known that he would accept a call from the party regulars at the Chicago convention. No such call ever came. Instead, the party let the keynoter, Ohio Senator Warren Harding, reconcile the Bull Moosers with his call for unity, and in a rather cut-and-dried affair the delegates chose Hughes. The Progressives made a brief try at another presidential campaign but were upset when Roosevelt turned them down and suggested they choose Senator Lodge. Ever hopeful, the Bull Moose "convention" nominated Roosevelt as its candidate, but Roosevelt's reply from Oyster Bay was not enthusiastic, so a die-hard group sought another convention to legitimize the nominating process. The result was that the burned-out Roosevelt again had to say no, and the Progressive movement petered out. Some Bull Moosers returned to the Republican fold, and others defected to Wilson.

Wilson was easily renominated and stayed close to the White House, while the Democrats ran on the theme "He kept us out of war" until it became a tiresome cliché. Hughes hit the road making sensible speeches from the platform of the observation car but was unable to crack any jokes. The curious crowds came but were far from enraptured after Hughes spoke. In that blessed time before opinion polls created their own results, the consensus among reporters following the two candidates was that the race was almost a dead heat.

The situation in California needed deft handling, for Governor Hiram Johnson was still a power in Republican circles despite his defection to the Bull Moosers in 1912. The *Los Angeles Times,* owned by the archconservative Harrison Gray Otis, was unforgiving, however; Otis wanted no part of Johnson and insisted that Hughes could win California on his own. Whether it was planned or not, Hughes and Johnson wound up in the same hotel on a hot summer night in Long Beach; but Hughes did not go out of his way for a perfunctory visit with Johnson, who was now the Republican candidate for the Senate. Nominally in charge of the Hughes effort in California, Johnson told supporters: "I don't know any reason why we should break our necks in this campaign." Later, Hughes said it was all a misunderstanding and apologized. Johnson snarled, ran a separate campaign, and had nothing good to say about Hughes.

The point may be overblown, but the fact is that when Hughes and Wilson went to bed on election night, it appeared that Hughes would be the next president. But during the night the California returns started coming in on the telegraph lines, and by Thursday noon it was apparent that Wilson had won California's 13 electoral votes, and hence the election. Had Hughes won California, he would have beaten Wilson, 267 to 264; but as it turned out, Wilson had 277 votes to Hughes's 254. Did the rift between Johnson and Hughes cost the Republicans an election? Look at the final figures: Johnson was elected to the Senate with a 300,000-vote plurality, while Hughes lost to Wilson by 4,000 votes.

In the popular voting, Wilson was ahead 9.1 million to 8.5 million. Also surprising was the third-party vote in some states, with Allan Benson, the Socialist candidate, winning as much as 15 percent.

Wilson "kept us out of war," but not for long.

CHAPTER TEN

~~~

An Era of Good Feeling—
Version II

W ilson's decision to seek war
with Germany, coming only weeks after his second inauguration,
left Republicans in a quandary. They could go along, and flaunt
their patriotism as well as the nearest Democrat; or they could
drag their feet and try to keep the United States neutral in a world
at war. In the House, Democrats held only a six-vote advantage;
in the Senate, 53 Democrats faced 42 Republicans.

Wilson jeopardized his program by going up to Capitol Hill
and confronting Congress directly. Since Jefferson, no president
had appeared in person before Congress. Wilson considered the
office of president akin to the British prime minister's post, and
he acted accordingly by going face-to-face with the Congress.
In January 1917 he told the Senate that the United States ought
to participate in a postwar plan for collective security, an idea
that Senator William Borah at once denounced as "madness."
More than a few Republicans who were imperialists in 1900 had
changed spots and were in 1916 speaking in isolationist terms.

Germany's resumption of unrestricted submarine warfare and
the disclosure of the "Zimmerman note," a diplomatic gaffe in
which Germany hinted to Mexico that there might be territorial
returns for aid against the Allies, switched public opinion. Wilson
sensed this change and came to Congress with his war message.
Only the remnants of the Progressives were saying "Slow down!"
After a few days of aimless debate—exactly 100 speeches in the

House—they surrendered and Congress passed the war resolution. Among the fifty House dissenters was the first woman ever elected to Congress, Representative Jeannette Rankin. Rankin, a Montana Republican, gave her maiden speech, which, the *New York Times* reported, "ended in a sob." The Senate vote was 82 to 6 for war, with Senators La Follette and Norris in the minority.

The isolationists justified their war vote on the grounds that Germany was a threat to the United States's territory. Senator Lodge, who had supported plans a year earlier for a kind of world organization with Franco-British leadership, voted for war without qualms.

During the war that followed, Republicans supported Wilson's requests for money, troops, and arms, and after a tactical blunder most members of the GOP in Congress supported a draconian measure that gave Wilson extraconstitutional powers to mobilize the nation for war. There was no truce, however, between Wilson and the Republicans on the matter of appointments as the bureaucracy in Washington and around the country grew at a spectacular pace. The dangers of a president interfering in local races became obvious when Wilson tried to discipline a Wisconsin Republican running in a by-election for the Senate. The butt of Wilson's attack beat his Democratic opponent handily; a chastened Wilson stayed clear of other local battles during the rest of his second term.

The Armistice of 1918 came shortly after the fall by-elections had whittled the Democrats' Senate lead to two votes and dramatically overturned the House. The Sixty-sixth Congress, which would settle the terms of the victory, was a belligerent Republican-dominated body, with the House lineup measuring 240 Republicans and 190 Democrats. Republican gains in the Midwest followed harsh criticism of price ceilings on grains, which farmers resented because cotton (produced in the solidly Democratic South) had not been affected by the price freeze and had climbed to record heights.

The German army was in retreat by September, and when voters went to the polls, it was common knowledge that victory was near. So voters must have realized that they were voting for a control on Wilson's foreign policy—whatever it was. Rarely in American history have voters been concerned about foreign affairs—a depression or prosperity can touch everybody, but a border squabble in the Balkans cannot arouse the average voter's interest.

The apathy toward foreign policy has been further augmented by the basic reality that the United States has not had a sustained, farsighted foreign policy since 1796. For two centuries the country's leaders have followed ad hoc policies of expediency, humanitarian in form sometimes, brashly overbearing in others, ideological when it seemed appropriate, but nearly always of a moralistic suasion. Repeatedly, American leaders have defined their foreign policy as "whatever serves the best interests of the United States," usually without an articulate statement to clarify the pronouncement. With elections every four or eight years, foreign policy directions have swung around 180 degrees more than once, but never as dramatically as in 1919 and 1920.

Trying to mend fences after a triumphant tour of Europe, Wilson invited the Republican Senate leaders to the White House for a dinner party that was intended to be a "bury-the-hatchet" session. Instead of reconciliation, the evening's theme seemed to be a declaration of war. One senator, questioned by a reporter, characterized the evening as like "having tea with the mad hatter."*

With an unpopular president and a squabbling Congress, the postwar political situation was made to order for a Republican sweep in 1920. The mood of voters was distinctly anti-Wilson, a discord perceived by Senator Lodge as he began to shape up opposition to the League of Nations (which he had once said he would support). The turn of public opinion against Wilson after a victorious war was to be repeated in the outspoken opposition evinced toward Harry Truman after World War II. But in 1920 an ill Wilson could not fight to save his pet project from Senate rejection.

Wilson went to Europe for the final Allied meetings that created a peace treaty and organized an international peacekeeping council, to be known as the League of Nations. Back

*Quoted in Mayer, *The Republican Party,* 356.

home, Wilson sent the treaty to the Senate. Lodge, who was now the national spokesman for the Republican party as well as the Senate Foreign Relations Committee chairman, had been waiting like a hunter in a duck blind. Moreover, Lodge was in command of the situation, for he was the acknowledged Senate leader and Roosevelt was suddenly out of the picture, having died in January 1919 just as the rhetoric was becoming overheated. The other senior senators—Boies Penrose of Pennsylvania, Reed Ogden Smoot of Utah, Francis Warren of Wyoming—were ready to go along with whatever strategy Lodge proposed to maneuver the party back into a position to win in 1920.

Senator Borah was a maverick, bothersome but without a following. To make Lodge's problems more complicated, former President Taft came out in favor of the League of Nations. A few loyalists supported Taft, but they were an undisciplined lot, while Lodge knew he had forty reliable votes in his pocket. Lodge probably did not want to kill the league, but he wanted to show his strength to the nation as a preliminary for the 1920 election. Increasingly, Wilson grew testy as the Senate hemmed and hawed.

At last, the gloves were off. Wilson decided to take his message to the people and scheduled an East-West swing on a presidential train. The frenzied approval Wilson hoped to see was not there, nor were the crowds. By the time he reached Colorado, Wilson was gravely ill, and a paralytic stroke brought the tour to an abrupt halt. The president was hurried back to the White House, with cryptic bulletins on his health released that gave the impression Wilson was in far better condition than the facts merited.

Meanwhile, Lodge attempted to outfox Wilson by sending a much-amended treaty to the Senate while Wilson was still haranguing the crowds. In Lodge's mind, the president was out on the grand tour to set up his renomination for president and a crack at the no-third-term tradition. Then a telegram sent the Senate and the treaty into a tailspin. Wilson was ill—*very* ill.

Wilson's true condition was not revealed to the public, but the senators knew the president was not physically capable of doing anything to support his idealistic program. The Democrats who tried to rally support could not, or would not, arouse public opinion by playing on public sympathy—after all, the public did not know how seriously ill Wilson was. After much backing-and-filling, the Senate coalition of Republicans and antitreaty Democrats rejected the Treaty of Versailles by a vote of 53 ayes to 38 nays, just short of the two-thirds majority necessary for passage.

There is much evidence that Lodge hoped to separate the League of Nations membership from the treaty rejection, and a House resolution to that effect was ready for passage if Lodge said the word. But jealous House members rebelled, and after Congress adjourned it was apparent that the public was indifferent to the whole "treaty mess." A business recession, the enforcement of the Prohibition amendment, and the opening of the 1920 baseball season were of far more interest to voters. When the treaty came up again for a final vote in March 1920, the ayes fell to 49 and the nays went up to 35. The treaty that included membership in the League of Nations was dead; technically, the United States remained at war with the Central Powers.

The Nineteenth Amendment was ratified in 1920, giving women, at last, the right to full citizenship in the voting booths. But it was the Eighteenth Amendment and the clamp on booze and beer that received the most attention—that is, if we discount the popularity of Charlie Chaplin and the Model-T Ford. The postwar culture was different; women were liberated not only at the polling place but also by fashion, which dictated short skirts, shorter or "bobbed" hair, and less cumbersome bathing suits. The country was on a binge of sorts, for bootlegging became a national pastime, jazz bands from New Orleans invaded Chicago, and phonograph records made every parlor a potential dance hall.

The Old Guard did not fit into this so-called Jazz Age with éclat. Lodge was up in years, Roosevelt was gone, Root was an old man, and General John Pershing (the logical choice for old-timers who loved military men) had no political pretensions. General Leonard Wood, who was more of a desk soldier than a field commander, had some following among the old Progressives. But in the late spring of 1920, there was no front-runner for the Republicans to start promoting.

Democrats were in no better shape. Wilson was too ill to be contemplated, although a few diehards believed Wilson could break the third-term tradition if given the chance. Governor James Cox of Ohio looked good to the party regulars, who did not want to be saddled with a southern senator.

If political campaigns made good motion picture plots, the GOP convention of 1920 would be the perfect vehicle. Except that the story is so well known, all the suspense has been sucked out of the plot. The smoke-filled rooms are there, the conniving politicians are there, and so is the handsome but somewhat confused senator who is the pawn of all the power brokers, hangers-on, poker pals, and just plain opportunists.

The strange cast came together in Chicago in June 1920 to choose a Republican presidential candidate. Governor Frank Lowden of Illinois thought he had a chance; so did General Wood, and even the president of Columbia University, Nicholas Murray Butler, had his band of horn-tooters. The weak-but-forgiven Progressives looked longingly at Senator Hiram Johnson.

Planks for the platform were easily moved into place, the usual call for higher tariffs was made, the oft-repeated strictures on unrestricted immigration were resurrected, and the League of Nations issue was sidestepped neatly with a statement favoring further efforts to ensure world peace. With all the platitudes safely in place, the delegates turned to the main business and hit a logjam of favorite-son votes. Chairman Lodge adjourned the convention after a few inconclusive ballots.

Truth can be stranger than fiction; indeed, the way Senator Warren Harding came out of the closet and walked away with the nomination late that Saturday night is one amazing story. The best evidence indicates the weary delegates gave in to the power brokers, who had convened at a nearby hotel and in a blue haze of tobacco smoke decided around two o'clock on Saturday morning that Harding could win because "he looked like a president" and was a member in good standing of the Senate's old-boys club. So the assembled senators sent out the word, and the switching began and continued until four o'clock the next afternoon, when the delegates recessed to take stock.

When the ninth ballot was called, the bandwagon began to roll. State after state abandoned its favorite sons and voted for Harding. On the tenth ballot, Warren G. Harding was nominated.

There were a few disappointed Republicans who did not exercise their lungs in the demonstration that followed. William Allen White, the Kansas editor who still had status, looked on with less than enthusiasm, for the party had been taken over by the Senate brokers and was, to White, no longer the organized talent agency it had been. In the heyday of Republicanism, White ventured, the Midwest had provided the party's heartbeat:

> Under the genesis of Republican federal leadership the major enterprises which welded those states into a homogeneous civilization were conceived and established. The railroads, the telegraph wires, the pipelines, even the newspapers and most of the western statemen were Republicans. Protesting Democrats were political second fiddlers . . . strangers in a strange land, which was on the whole a happy, diluted Republican plutocracy in its ideals and achievements.

That era was over, White concluded, because when Roosevelt came on the scene with ideas for change and progress, the Old Guard turned away. By nominating Harding, the Republicans admitted they were "interested chiefly in amassing wealth. . . . liberalism . . . was a negligible minority." And so it was, but not many Republicans joined White in his lament for old values and ideas.

Not that the delegates in 1920 were ready to roll over repeatedly when the whip was cracked. The Senate caucus might name a presidential nominee, but the delegates were tired of handpicked candidates, and they rebelled at the vice presidential nomination of still another midwestern senator, Irvine Lenroot of Wisconsin. From the floor a delegate from Oregon nominated Calvin Coolidge, governor of Massachusetts, and before the party managers could react, the taciturn New England Republican had swamped Lenroot and was on the ticket. A discerning observer said the delegates simply were tired of being stampeded. "The Senate bosses were gone," reporter White recalled, so for the first time in four days "the Convention was to have its own way."

Coolidge's credentials were impressive, for he had a reputation as the governor who had broken the police strike in Boston in 1919. As Harvard students were enrolled to police the streets, Governor Coolidge became a hero of sorts to a nation that was fed up with the wave of postwar strikes that plagued mines and factories across American in 1919–1920. "There is no right to strike against the public safety by anybody, any time, any where," Coolidge said when he ordered the strikers back to work. A tough-talking man, Coolidge was, when he talked.

Neither Coolidge nor Harding needed to say much in the 1920 campaign. The Democrats picked Governor Cox for the presidential nomination and placed young Franklin D. Roosevelt of New York on the ticket in second place. Thus a newspaper publisher from Ohio was on both tickets, for Harding had run the *Marion (Ohio) Star* before his political fling. In short, a businessman-turned-politician was bound to be the next president, regardless of which party won.

Harding spoke of a return to "normalcy," which sounded good to voters who had no clear idea of what normal times really entailed, inasmuch as bootlegging and rum-running were among the leading national industries in a country indulging in the "noble experiment" of forsaking strong drink. The Volstead Act, passed over Wilson's veto, listed as intoxicating any beverage containing more than an eyedropperful of alcohol and left enforcement up to federal agents or local authorities. The lid that had been clamped down in January 1920 was pried loose for the two party conventions and never was replaced in the speakeasies and gin joints that soon dotted the landscape and flourished in the cities.

Republicans figured they would win in November, but few could have foreseen the landslide that hit the Democrats. Harding won 16.1 million votes, almost twice the number the Cox-Roosevelt ticket received, and in the electoral college it was Harding 404, Cox 127. Not since Grant smothered Greeley had the Republicans won so easily and decisively.

Everything went Harding's way for a while. He made several outstanding cabinet appointments in selecting millionaire Herbert Hoover (noted for his war relief expertise) as secretary of commerce and banker Andrew Mellon as secretary of the treasury. The choice of Charles Evans Hughes as secretary of state was brilliant, as was the selection of Henry Wallace, the editor of the conservative *Wallace's Farmer,* for the agriculture post. Less dazzling was the place picked for Senator Albert B. Fall of New Mexico, who was known to be hostile to the conservationists and yet was made secretary of the interior. Harry Daugherty, Harding's sidekick from Ohio, was placed in the attorney general's seat, and a key post in the Veterans Bureau went to another poker buddy of mediocre talent.

By the time Harding was settled in the White House the farmers were feeling the pinch of a postwar recession. Price supports for wheat, artificially inflated during the war, officially ended in May 1920. Thereafter wheat prices tumbled, as did some other commodity prices. Farmers, with less money to spend, stopped buying cars and tractors, and before long a mild recession was taking shape. Shortly before Harding took office, wheat sold for as little as 67 cents a bushel. If this was "normalcy," the farmers wanted none of it.

Pushed by Senator Borah, the State Department called for an international conference to reduce naval rearmament. Here was a device that allowed the United States to bypass the League of Nations, and Republicans supported Borah's idea for its statement about sovereignty rather than for its merits. When its business was finished, the Washington Naval Conference of 1922 had set limits for the major powers that seemed to augur well for postwar arms control. The Republicans also created the Bureau of the Budget, to give system to the federal finances, and turned over to the director an awesome task. Harding appointed Charles Dawes, a Chicago banker, to the new position, and within six months Dawes had proved capable enough to suggest a budget surplus was within reach. A soldier's bonus bill, which the business community thought would require new taxes, drew Harding's veto; but an excess-profits tax enacted during the war was repealed so that Mellon could return $3.5 billion to wealthy businessmen and corporations during his tenure at the treasury.

The 1920 platform had promised to give attention to the tariff, and Congress soon fell in step with the Fordney-McCumber

Act of 1922, which raised duties to an all-time high. The art of logrolling came into play, for Senator Johnson of California wanted fruit and nuts protected from foreign competition; once the duty list included his favorite products, Johnson's opposition disappeared. On the final vote, the only Republicans voting against the act were La Follette and Borah.

The Lincoln Monument was finally finished and dedicated in 1922 as a secular temple for the Republicans' greatest hero. The ceremonies on Decoration Day were marred by the rudeness of guards toward the main speaker, the president of Tuskegee Institute, and toward other blacks who were herded into a segregated area at the event. But the magnificent building filled out the west end of the Mall, and Daniel Chester French's marble statue of the Great Emancipator was simply awesome. Harding's appointee as chief justice, William H. Taft, was among the assembled admirers who paid homage to the man who had led the Republicans in their first successful quest for national power.

Senator George Norris, distressed at the way the Mussel Shoals Dam project was being handled, tried to prevent the leasing of the wartime nitrogen plant to industrialist Henry Ford. In 1921 Ford said he wanted to make low-cost fertilizer using the government-built facility on the Tennessee River, but Norris insisted that the huge generators be used to electrify a region where few farmers had ever turned an electric light on in their homes. The Wilson Dam was completed to finish the original plan, but all Norris could do was stop Ford from taking over. Two of Harding's successors would veto legislation the Nebraska Republican introduced to create the Tennessee Valley Authority, leaving private utilities in charge until 1934.

Ford lost his TVA battle but kept busy making Model Ts. The steel Ford needed was coming from the huge blast furnaces around Pittsburgh, where a twelve-hour workday was normal. In the spring of 1923, the head of U.S. Steel justified the mill conditions and seemed to challenge anybody—union steward or the Congress—to change a tradition that defied the shift to an eight-hour day in other industries. Somehow, Harding got wind of the steel mogul's defiance and wrote him a personal letter asking for an end to an "obsolete" practice, and during the summer there was a quiet announcement that steelmakers were ready to negotiate for a shorter workday.

Harding's successes were few, however. Cracks in the administration's facade began to appear when Jess Smith committed suicide. Smith had been the close friend of Harry Daugherty, and in time it was disclosed he had been taking bribes in an alien property scam. Then news from the Veterans Bureau leaked out that Colonel Charles R. Forbes was in trouble, and he resigned. Gossip in the Capitol corridors also concerned shady lease deals involving the Teapot Dome petroleum reserves. Harding began to perceive that his poker-playing pals were taking advantage of their political powers, and he grew distressed. The Kansas editor, William Allen White, was invited to the White House and there heard the president bemoan his crumbling "kitchen cabinet." "I can take care of my enemies all right," Harding told White, "but damn my friends . . . they're the ones that keep me walking the floor nights!" *

The worst was yet to come, but Harding never learned of it. Tired of the strain, Harding set out for Alaska on a trip that would include a stop in San Francisco. Upon reaching San Francisco, Harding went to the Palace Hotel complaining that he did not feel well. Doctors were summoned, and the president seemed to rally. Then Harding sank into a crisis and died on August 2, 1923.

A national day of mourning would attest to Harding's popularity, as the baton of leadership was passed across the continent. Early on August 3, a messenger carried the news of Harding's death to a dark farmhouse in Plymouth Notch, Vermont. Before daybreak, Calvin Coolidge took the presidential oath and headed for Washington as the morning newspapers told readers: "President Harding Dies!"

Coolidge came into office with a clean slate, which is what the nation badly needed. Disclosures of wrongdoing would continue

*Quoted in Malcom Moos, *The Republicans: A History of Their Party* (New York: Random House, 1956), 334.

to surface for the next six years, but the new president was untainted by all the scandals that had occurred during the Harding administration.

Coolidge brought to the White House another invaluable asset. His wife, Grace, was a fashionable, articulate first lady who would be remembered by the executive mansion staff for generations. She was thus the perfect counterfoil for her taciturn, shy husband.

Because Coolidge barely had time to move into the White House before the 1923 Christmas season, he knew that the Sixty-eighth Congress would want to know where he stood on the tariff and other issues. Coolidge grouped his family in a holiday mood, set some ground rules, and adopted the policy he would stand by until March 1929: don't talk but listen for the quiet voice of public opinion.

Newsmen soon learned that Coolidge could not be quoted directly, so they wrote stories giving their source as "a White House spokesman." *Time* magazine was barely two years old and ready to tell readers what Coolidge ate for breakfast, lunch, and dinner. Radio was making fast headway, but not as a news media, so Coolidge was not pestered with microphone-ladened reporters; but tabloid newspapers were becoming more popular, and to their headline writers the president was "Cal" (because "Coolidge" would not fit their half-page format).

Thus in a media climate that was unfamiliar to him, Coolidge retreated and became "Silent Cal" to a nation that came, more and more, to like the president for his shunning of the limelight. On a fishing trip to Vermont, the president did permit a photographer to snap him as he held a fly rod. The resulting picture of a grim gentleman, wearing a boater hat and a necktie as he tried to fish, amused the nation and helped fix in the public's imagination the idea that Coolidge was all business.

Indeed, that was Coolidge to a tee. His tenure is often recalled in the single phrase he repeatedly used, until it became a cliché. "The business of America is business," the president told a conference of assembled industrialists and financiers, and that seemed to say it all. The comedian Will Rogers figured he had it right when he told amused audiences at the Ziegfeld Follies,

"This guy Coolidge don't do nothin', which is just what the American people want him to do."

The Republican party had come into being to smash slavery, and by 1923 the party was still single-minded. The driving impulse of the party Coolidge headed was that government should help business and industry maintain a level of prosperity with as little outside interference as possible. The leading newspapers in nearly every city of any size accepted this philosophy, and thus an alliance between the major medium of daily newspapers and the Republican party was confirmed each day. From the *New York Herald-Tribune, Chicago Tribune, Des Moines Register,* and *Los Angeles Times* came a daily stream of news and opinion that reinforced their readers in their Republican convictions. Outside the South, few major newspapers made a pretense at being either independent or Democratic.

During Coolidge's tenure the major focus of news shifted to New York, because there wasn't that much going on in Washington. Coolidge decided to be an executive who was not an initiator of laws but an enforcer. A grateful Senate understood perfectly, and during Coolidge's tenure the number of vetoes was small (twenty by signature, and thirty "by pocket"). At the same time, the number of White House initiatives was also minimal. Coolidge was a caretaker president who found the country prosperous and intended to leave it that way. Except for the farmers, the country in 1924 was heading into new economic ground every month. And to assure farmers that the Republican party was still their friend, Congress had passed in 1922 the Capper-Volstead Act, which exempted farm cooperatives from antitrust laws so that marketing (of oranges, for example, through the "Sunkist" cooperative) could stabilize prices and prevent overproduction.

Rarely in American history have political parties lost elections when the country was in a business boom; this is the other side of the coin from the party debacles suffered during depressions. So how could Coolidge lose in 1924?

He couldn't. For comic relief, the nation turned to the Democrats. The Democrats conducted a farcical convention in Madison Square Garden and, after a staggering 104 ballots, nominated a Wall Street lawyer, John W. Davis, for president. Coolidge had no serious rival for the GOP nomination; La Follette made his usual call for a Progressive gathering, then went before the Cleveland convention to accept the third-party nomination with all the zest of a schoolboy (he was pushing seventy-one). La Follette's running mate was a Democratic Senator, Burton K. Wheeler, who was known for his disdain of party discipline.

The La Follette candidacy provided an exciting sideshow for the 1924 election, but in general voters seemed bored by the whole thing. Coolidge won by a landslide, with 15 million votes to 8.3 million for Davis and 4.8 million for La Follette. More voters would have turned out, but the results seemed so obvious in October that millions of voters in November simply preferred to "go fishin'." Coolidge's electoral vote was even more impressive, as he had 382 votes to Davis's 136. La Follette won only the electoral votes of his home base, Wisconsin. Voters also sent a Republican Congress to work with Coolidge. In the Senate, 56 Republicans overmatched 39 Democrats, while the GOP held the House by a margin of 247 to 183.

Death administered its inexorable call where the voters would not. Lodge died, and La Follette was soon in his grave too, as was "Uncle Joe" Cannon. A new generation of Republicans was moving in, led by "Nicky" Longworth, Theodore Roosevelt's son-in-law and an Ohio congressman who became Speaker of the House. The new Senate majority leader was the phlegmatic Charles Curtis of Kansas.

Coolidge did not clean house in his cabinet, but changes were made. Secretary of State Hughes left to become a judge on the World Court in Hague and was succeeded by former senator Frank P. Kellogg. Harlan Fiske Stone, an Amherst classmate of Coolidge's, was installed as attorney general. (Eventually, Stone wound up on the Supreme Court.)

With this team in place, Coolidge was committed to a simple policy: stand aside and let prosperity roar ahead. Coolidge sought only to keep his house in order and let the country run itself. If the farm depression had not deepened, this hands-off policy might have worked. The farm-bloc senators, however, would not see their constituents slide down the economic scale without a fight. They brought forth legislation designed to guarantee farmers a price for their commodities roughly based on the free-market price plus a subsidy tied to the tariff laws. Four versions of what was known as the McNary-Haugen bill came before Congress. Two failed because of sectional animus, but in 1927 the third version went to Coolidge's desk for signature. In his veto message, Coolidge scolded the "sons of the wild jackass" (farm-bloc senators so named by an offended colleague) for singling out certain commodities for assistance. The fourth version of the bill, passed in 1928, also drew Coolidge's rebuke. In both cases, the farm bloc was unable to muster enough votes to override the presidential veto.

With his coldhearted approach to farm problems, Coolidge relied on a fixed principle in his political philosophy. The McNary-Haugen bill provided for a bureaucracy and some price-fixing that would be monitored, and Coolidge saw this as unwarranted federal interference in the workings of the marketplace. The government could "help farmers to help themselves," historian John D. Hicks observed, but farmers had no business asking the government "to do what government had no right to do."

Farmers in the Midwest felt betrayed, but most remained loyal to the party that was behind Coolidge almost 100 percent. On the one hand, the courage of midwestern Republicans in supporting the president when their constituents were threatened with bankruptcy is commendable. On the other hand, the Republican credo of withholding assistance to marginal producers of grain and cotton was bound to haunt candidates if and when the whole economy sagged.

The economy did not sag in 1926, but the declining fortunes of the farm belt hurt Republican candidates in the off-year elections. The number of Republican in the Senate slipped to 49, as Democrats gained until they held 46 places. In the House, Republicans still held a majority, 237 to 195, but had lost 10 seats. To help the Republicans keep their Senate hold, Senator Henrik Shipstead of Minnesota was invited to join the Republican conference and accepted. An outspoken Republican champion of isolationist foreign policy, Gerald P. Nye, was elected to the Senate from North Dakota.

Stocks continued to spiral upward in 1927 as Babe Ruth kept hitting home runs and "Silent Cal" Coolidge was almost as popular as the baseball hero. But nobody was as popular as Charles A. Lindbergh, after his flight to Paris. The boyish aviator was almost as unwilling as Coolidge when it came to talking in public, and that attribute seemed to thrill an adoring public all the more. Will Rogers, his name a household word, took time off from work at the Ziegfeld Follies when he was invited to spend the night at the White House. The nation laughed at Rogers's account of the presidential living quarters; but some months later when the comedian mocked Coolidge's nasal twang on a faked radio interview, the president was not amused.

Inevitably, Coolidge's supporters decided that an early statement on the 1928 presidential election would be helpful, but the president beat them to the punch when he issued a terse announcement about his intentions. "I do not choose to run" was all the supporters needed to hear to decide on a draft-Coolidge movement. Perhaps Coolidge would have accepted a draft, but the Old Guard insiders had already considered the field and picked their man: Herbert Hoover.

Hoover had won international acclaim for his work in postwar Europe, where he headed a relief agency that did outstanding work. Then, as secretary of commerce in the Harding and Coolidge cabinets, Hoover had business leaders falling all over themselves in testimonials to his fitness. Secretary Hoover had encouraged American businesses to make European loans when the balance of trade made Germany, France, and other nations short of the cash needed to buy American commodities. Eventually, American bankers and investors lent $7 billion to prop up these foreign sales; when a depression hit, most of these loans would be in default.

In 1928, however, Hoover represented that epitome of a good candidate: a solid businessman who had successfully competed in the marketplace. Did he not speak highly of "the emery-wheel of competition" that had made America the greatest consumer nation in history? A self-made man, Hoover had wealth from his mining ventures, and his California background helped party leaders decide his presidential credentials were well-nigh perfect.

Perhaps, as Wilfred Binkley suggested, the Republican party by the mid-1920s "was growing flabby for lack of stiff opposition." Perhaps the drum thumpers were too strident. The head of General Motors told a cheering audience that "the United States has reached a level of permanent prosperity." The chief of one of America's largest corporations was on record as predicting that the era of boom-and-bust cycles was over. The old-time Republican promise of "a full dinner pail" was no longer adequate.

Hoover, like Grant behind him and Willkie ahead, had never been elected to any office. He was a political novice, but he had high connections in every boardroom on Wall Street. Slight of stature and full of energy, Hoover radiated confidence in cabinet meetings and at party conferences. Only the farm-bloc senators were wary of Hoover, because they remembered that in 1918, when he was in charge of the War Food Administration, Hoover favored a cap on commodity prices. After four floor fights, and losses, on the McNary-Haugen bill, the farm bloc's influence in party councils was at low ebb, however.

Hoover had a natural reserve that was misinterpreted by casual acquaintances. A churlish reporter told readers that Hoover was a far cry from Lincoln—Lincoln split rails, he said, and Hoover split infinitives. As first lady, Lou Henry Hoover graciously invited a black congressman to the White House for tea in the summer of 1929, and in the South the sparks flew. Outraged members of the Texas legislature discussed a call for Hoover's impeachment, but the president consoled his wife by saying, "one of the advantages of orthodox religion is that it provides a hot hell for the Texas legislature."*

Prohibition was also coming up as a national issue, in part because the most vocal Democratic candidate for nomination was Governor Al Smith of New York. Smith wanted the Eighteenth Amendment repealed and was not backward in saying so. Smith was also a Catholic, and the prospect of a "wet" Catholic on the Democratic ticket brought smiles of relief to comfortable gentlemen seated in New York's Union Club.

---

*Quoted in Frank Friedel et al., eds., *The White House: The First Two Hundred Years* (Boston: Northeastern University Press, 1995), 41–42.

In some desperation, the farm bloc caucused and announced that it would enter its own candidate in the 1928 presidential primaries. The mavericks picked George Norris, the Nebraska senator, as their candidate and planned to make the rejected McNary-Haugen bill an integral part of their platform. Hearing this, the normally silent Coolidge let reporters know that he would consider votes for Norris as a personal repudiation. Meanwhile, Hoover's poor showing in a few state presidential primaries did nothing to help his chances.

Hoover needed the California delegation, but Senator Hiram Johnson was no admirer of the Palo Alto resident (for Hoover was now an official Californian). Johnson could not afford to fight the Old Guard any more, because he was facing a strong challenge at home and any kind of split would hurt his own reelection campaign. So Senator Johnson managed to climb on board the Hoover bandwagon, if the staid vehicle deserved such a spectacular title, and the Republican convention in Kansas City was a kind of love feast for the anointed candidate.

A tone of hypocrisy crept into the proceedings when the farm bloc tried to disrupt the proceedings and got nowhere. Senator Curtis of Kansas, representing a state where wheat prices were crumbling, singled out Hoover as a part of the problem facing the nation. Mentioned as a possible vice presidential candidate himself, Curtis flushed and renounced a Hoover-Curtis ticket as a charade. Yet, in the early morning light around Kansas City, the inner circle had prevailed, and the candidates were Hoover and Curtis. The party platform hedged on aid to suffering farmers but promised to tighten the screws on federal enforcement of the Volstead Act. The "drys" were delighted, as were the isolationists with the usual denunciation of the League of Nations.

Democrats obligingly chose Al Smith as their nominee, thus alienating the solid South in one blow. The Ku Klux Klan was ebbing in some states, but anti-Catholic sentiment was still a fact of life in Protestant America in 1928. The "No Popery" slogan worked in England in 1628 and would work again in the United States three hundred years later. Kingdoms and republics can have a lot in common when bigotry is on the table.

Republicans campaigning for Hoover did not bang on "the full dinner pail" but substituted an updated version: "A chicken in every pot and a car in every garage." Now we are talking business! And business loved the talk! When Hoover made his speech thumping for "rugged individualism" as a cure for any social ills, his audience was overwhelmed.

Smith proved to be a New Yorker to the core. When a reporter asked the Democratic candidate how he expected to do in the western states, Smith's reply was: "What are the states in the West?"

The *Literary Digest* poll, not scientific but better than a wild guess, predicted a Hoover victory. Why not? Under Harding and Coolidge unemployment was down, factory jobs were up, new cars crowded the narrow highways, and radio antennae filled the skies over all the major towns and cities. Smith supporters wore neckties emblazoned with "Smith and Beer in '28." Republicans conceded that changes in voting patterns would occur, but they hoped that dry-throated voters in Kansas and Nebraska would offset the Irish "wets" in Boston and New York.

As it turned out, the drys beat the wets by 6.4 million votes, enough to qualify the election as a "Hoover landslide." In the electoral college, five southern states joined with Republicans to give Hoover a 444-to-87 edge. The Hoover avalanche brought in a new crop of senators, some from the South or Southwest, so that Republicans would dominate the Senate 56 to 39. In the House, the GOP margin was an even 100 votes over the Democrats.

On the day following Hoover's victory, disconsolate Democrats reviewed their party's history and found little cause for joy. Since 1860 they had lost all but four elections, control of Congress was in Republican hands again (as it had been for most of the past sixty years), and Smith's defeat appeared to indicate that only a Protestant could be elected president of the United States.

Indeed, for Democrats the only bright spot was in New York State, where the crippled Democrat with a blue-blood name and Harvard law degree had been elected governor in a tight race.

Franklin D. Roosevelt was going to Albany, but the party itself seemed to be going to pieces.

Meanwhile, the Empire State Building was rising on Fifth Avenue, interest rates were also going up, and the atmosphere in Washington was even headier. A car in every garage? Shucks, why not two? And why settle for a chicken in every pot, when General Electric common stock was splitting four for one?

CHAPTER ELEVEN

"The Republic Survives!"

As the Great Depression fades into memory, allusions to Black Friday, Black Tuesday, and the "Crash on Wall Street" and the plaintive tune "Brother, Can You Spare a Dime?" have become but dim markers in the American consciousness. Despite the dramatic stock market plunge on the autumn of 1929, the Depression did not strike, like a tornado, with sudden fury. The economic blight came on slowly, like a dust storm on the Plains that appears on the horizon, then moves insidiously until it has surrounded everything in a cloud of reddish particles that torment, choke, and stifle all living creatures.

In tornadoes, one reacts quickly and intuitively. In a depression, the confusion tends to grow as things slide from bad to worse. Inaction is justified by the slow pace of events.

Herbert Hoover was in many ways one of the most able administrators ever elected to the presidency, but when the depression hit, he was philosophically incapable of giving the country what it needed—firm leadership. Democrats have taken advantage of the public's short memory with the old saw, "Hoover brought on the Depression and was broken by it." In fact, the tragedy of the Depression was that Hoover and his party were unprepared for an economic earthquake and thought this recession was like so many others, a minor tremor that would fade away in a few months or a year at the most.

Later, the explanation was easy. Housing starts slowed in 1927, and inventories started piling up at factories in 1928. The average annual income of the American farmer in 1932 fell to $304; in 1920 it had been $1,196. Reduced payrolls led to cuts in consumer spending, but the price of a new Ford went up in 1929, as did the cost of a new "Frigidaire." A new Buick sold for $1,295, delivered from Detroit, but a two-door Oldsmobile could be bought for $875. A *Ladies' Home Journal* article titled "Everyone Ought to Be Rich" advised readers to invest $15 a month in common stocks so they could retire in twenty years with an $80,000 nest egg.

The market crash on October 29, 1929, was a wake-up call with a nightmare crescendo. Within a matter of hours, unprecedented downside volume on Wall Street wiped out almost $30 billion in "paper profits." Margin calls ruined small speculators; tumbling prices caused banks to totter, spread panic in the marketplace, and jeopardized the savings of millions of American wage earners.

Ironically, Albert B. Fall's trial on bribery charges ended as the Wall Street debacle unraveled. On November 1, as the stock market continued downward, Fall was fined $100,000 and sent to jail for a year. Temporarily, a memento of the Harding era grabbed the headlines away from the canyons of Wall Street.

Wall Street is usually a more honest predictor of future events than are politicians. And since 1870, an informal alliance between Wall Street leaders and the Republican party had been no secret. Nobody expected J. P. Morgan or John D. Rockefeller to support the Democratic ticket. So the focus of millions was on both the White House and Wall Street as the crisis deepened during the Christmas season of 1929.

Not that many Americans owned stocks in 1929, probably less than 8 percent of the nation's population of 115 million. But the market plunge escalated the farm crisis, the factory closings, the rising bankruptcy rate, the banks' involvement in heavy speculation, and the tightening of monetary systems in Europe. The cheering squad in Washington was out of touch with reality as 1930 dawned.

Congress took action all right. Convinced that tariffs were the answer to most economic problems, the Republicans in the House and Senate whipped together the Hawley-Smoot Tariff

Act, which raised duties to their highest peak in American history. In truth, the bill had been written during a special session Hoover called in the summer of 1929, when the economy seemed to be humming. But with the Wall Street disaster clearly on the table, Congress passed the high-tariff bill into law and in June 1930 Hoover signed it, almost like a death warrant. European debtors found American markets closing, so they could not meet their payments, and American farmers saw their foreign markets dwindle because there was no cash available aboard.

Amid the economic distress one comic note was supplied by the same senator who gave his name to the high-tariff bill. Reed Ogden Smoot, who had been in the Senate since 1903 and therefore had tons of seniority, became interested in his fellow senators' efforts to block the censorship of books imported from Europe that were classified as "obscene." The ban involved such works at James Joyce's *Ulysses* and D. H. Lawrence's *Lady Chatterley's Lover,* which the Utah senator denounced as unfit for American readers because of their explicit sexual content. The humorist-poet Ogden Nash gave Smoot immortality (of a sort) when he wrote a widely read piece of doggerel headed " 'Smoot Plans Tariff Ban on Improper Books'—News Item." After tongue-in-cheek praise of the Utah lawmaker, Nash's poem went on:

> Senator Smoot is an institute
> Not to be bribed with pelf;
> He guards our homes from erotic tomes
> By reading them all himself . . .
> Smite, Smoot,
> Be rugged and rough,
> Smut if smitten
> Is front-page stuff.

The customs ban continued in 1930, but sophisticated readers found ways around the ruling, and Smoot professed to believe justice had prevailed.

Humor is hard to find in dreary economic days, however. The dismal story of the Depression can be told in one set of statistics. Unemployment rose to 5 million in 1930, to 9 million in 1931, and reached 13 million in the 1932 election year. The

1930 off-year elections told the story of a confused nation. In the House elections, Democrats won a majority with 220 seats, but a slender majority it was—the Republicans had only 7 fewer seats. Republicans still held the Senate, but by a single vote.

Hoover tried to keep up the nation's morale. He spoke on the radio and appeared in motion-picture newsreels (a prominent part of every cinema's daily program), but the talk seemed hollow when the audiences walked out onto the streets and saw grown men selling apples from stands made of shipping crates, sometimes with signs that pleaded: "Help a Vet, Apples 5 cents." Hoover held a series of White House conferences, bringing industrial and business leaders to the capital for pep talks from a president who exuded confidence. In New York State, the weekly relief checks for needy families averaged $2.39.

Taft died, and Charles Evans Hughes was Hoover's choice to be chief justice. President Hoover promised to work with the next Congress and gave much attention to the legislation that would establish the Reconstruction Finance Corporation to assist businesses that needed low-cost loans to stay solvent. The idea seemed to be that if large corporations could keep afloat, they would revive prosperity through their sales and payrolls. To critical Democrats the plan sounded like a "trickle-down" theory of economics, and in the 1932 campaigns they sharpened their knives. Meanwhile, Congress gave Hoover his RFC bill in January 1932, with its $500 million price tag attached. A Democratic bill calling for federal funding to construct public buildings went against Hoover's grain, however, and was vetoed in a clear-cut message to Congress; no Republican president was going to try make-work programs to create "phony jobs."

Always ready to sound cheerful, delegates to the Republican National Convention met in Chicago on a warm June day in 1932, renominated Hoover, and then wrote a platform that predicted a fast recovery for the economy and praised Hoover for his devotion to party principles. Two weeks later, a noisy gathering of Democrats in Chicago blamed Hoover and the Republicans for the nation's economic woes and drew the line on the issue of Prohibition (which the GOP plank still halfheartedly supported). Democrats said they wanted the Eighteenth Amendment repealed with no ifs, ands, or buts. A "Stop Roosevelt" movement against the New York governor fizzled, and on the fourth ballot Franklin D. Roosevelt was nominated.

Both conventions appealed to the veterans, but the men who had fought at Chateau-Thierry had other ideas. A bonus bill for World War veterans was debated in Congress in June, although Hoover spoke persuasively against the measure at an American Legion national convention. Further unemployment brought angry veterans into a "Bonus March" on Washington, with 11,000 penniless men straggling into the capital and camping in a makeshift compound. Vowing they would stay in Washington until the president and Congress met their demands, the veterans erected "the kind of 'Hooverville' that had appeared during the hard times on the outskirts of every sizable American city," historian John Hicks wrote.

The House passed a bonus bill, but it was stymied in the Senate. Late in July 1932 local police tried to clear protesters from some buildings in downtown Washington and two veterans were killed. Hoover's reaction was to order troops commanded by General Douglas MacArthur to rout the former soldiers and destroy their shabby encampment. The orders were carried out, but the nation's reaction was one of mixed pity and disgust over the treatment of the hapless veterans.

Public confidence in Hoover eroded after the Bonus Army incident, despite the president's repeated assurances that the economy had bottomed out and would soon show signs of a vigorous recovery. The presidential campaign of 1932 was unique, for a national radio hookup became the main means of reaching the voters. Some radio campaigning had been introduced in 1928, but in 1932 the nation heard a smooth-sounding Democrat assure them that a change in Washington was the tonic America needed. Hoover's voice was not as pleasing to the ear, but the president talked with facts while Roosevelt talked with emotion about the little man whom big government had forgotten.

The voters became the ultimate jury, and their verdict favored the Democrats, starting with Roosevelt and going down to the local sheriff in many communities that had not voted Democratic in half a century. The Democratic landslide of 1932 bespoke the nation's desperation. In the popular vote, Roosevelt led Hoover 22.8 million to 15.7 million; Democrats carried forty-two states, while Hoover won six. In the Congress, the new House would have 313 Democrats across the aisle from 117 Republicans, while the Senate had a Democratic majority of 59 to 36.

A constitutional amendment introduced by Republican George Norris was gliding along in the state legislatures but had not been ratified. The incipient Twentieth Amendment would eliminate "lame-duck" congresses and start the wheels of government early in January, with the presidential inauguration moved up to January 20. The last Republican president to leave office on March 4 was not a happy man. Hoover believed Roosevelt had won by misrepresenting his administration, so he tried to make a series of moves that would tie Roosevelt's hands once the Democrat took office. These included an effort to place the gold standard beyond recall and endorsements of Hoover's commitment to international disarmament. A meeting between the president and the president-elect was inconclusive. When the two silk-hatted gentlemen rode in a limousine to the inauguration on March 4, 1932, the pleasantries were overlooked.

Those who periodically pronounce the two-party system dead have little sense of history. The Democratic victory in 1932 came after the party founded by Jefferson had been buried many times, but its resurrection in 1933 marked a major turning point in the nation's history in the same way that 1860 had been a landmark Republican year. Franklin D. Roosevelt's whirlwind government, with its famous hundred days of new programs, startling legislation, and a new approach to the Great Depression, signaled a new beginning for a party that had grown tired after two generations of being the underdog.

Roosevelt and his New Deal brought a philosophy to Washington that shocked the Republican Old Guard with its audacity. With a turnover in the bureaucracy that placed "brain trusters" from Harvard and the University of Chicago into critical cabinet or high-level positions, Roosevelt's response to the Depression was to make the federal government an agency for change, not a passive observer of turmoil. In one of his memorable speeches, Roosevelt said, "Thank God, our problems only relate to money." If money could bring an end to the Depression, Roosevelt and his obliging Congress were ready to spend it.

Federal spending for public works, unemployment insurance, the Civil Conservation Corps, the National Youth Administration, the federal crop loan program, and other relief agencies soared. The national debt went to unprecedented peacetime levels, making Republicans who survived in the off-year elections of 1934 insist that the nation might be bankrupt if Roosevelt's programs were not discontinued. Voters did not share that concern, however, as they increased the Democrats' domination to a 69-to-25 majority in the Senate and to a 319-to-103 ratio in the House.

Clearly, the Republicans were on the defensive as they lost more statehouses in the deepening depression. With New Dealers in control of the domestic scene, Republicans in the Senate shifted the limelight to an investigation of war profiteering in 1917–1918. Headed by Senator Nye, the North Dakota Republican, an investigative subcommittee sought evidence to support a widely held theory that munitions makers had orchestrated the American entry into the European conflict. Mountains of testimony produced no conclusive charges, but in Republican circles suspicion was tantamount to proof. A strong isolationist urge was nurtured by the Nye investigation, particularly in the Midwest, and the organization of pacifist groups on college campuses often drew support from Young Republican clubs.

Adding fuel to the Republican criticism of the New Deal was the fact that the Depression hung on tenaciously. Jobless rates did not improve, farm prices remained low, and factory output was less than 50 percent of capacity in some industries. General Motors stock fell from its pre-Depression high of 91 3/4 to 8, and most of the nation's largest corporations were similarly in disfavor with investors. The Securities and Exchange Commission was created to prevent another 1929 debacle, but critics said it was another case of overregulation, and "too little, too late."

One tiny gleam of light came from the rural electrification program, which Roosevelt created by an executive order. Millions of farms were extended electrical service from 1935 onward, with the building of power plants to provide low-cost power. And organized labor benefited from the Wagner Act, which upheld the rights of workers to organize and seek wage levels through collective bargaining. The Supreme Court struck down the National Recovery Administration (charged with promoting wage and working-hour "codes") but upheld the Wagner Act, and the conservative high court was believed by some Republicans to be their last bastion of hope. If the Supreme Court would not uphold laissez-faire principles as a governmental philosophy, who would?

Not the New Deal. In the summer of 1935 Congress passed a revenue bill that Roosevelt called "tax fairness" and many Republicans insisted was a "soak-the-rich" bill. The bill aimed to increase taxes on incomes over $50,000 with higher percentages adjusted as the amount went up—75 percent on incomes of over $5 million. Few Americans made that kind of money, but conservatives disliked the principle of the thing. Congress also enacted an excess-profits tax, which many corporate leaders denounced as "economic strangulation."

Roosevelt's popularity was boldly contested by Republicans at the Cleveland nominating convention in June, when conservative Governor Alfred M. Landon of Kansas was picked to head the ticket. The keynote speaker and all who followed him denounced the New Deal as a usurpation of the powers of the federal government, and much praise was heaped on the Supreme Court for its decisions that had sidetracked a few of Roosevelt's favorite programs. Soon campaign buttons shaped like sunflowers (the Kansas state flower) blossomed in Republican campaign quarters, and an unlikely ally appeared when Al Smith, the 1928 Democratic presidential candidate, broke with Roosevelt and endorsed Landon, as did hundreds of daily and weekly newspapers. In the late fall, the *Literary Digest* poll confidently predicted Landon would beat Roosevelt in November.

With bands tooting "Happy Days Are Here Again," cheering Democrats met in Philadelphia. Roosevelt was renominated by his party, and the Democrats went a step further and voted out the two-thirds rule that had led to so many endurance contests since it was adopted in 1832. Also in the race were the

Union party, with a Republican congressmen as its candidate, and the Communist Party U.S.A., with its candidate Earl Browder. Like Landon, Browder was a Kansan, but there the resemblance ended.

As the red-faced *Literary Digest* acknowledged, Roosevelt won in landslide fashion. Landon carried only Maine and Vermont in what was the most lopsided presidential election since Monroe won virtually unopposed in 1820. The electoral college vote said it all—523 for Roosevelt, 8 for Landon. In Congress, the Republican losses were significant. The new House had 331 Democrats, while 89 Republicans answered the rolls in January 1937. The Senate Democrats had a 76-to-16 majority.

A confident president took office on January 20, 1937, as the term began under the Twentieth Amendment for the first time. Democrats lost none of their enthusiasm in the Seventy-fifth Congress, but the Depression would not go away. Republicans relished the intraparty battle as Democrats accused each other of "Supreme Court packing" when a bill to increase the membership of the high court was introduced. Senator Wheeler, still a bumptious thorn in the side of his party, denounced the bill and was heartened when Chief Justice Hughes sent him a letter assuring the Montana lawmaker that the court needed no new justices for its workload. As the debate continued, however, the high court softened its restrictions on New Deal legislation. A rewritten bill, taking out the expansion provision of the first bill, finally passed and Roosevelt signed it. The membership of the Supreme Court stayed at nine.

By the end of 1937 the New Deal had brought in the eight-hour day, a minimum wage, and collective bargaining, much of it over the protests and votes of Republicans in Congress. The farm bloc still was Republican in membership but had come out for such New Deal measures as parity prices for commodities and farm-loan programs. Farm voters responded with confused loyalties. A Democrat, Guy Gillette, was elected to the Senate by Iowa Republicans; in Nebraska, Republican George Norris campaigned on his record of support for the New Deal. Gillette was reelected; Norris was not, despite a campaign plea from Roosevelt for his Republican supporter.

Western Europe was experiencing a depression as deep as that which had struck America, and in Germany the jobless problem was acute when Adolf Hitler strutted onto the political scene. In a series of daring moves in violation of treaty obligations, Hitler reoccupied the Saar basin, rearmed Germany, seized Austria, and in 1938 made gestures patently designed to annex Czechoslovakia into what Hitler styled his "Third Reich." By 1938 the German Nazi party led by Hitler was also flaunting its anti-Semitic tactics, and in the fall of 1938, with British and French collusion, Germany absorbed the Czechoslovakians without a shot fired.

The brazenness of Hitler's advances startled some Americans, but Congress was more concerned about internal weakness than about the growing war clouds abroad. In May 1938 the House established the House Un-American Activities Committee charged with seeking out and exposing subversion in the United States supported or abetted by any foreign power, but the chief target by implication was the Soviet Union and its American counterpart, the Communist Party U.S.A. Republicans served as minority members on the committee and learned lessons on conducting investigations and hearings that they would use in the decades ahead. The Depression abated hardly at all, and voters showed mild dissatisfaction by punishing the incumbent Democrats, who lost seven senate seats and a hefty eighty in the House in the fall by-elections.

Despite the threatening posture of Hitler in Europe, the American people and their representatives in Congress remained preoccupied with the floundering economy. President Roosevelt's radio "fireside chats" were becoming a frequent part of American home life as over 26 million homes possessed at least one set and programs such as *Amos n' Andy* and *One Man's Family* were a part of the nation's morning conversation. How many millions were listening on September 1, 1939, when World War II began with Hitler's invasion of Poland cannot be guessed, but the nation grew somber when England, France, and the Soviet Union were soon involved. After a winter of "phony war," the dreadful May 1940 invasion of the Low Countries by crack German armies, followed by the fall of France in May 1940, sobered the American people. Congress passed the first peacetime conscription law in history, and President Roosevelt called for a billion-dollar rearmament program that slowly generated a business recovery in the election year of 1940.

During the fall of 1939 President Roosevelt had looked ahead to the election and decided to bring Republicans into his cabinet. Governor Landon and Frank Knox, a Michigan newspaper publisher with liberal Republican credentials, were approached, and a bipartisan appointment for both was discussed. But Landon gave Roosevelt an ultimatum—the president would have to promise not to run for a third term before Landon would join the official family. Knox said he would not be the only Republican serving, so Roosevelt kept looking and finally settled on Henry Stimson, who had served in the Taft and Hoover cabinets. As the Republican nominating convention was about to convene in June 1940, the president announced that Knox would be his secretary of the navy and Stimson would hold the War Department portfolio.

Roosevelt's gesture brought a mixed reaction in Republican circles. In New York, the thirty-eight-year-old district attorney, Thomas E. Dewey, a Republican, gained a national reputation for his conviction of various gangsters who had taken over the rackets operating in Manhattan. Widely hailed as a "gangbuster," Dewey ran a good race for governor and despite his loss was described in news magazines as a possible presidential candidate. As a favorite son from New York, with its huge electoral vote, Dewey was confident as the Philadelphia convention opened. Senator Robert Taft of Ohio had former President Hoover's blessing and was probably the favorite with the banking community on lower Manhattan. A whole raft of favorite-son candidates, including Senator Arthur Vandenberg of Michigan, brought up the rear.

Then something happened. An amateurish effort by some New York editors and lawyers who longed for a new face settled on Wendell Willkie, a corporate lawyer who displayed great charm on a popular radio show and was soon invited to speak at various Republican meetings, always professing not to be a candidate but only a citizen concerned about the future of the Republican party. Governor Landon initially thought Willkie could not be taken seriously, for he admitted that as late as 1936 he had been a registered Democrat. But *Fortune* magazine, and then *Time*, both owned by Henry Luce, began publicizing Willkie, and by the time of the June meeting in Philadelphia the noncandidate was probably the best-known Republican in America.

Although Landon was still the titular leader of the party, he was swept along by events like everybody else. After Minnesota's youthful governor, Harold Stassen, gave a spirited keynote speech, the groundswell began. The galleries were packed with chanting crowds whose chorus of "We Want Willkie!" went out on the national radio hookups and seemed to indicate a grassroots surge for the Indiana native with his tousled hair and beaming smile. Petitions pleading for Willkie's nomination came to Philadelphia by the bale and were delivered to delegations; Willkie posters and buttons appeared out of thin air; and after six ballots the Willkie "grassroots" movement (or maybe "Madison Avenue" movement would be more correct) triumphed, leaving supporters of Dewey and Taft stunned on the sidelines. The professional politicians were not pleased, but they had not calculated the force of a series of demonstrations that seemed spontaneous and refreshing to the amateur delegates. If Willkie was a former Democrat, so had been Grant, much of Lincoln's cabinet, and for that matter—who cared?

On the platform committee, the old-timers had more control. At first, there was talk of a foreign-policy plank calling for aid to the European democracies that were hard-pressed by the German army. But many standpatters resented Roosevelt's selection of Knox and Stimson as a grandstand play, and they nearly passed a resolution that would have expelled the two new cabinet members from the Republican party. The punitive resolution was shelved, but a plank critical of Roosevelt's foreign policy was adopted, although a few senators would have favored one that was distinctly isolationist in tone.

Willkie proved to be an enthusiastic campaigner, but he was outmatched by Roosevelt, who won his third-term nomination after the convention heard the president's message of reluctance to run, which left the door open for a draft. The delegates responded by pointing to the national emergency that made the third-term tradition cumbersome rather than embarrassing. Secretary of Agriculture Henry A. Wallace, the son of a Republican who had served in the Harding and Coolidge cabinets, was nominated for vice president.

Even though he was an amateur who had never held elective office, Willkie won thousands of new voters, but his inexperience showed at times, and the war in Europe (rather than homegrown problems) commanded his attention. Indeed, while the isolationist wing of the Republican party was gritting its teeth because he was on the ballot, Willkie seemed intent on outdoing Roosevelt in his admiration for the democracies trying to hold Hitler at bay. Later reminded of some extravagant statements, Willkie excused his excesses as mere "campaign oratory."

Roosevelt did not repeat Wilson's canard, "He kept us out of war," but he did promise voters that he would never send an American boy to fight abroad. Willkie's main message was that it was time to give Republicans a chance and retire Roosevelt along with the New Deal to the history bin.

A sideline to the political campaign was the noise made by a group of isolationists who took the name *America First* for their drive to renounce the nation's involvement in foreign wars. Colonel Charles Lindbergh joined Republican senators Gerald Nye and Robert La Follette Jr. and other critics of Roosevelt's foreign policy in pleas for an isolationist policy. At a series of mass meetings the America Firsters, often supported by seasoned Roosevelt haters, echoed the disillusionment that followed World War I as George Washington's warnings against "entangling alliances" were repeated in impassioned tones. The movement had some support in the Midwest, but except for the extensive media coverage it had little impact elsewhere.

Prior to the election, a national "get out the vote" campaign assured citizens it was their patriotic duty to vote; thus the total number of ballots reached a staggering 50 million, counting the various "also-ran" candidates. But Roosevelt broke the third-term bonds with 27 million votes to 22 million for Willkie, and in the electoral college the president led, 449 to 82. Soon, Roosevelt sent Willkie to meet with the Allied leaders in Europe, and Willkie's book growing out of that trip, *One World,* became a propaganda forerunner of the drive to create a United Nations.

A growing number of Americans feared that the nation was headed down the same path taken in 1917, when a strong leader was trying to stop German aggression while also being friendly toward England and France. Early on, Roosevelt warned against historical parallels and insisted that what he wanted was an America (as he said during the Christmas season of 1940) that would be "the great arsenal of democracy." But German submarine attacks were forcing Great Britain to tighten its limited food and petroleum supplies as the German Luftwaffe pounded the English with devastating air raids.

In June 1941 the German-Soviet alliance was broken as the *Reichswehr* swept eastward with Moscow as its objective before the winter snows. Suddenly a two-front war spread the destruction but also made American aid to the Soviet Union seem advisable, despite a strong conservative bias against the communist government. (Not a few Republicans still held it against Roosevelt that he, unlike presidents Harding, Coolidge, and Hoover, had recognized the Soviet Union and set up a diplomatic channel in 1934.) Within weeks, the Japanese occupied French Indochina, and Roosevelt ordered the freezing of Japanese credits in the United States. Tension between the Americans and the Japanese was not the main thing worrying Congress, however, when a vote to extend the peacetime draft was debated in August 1941. The isolationist wing of the Republican party fought doggedly to defeat the measure, and the draft ultimately was saved by only a single vote, 203 to 202.

Then came the "day of infamy"—December 7, 1941. Pearl Harbor changed the political spectrum less dramatically than it did every other aspect of American life, but the dictum of "politics as usual" was a wartime casualty. Roosevelt appeared before Congress on December 8 and asked for a declaration of war against Japan. The Senate responded with a unanimous vote, but in the House the vote was 388 to 1, the lone dissenter being Republican Jeannette Rankin, returned to the House (after a long hiatus) in the 1940 election. A model of consistency, Rankin had also voted against war in April 1917.

From December 7 until the end of the war in both Europe and the Pacific, Republicans in Congress and in courthouses and on school boards were eager to serve a nation fighting for its democratic life. In the by-election year of 1942, the Senate remained Democratic, 58 to 37, as nine new Republicans gained seats; in the House, Republican gains were more significant as the Democrats lead was cut to ten votes (218 to 208). Criticism of the New Deal and Roosevelt was muted as the war changed society in fundamental ways. In 1939, fewer than 4 million workers paid income taxes; in 1945 the number of taxpaying workers rose to 42.6 million—a tenfold increase that poured $35 billion into the federal treasury in the last year of the war. The imposition of income-tax payroll deductions in 1943 eased the strain of financing the war. At the war's end, the national debt had reached $260 billion and was still climbing.

Throughout most of the war, Republicans were split into two camps. At the national level, GOP leaders in Congress generally supported the president's requests for more arms, men, and aid to America's allies; but at the state and local levels, Republicans continued their criticism of Roosevelt's policies and won more statehouses in the 1942 elections. In 1944 President Roosevelt called for a new bill of rights for postwar America that included the right to a job, to a decent home, and to education. Hardline Republicans viewed these proposals with skepticism, and some bitter opponents of "that man in the White House" had become so estranged from the political process they gripped their copies of the *Wall Street Journal* and concluded the nation was on the pathway to ruin.

Less pessimistic Republicans in Congress voted for the so-called GI Bill of Rights in 1944, providing education, medical care, and housing loans for returning veterans. Politics heated up, however, when the "No Third Term" opposition to Roosevelt resurfaced as a "No Fourth Term" movement determined to prevent his reelection. Democrats nominated Roosevelt without major qualms, but they did take Henry Wallace off the ballot and replace him with Senator Harry Truman as vice president.

Readers of *Time* may have thought the 1944 Republican convention would rubber-stamp Willkie again as the party's candidate. In no mood to be stampeded a second time, however, regular Republicans disciplined Willkie by soundly trouncing him in an early primary contest, a disappointment that soon led to Willkie's withdrawal from the race. General Douglas MacArthur and Harold Stassen, also entered in the Wisconsin primary, were readily trounced by the front-runner, Thomas Dewey, now governor of New York. After that, there was no stopping Dewey, who won on the first ballot at the Republican nominating convention by the astonishing count of 1,056 to 1. Senator John Bricker of Ohio, an original supporter of fellow senator Robert Taft, was given the vice presidential spot in a conciliatory gesture to the ultraconservative delegates.

Bricker, turned loose, became something of a liability. He put his foot in his mouth when asked about support coming from a notorious anti-Semitic, right-wing extremist. Bricker blithely said he welcomed all support, then had to back down when Dewey called the extremist a "Hitler-like rabble-rouser." Speaking in Dallas in October 1944, Bricker vented his wrath on political action committees (the PACs were a brainchild of the CIO union leadership, created as a funnel for campaign contributions) and took a swipe at Roosevelt. "To all intents and purposes the great Democratic party has become the Hillman-Browder Communistic party with Franklin Roosevelt as its front," Bricker said as he named seven federal employees linked to the CIO-PAC. Their PAC connection, Bricker said, "conclusively proved that Franklin Roosevelt and the New Deal are in the hands of the radicals and the Communists."

Calling Roosevelt a communist sympathizer became standard campaign jargon, but nobody had the temerity to mention Roosevelt's health as an issue in the campaign. Newspaper reporters surrounding the president kept their discretion intact and never told voters of Roosevelt's need for physical assistance in nearly every movement. Photographers would not take pictures of the president in a wheelchair or being supported in his painful moves on a brief campaign skirmish. Truman, added to the ticket because of his judicious handling of a probe into wartime industry, remained in the background. Indeed, Roosevelt all but ignored his running mate.

The 1944 presidential election proved that the war veteran FDR was as popular as the early Roosevelt, each in his own way winning the nation's affection by creating the perception of strong, determined leadership. In the popular vote, Roosevelt beat Dewey by 3.5 million out of 48 million votes cast; in the electoral college, the difference was 432 to 99. Roosevelt carried every industrial state and every large American city. Only in the midwestern grain belt were Republican loyalties left intact. The elected Seventy-ninth Congress had Democratic majorities in both houses, without much change from the previous lineups.

The only issue that aroused much interest was the discussion of the postwar world, and Republicans generally eschewed any comparison with the anti-League battles of the Wilson-Harding years. The most notable case of a turnaround was offered by Senator Vandenberg of Michigan, who dropped his isolationist stand and became a kind of spokesman for a bipartisan foreign policy that would include American entry into a postwar organization to preserve world peace. When the United Nations was formed in 1945, the Senate confirmed the treaty that took the United States into the international organization by a vote of 89 to 2. The opponents were Republicans William Langer of North Dakota and Henrik Shipstead of Minnesota.

Roosevelt's death on April 12, 1945, brought a temporary halt to the buildup of rancor that four successive defeats had developed among loyal Republicans. For the moment, Harry Truman had the support of both sides of the aisles in Congress as the war came to an end early in May with Germany's surrender and in August with the Japanese capitulation. The San Francisco meeting of the Allies to create a United Nations proceeded smoothly, although conservative newspaper columnists had some reservations concerning the Soviet Union's postwar intentions. A demobilization of 12 million servicemen and women proceeded apace, and by early 1946 many economists were warning of a postwar depression. Stock prices stood still, as Americans feared a wave of unemployment would knock wartime dreams of a booming America into limbo.

Nothing of the sort happened, of course. The pent-up consumer demand kept the auto industry puffing to keep cars rolling off assembly lines, steel consumption rose, and once the wartime price controls were lifted, a genuine boom ensued. Long waiting lists accumulated at car dealerships as buyers clamored for a Chevrolet sedan with a list price of $1,265.

The good news of the economy did not lap over into Truman's administration, however. After their long stretch of congressional control, the Democrats were criticized as "tired," and a listless Congress wrestled with the problems of atomic control, rising suspicions of the Soviet Union, and inflationary pressures created by price boosts in key industries. A deluge of postwar strikes, including a devastating railroad walkout, forced Truman to threaten a federal takeover of the tracks. A similar confrontation with John L. Lewis of the coal-miner's union brought Truman into the labor arena again, but seizure of the mines mainly polarized public opinion and did little to settle labor unrest.

Truman's approval rating went down in the polls, and Republicans seized on national discontent in the fall of 1946 with a bumper-sticker slogan, "Had Enough? Vote Republican." Democrats who had pledged their loyalty to Truman in April 1945 shifted uneasily. Hundreds of veterans made their first bid for office, including former naval officers Richard M. Nixon in California and John F. Kennedy in Massachusetts and former Marine airman Joseph McCarthy in Wisconsin. The first two won House seats, while McCarthy became the Republican junior senator from Wisconsin.

Republicans capitalized on the anti-Truman sentiment, the ennui of postwar disillusionment, and the rise in grocery prices as they won control of Congress for the first time since 1928. In the Senate, the GOP advantage was a thin 51-to-45 margin, but in the House the Republican majority was 246 to 188. Voters, it seemed, demanded laws to curb wildcat strikes, hold prices down, and dismantle some New Deal programs still funded for a Depression era that was fading into memory.

Flush with their triumph, the House Republicans elected Joseph Martin of Massachusetts their Speaker and proceeded to "whip labor into line" with passage of the Taft-Hartley Act that overturned some New Deal labor legislation. The act outlawed the closed shop, restricted union participation in election financing, and gave the president power to order a cooling-off period in strikes threatening the nation's welfare. President Truman's veto was easily overturned, but organized labor resented the law and ended a brief flirtation with Republicans in Michigan, Pennsylvania, and Ohio. Republicans did find that their tenuous alliance with conservative southerners in Congress gained strength in postwar elections. Truman's executive order for full integration of the armed services was particularly galling to many congressmen from the old Confederacy.

Dealing with Congress proved difficult enough for Truman, but more worrisome was the Soviet Union's aggressive policy in eastern Europe, which obviated all thoughts of a postwar world where democratic governments might exist in Poland, Hungary, Czechoslovakia, Romania, and Yugoslavia. Winston Churchill's "Iron Curtain" speech in Missouri set the tone for a new kind of skirmish, a "cold war" in which the Soviet Union used intimidation to subjugate democratic governments and convert them into communistic states. East Germany soon became a Soviet satellite as the tension between East and West heightened. The inroads of communist armies in the Chinese civil war drew particular attention from West Coast Republicans, who predicted a "Truman sellout" of Chiang Kai-shek's nationalist forces. Senator William F. Knowland of California became so critical of the Truman policy toward the Orient that his detractors called the Oakland Republican "the senator from Formosa."

Knowland and other Republican critics accused Truman of being "soft on communism," but the president's announced policy for containing the growing Soviet sphere of influence marked the limits of Soviet expansion. The Soviet Union had, meanwhile, proved its own atomic-weapon capability, intensifying concern that a third world war might involve unspeakable damage to civilian populations. Undaunted, Truman supported a plan broached by Secretary of State George Marshall for American support to aid in the reconstruction of war-torn Europe. Marshall said American financial aid would support a program not aimed at "any country or doctrine but against hunger, poverty, desperation, and chaos." The Soviet bloc at once denounced the program, leaving the United States free to help ailing former allies and the people of West Germany and Italy rebuild their devastated countries.

Senator Vandenberg, who had become the leading Republican involved in foreign policy, announced his bipartisan support for the Marshall Plan, thus ensuring its passage through Congress. This would be one of the last pieces of bipartisan legislation to pass Congress for the next generation; but in retrospect, the $18 billion price tag for the Marshall Plan proved to be money well spent. Candid Republicans admitted Marshall's plan had prevented further communist exploitation of the postwar economic disorders affecting the Western democracies.

Goaded by charges from Republicans that his administration was not taking a hard line on communist sympathizers in governmental positions, President Truman in March 1947 ordered a loyalty check of employees suspected of subversive activities. Critics of Truman's policy said it initiated a witch-hunt, but the accusations against Alger Hiss, a State Department employee, led to a sensational trial that projected Representative Richard Nixon into the spotlight and, eventually, led to Hiss's conviction and imprisonment.

Perhaps more sensational were the 1947 hearings of the House Un-American Activities Committee, now chaired by Republican J. Parnell Thomas of New Jersey. As the committee investigated rumors of communist influence in the film industry, a long list of film stars were subpoenaed. From stars to bit players, they were asked to testify about their knowledge of red-tinged movies and actors. Before the highly publicized hearings ended, a group of screenwriters that the press called "The Hollywood Ten" were sentenced to jail for contempt of Congress. As president of the Screen Actors' Guild, Democrat and screen star Ronald Reagan played a passive role until the hearings ended.

Two years of war between the executive branch and the White House led Republican leaders to believe that finally, in 1948, the presidency would swing back their way. All the polls showed Truman was highly unpopular. Some high-ranking Democrats even talked of abandoning the president and nominating Secretary of State George Marshall to lead their ticket. But in the end, the state preferential primaries were avoided (incumbents can do that, outsiders can't) and Truman applied enough pressure on the big-city machines and labor leaders to give him the nomination. After a "hell-raiser" of a keynote speech, Senator Alben Barkley of Kentucky was made Truman's running mate.

Opinion polls led Republicans to feel a sense of euphoria when they gathered in Philadelphia to pick a nominee and, the Lord willing, the next president. The Gallup, Roper, and other leading polls all reported an enormous decline in Truman's popularity, in some cases to less than 30 percent, so how could they lose?

Sad-faced Democrats grudgingly admitted the Republican nominating convention would probably choose the nation's next president. Thomas Dewey was available, but he bore the scars of 1944 and would have to overcome the historic snub given by all past Republican conventions to previously defeated candidates. Perhaps Senator Taft of Ohio was the betting favorite, because the hard-core conservatives trusted this son of former President Taft.

Taft was a thinned-down version of his presidential father, with an Ivy League background, a solid conservative record in Congress, and a speaking acquaintanceship with almost every major Republican in the country. But neither Taft nor Harold Stassen had counted on the organizational skills of Dewey's campaign team, and when the first ballot gave the New York governor 434 votes, alarm shifted to panic; after the second ballot it was all over. Dewey was defying tradition and would be the 1948 standard-bearer, with California Governor Earl Warren as the vice presidential nominee.

Postmortems of the 1948 election have occupied academicians for more than forty years as they have used statistics, charts, slide rules, and computers to explain how, although Truman did not win, Dewey lost the election. The infusion of the race issue into the campaign by the States' Rights party of Democratic dissidents seemed to give Dewey the election on a silver platter; but the embattled Truman stumped the country in a railroad car denouncing "the good-for-nothing Eightieth Congress" to cheering crowds. Dewey, believing he had the election sewed up, spoke in generalities and talked repeatedly about a "housecleaning in Washington come next January." Dewey's demeanor also hurt his chances, for he could not warm up to crowds, called the engineer who accidentally lurched his observation car an "idiot," and plainly disliked the whistle-stop method of campaigning that Truman was enjoying to the hilt.

Democrats were ready to send Truman their condolences on election night, as the first returns from the eastern cities bespoke a confirmation of the pollsters' predictions. But as the midwestern and western returns dribbled in, Truman showed surprising strength in areas that were normally Republican. On the morning following the election, uncertainty reigned. The States' Righters took four southern states, and Dewey's chances looked better. Then an avalanche from the West rolled in, signaling an upset of monumental proportions. Two days after the voting, the Republicans learned they had lost the Midwest, the Rocky Mountain states, Texas, California, and Washington. The greatest political upset in American history had resurrected the man whose haberdashery business went bankrupt after World War I.

Truman joked as he held up the journalistic blunder of the century, the *Chicago Tribune*'s premature headline: "DEWEY DEFEATS TRUMAN." Red-faced poll-takers professed their shock. Obviously, said one embarrassed pollster, "voters did a lot of last-minute switching." No kidding!

Stunned Republicans hoped for some solace from the congressional races, but none came. Instead, the Democrats had recaptured the Senate, 54 to 42, and held a majority in the House, 263 to 171. The Dewey buttons were discarded, the telephones at campaign headquarters were disconnected, and saddened Republican diehards made only one vow that would be carried through—Governor Dewey was still "young" at fifty-five, but politically, he was finished as a presidential prospect.

Republicans in Congress picked up the pieces, and a few came out swinging belligerently. The most notable angry Republican was Senator McCarthy, who discovered that any speech hinting at subversives in federal jobs caused audiences to beg for more. McCarthy revived the "soft on communism" campaign against the Truman administration early in 1950 with his charge that he knew of "205 men that were known to the Secretary of State as being members of the Communist Party and who nevertheless are still working and shaping the policy of the State Department." Newspapers repeated the sensational charges, forcing Secretary of State Dean Acheson to issue a denial. His ire raised at a press conference, Truman told reporters McCarthy's claims were simply "lies, slanders, [and] character assassination." But television networks were now part of the journalistic scene, and McCarthy was soon seen on America's living-room screens as the Republican avenger.

Other events in 1950 made the shadow of the Soviet Union seem omnipresent in American life. The invasion of South Korea by the communist regime in North Korea in June 1950 forced President Truman to make a quick decision. Truman ordered American troops to the battle zone, in support of a "police action" authorized by the United Nations. Congress was not in session when the fighting began, but in general both parties supported Truman's initial reaction. An exception was Senator Robert Taft, who claimed the president had exceeded his executive powers by committing American forces to the fray. An opinion poll in July 1950 gave Truman's action a 77 percent approval rating, however, and Taft's criticism was not echoed by other Republicans. Indeed, haunted by the memories of Franco-British apathy when Hitler first started his invasion tactics, politicians did not want to be labeled as "appeasers" in the climate of anticommunist opinion prevailing in the land.

The Korean War went badly until September, when General Douglas MacArthur executed a brilliant land-sea maneuver that sent the North Korean army into a near-panic retreat. MacArthur promised Americans he would have "the boys home by Christmas," but he had not counted on the intervention of communist China's People's Army. MacArthur's boast that his goal was "a unified . . . democratic Korea" was taken seriously in Peking, and the Chinese counteroffensive started right after Thanksgiving Day.

Crossing the Yalu River in massive force, the Chinese routed the United Nations troops made up primarily of American soldiers. After much retreating and recapturing, a stalemate developed. Volatile Americans who supported the war six months earlier decided in January 1951 it was time to pull out of Korea, and 49 percent of those polled said American involvement had been a mistake in the first place. At home, the generals who had won World War II advised the president to avoid enlarging the Korean War, but MacArthur disagreed and went to Taiwan seeking more manpower. The last straw was a letter MacArthur wrote the House minority leader, Republican Joe Martin, in which he deplored the stalemate. MacArthur, apparently willing to use the atomic bomb on tactical targets inside China, appealed for Republican support. Martin made the letter public, and a controversy immediately erupted.

A chorus of Republican critics now took aim at Truman, led by Senator Taft, with McCarthy not far behind and Martin bringing up the rear. Truman's conduct of the war was the issue, and GOP critics claimed the commander in chief was in over his head. Whether MacArthur should have his way completely was not the main issue.

Truman chose to make MacArthur's letter to Martin the issue. He fired MacArthur five days after Martin released the explosive letter, and a firestorm of public protest followed. Confusion among the Democrats allowed the Republicans to pass a resolution inviting MacArthur to address Congress. Back on American soil for the first time in fourteen years, MacArthur had a hero's welcome in Washington as he ascended Capitol Hill. At the joint session, MacArthur implied that he had been a caged tiger, not able to do his utmost to win in Korea. Then he ended his remarks with a line taken from a West Point song: "Old soldiers never die, they just fade away."

Television cameras and newspapers featured the tiff between MacArthur and Truman as some Republicans began to talk about running "the old soldier" for president. Meanwhile, the war in Korea dragged on, the casualty lists lengthened, and the monthly draft calls reached 47,000. Truman's popularity again took a nosedive. Democrats sent up a trial balloon for a national health insurance program; angry medical organizations, including the one most doctors belonged to, denounced the plan as "socialized medicine," and it was dead on arrival in the House. Nor was the Truman administration able to bring about outright repeal of all the Taft-Hartley Act's provisions.

Minor scandals with charges of "influence peddling" haunted the White House.

With the approach of 1952, both major parties began a search for a presidential candidate. Truman was out of the running, and in the early presidential primaries Democrats seemed to favor Senator Estes Kefauver. Party leaders were not impressed with Kefauver, despite his demeanor on national television as head of a Senate committee investigating organized crime. In time, Governor Adlai Stevenson of Illinois was nominated in spite of his publicized sense of humor and (remember, this was 1952) the fact that he was divorced.

The Republicans had more of a problem, because the old loyalists were determined to see their man, Robert Taft, nominated. Taft's trouble was that Dwight Eisenhower, the commander of Allied forces in World War II, had finally cleared the air and announced he was a Republican (earlier, Democrats had made overtures, awaiting the general's decision). Eisenhower was back in military harness in 1952, after a brief stint as president of Columbia University, and he was commander of the North Atlantic Treaty Organization forces when the Republicans came calling. Once his name was on the presidential primary ballots, Taft's chances faded.

How much influence the so-called eastern crowd exerted in the nomination is uncertain. Western Republicans such as Richard Nixon believed the eastern establishment was not vigilant enough in its concern for anticommunist activities, and they feared that Thomas Dewey still had one more race left in him. Recently reelected governor of New York, Dewey was too realistic to think he could make a third presidential try, but he was interested in the party's future. Looking over the field of potential candidates, the party insiders apparently decided Harold Stassen was already (at the age of forty-four) shopworn, while Governor Warren of California was too liberal for conservatives who looked back longingly to the Coolidge-Hoover era.

Eisenhower's chief asset was the mystery surrounding his political past. So far as anyone knew, he had never bothered to register, had not voted in any presidential election, yet had made off-the-record statements critical of Truman. With that slight opening, the "eastern crowd" sent emissaries to Paris, where the NATO headquarters was located, and sought a statement from "Ike." In January 1952, with Senator Henry Cabot Lodge Jr. smiling in the background, the general told the world he was, in fact, a Republican.

From that time on, Taft forces fought a hopeless rearguard action but did not surrender. Eisenhower was granted a leave on June 1 and was soon back home, politicking with the best of them. His popular book on World War II was titled *Crusade in Europe*, and this campaign, Eisenhower vowed, was a crusade to preserve the Republican party. Some historians have compared the convention battle to the 1912 contest between Taft's father and Theodore Roosevelt, but the analogy is strained. From the outset, Eisenhower's popularity made it clear he was the choice of delegates from all the big states except Ohio, California, Michigan, and Pennsylvania, where favorite sons held fast.

In a crucial vote involving the seating of contested delegations, Taft's men lost. As the July convention moved along, some old-time Republicans foresaw a deadlock that would open the way for a dark horse. Senator Everett Dirksen of Illinois, perhaps Taft's closest adviser, came on the convention floor and pointed to the New York delegation and to the governor. Millions of television viewers watched Dirksen look directly at Dewey and shout: "We followed you before, and you took us down the path to defeat."* After losing another close fight on seating, the Taft forces gave way. Pro-Eisenhower delegations from Texas and Louisiana also were seated without a contest.

Taft's supporters clung to one last desperate hope that the favorite sons would release their delegations after the first ballot and begin a swing to the Ohioan. But miracles rarely happen during political conventions. On July 11 the first ballot gave "Ike" 595 votes; Taft had 500, and Warren trailed with 80. Stassen and MacArthur were brushed aside with token votes, and then Minnesota made the switch to Eisenhower and the booming demonstration vicariously drew in television audiences across America. The chant—"We Like Ike!"—seemed infectious.

*Quoted in Mayer, *The Republican Party*, 490.

To Eisenhower's supporters, the nagging question was: "Does America like Ike?" Painful memories of dismal battles and failing campaigns from 1932 to 1948 caused concern about the general's ability to look and sound presidential in an era when the television networks had added a new, powerful, and expensive dimension to national campaigns. Also waving a flag of caution were those who recalled how popular MacArthur had been a year earlier, and how that popularity had quickly faded.

Perhaps only one man in the convention hall listening to Eisenhower's acceptance speech shared none of these concerns. Senator Richard M. Nixon, chosen to be the vice presidential nominee, was confident of victory. His outstretched hands made the V-for-victory sign left over from the war. Surely, Ike was invincible, and his coattails were a mile long.

CHAPTER TWELVE

The Republican Resurrection

Eisenhower gave the Republicans a candidate who could stress the need for national unity without mentioning the New Deal. The Korean War was the chief campaign issue, and when "Ike" promised he would go to Korea and end the war, the Democrats had no viable alternative. Stevenson was locked into supporting the old, somewhat tired Democratic sloganeering, and when he promised to "clean up the mess in Washington" he not only offended Truman but also seemed to emphasize how a change might be healthy.

For his part, Eisenhower followed Truman's 1948 pattern and traveled across the country, speaking from the back of an observation car with his pat, short speech. His administration, he promised, would tackle the three problems that Democrats couldn't handle: Korea, communism, and corruption.

The campaign was rolling along, picking up speed, when a sudden hitch occurred. A reporter broke a story revealing that Richard Nixon had a secret "slush fund." Wealthy Californians had established the account to help the young congressman in his fight against subversives, or so it was explained. On national television, Nixon defended himself, alluded to his children's dog Checkers, and mentioned his wife's "Republican cloth coat" (a recent Democratic scandal had involved the gift of a fur coat). Republican leaders may have considered dumping Nixon, but the speech drew a raft of sympathetic telegrams and messages. Nixon stayed on the ticket.

Polls, still cautious after the 1948 embarrassment, forecast a narrow win for Eisenhower. "The election could go either way," newscasters parroted as they summarized the months of hard campaigning. The harsh fact was that almost 60 percent of the American voters either were registered as Democrats or considered themselves Democrats in 1952. Could Ike break down the coalition of blacks, union workers, Jewish city dwellers, and Catholics loyal to big-city machines in dozens of urban areas?

Returns on election night carried the answer. Eisenhower won a record-breaking 33.9 million votes, far outdistancing Stevenson's 27.3 million. Four southern states defected from the once-solid South, starting a trend that would continue through the rest of the century as the more conservative southern leaders abandoned their historic base and sought a new home in the Republican party. Increasingly, southern blue-collar workers were abandoning their past Democratic ties, in part out of resentment stemming from Truman's integration of the armed forces, but some of the disenchantment was deeper. Within a decade, George Wallace in Alabama would understand how deep that bitterness sank and would learn to exploit it.

Clearly, however, it was more than a blue-collar rebellion within the Democratic party. After the Eisenhower landslide of 1952, being a Republican in the South became more and more a mark of the gentility that was previously reserved for the Democratic upper crust.

That Ike won because voters trusted him, and crossed over party lines in droves, was affirmed by the fact that he did not pull off a earth-jolting landslide that brought in a Republican Congress easily under Republican control. The Senate had 48 Republicans, 47 Democrats, and the former Republican Wayne Morse, who had become an Independent. In the House, the Republicans won 221 seats, with 212 going to Democrats. In short, the Republicans controlled Congress, barely. But restless southern Democrats were ready to cooperate on conservative measures, so Ike could have had his way on any issue he had strong feelings about—but it turned out that strong feelings were not Eisenhower's style. He was a moderate, sometimes almost apolitical in his view of government, and never a rabid partisan like Theodore Roosevelt. Almost forty years would pass before another Republican Congress would convene to welcome a Republican president.

Eisenhower kept his pledge to go to Korea and went in early December, but nothing conclusive grew out of the visit. The Korean stalemate continued.

In office, Eisenhower took a military man's mind-set as his guide and Thomas Dewey as his mentor. He made the decisions, trusted subordinates, and demanded loyalty somewhat ahead of judgment. His secretary of state, John Foster Dulles, was considered an expert in foreign affairs but somewhat doctrinaire. Herbert Brownell, like Dulles a confidant of Dewey, was appointed attorney general. Banker George M. Humphrey became secretary of the treasury, and Charles E. Wilson left General Motors to head the Defense Department. Most of the cabinet and diplomatic posts went to Republicans with an industrial or business background. The exception was Ezra Taft Benson of Utah, who served as secretary of agriculture. The glamour was supplied by Texan Oveta Culp Hobby, wartime commander of the Women's Army Corps, who was named secretary of the recently created Department of Health, Education, and Welfare. No less glamorous, perhaps, was the new ambassador to Italy, Clare Booth Luce, a distinguished playwright and the wife of *Time* publisher Henry Luce.

From the outset Eisenhower told his cabinet he was concerned with keeping the Soviet Union contained, ending the Korean War, and slowing down federal programs relating to economic and social issues. Scholars who once considered Eisenhower a kind of Coolidge in disguise have backtracked in recent years to give him credit for his moderate, evenhanded approach to his major problems. A national superhighway system was constructed during his administration, the Korean War was finally ended, and despite some mild pressure the United States made no attempt to rescue France's failing military efforts to stop native communistic takeovers in Indochina.

In foreign affairs, Dulles became a hard-liner in his confrontations with the Soviet Union. The Berlin airlift, started under Truman, was a commitment to western Europeans that was discontinued when Hungary was invaded by Soviet tanks and became a satellite of the USSR. Dulles was accused of "brinkmanship" for making threats that brought the two major powers close to war. But if the climate between Moscow and Washington was frosty, it was only part of the cold war, and never turned into a shooting one.

The complete capitulation of the nationalist forces in China was a continuous source of regret to one group of Republican senators, led by William F. Knowland of California, who became majority leader in 1953 (after Robert Taft died in August). Sarcastically known as "the China lobby," these senators effectively kept the People's Republic of China at arm's length, so that tourism and trade between the two nations was minimal. War threats over the status of Formosa (now renamed Taiwan and the last refuge of Chiang Kai-shek's supporters), which was a "bone in the throat" of Chinese communists, would persist and carry over into the last decade of the century.

Republican candidates learned in 1952 that tough talk about communists helped nudge many marginal races in their favor. None had been more effective than Senator McCarthy as an anticommunist vigilante. Now that Republicans controlled Congress he pressed the advantage in nationally televised hearings where accusations were rife and the ordinary rules of judicial fair play were barely observed. Liberal Republicans looked to Eisenhower for some sign or word that would squelch McCarthy, who was running for reelection, but none came. Confrontation, particularly with others in his party, was hardly Ike's style.

McCarthy's list of communists shrank, but he persisted and created a climate of opinion that gave the English language a new word, *McCarthyism*. The term's connotations were of wild accusation and character assassination by innuendo rather than proof. The Korean War ended in a negotiated settlement in July 1953, but "fighting communism" was still *de rigueur* around McCarthy's office.

By 1954, McCarthy was ready to take on the United States Army. He lost credibility, made a hero out of the defense attorney, and disgusted television audiences with his broad-brushed accusations. In time, McCarthy's Senate colleagues had enough and voted to censure his conduct. Republicans joined Democrats for the 67 to 22 vote. Perhaps novelist William Faulkner said it best when he looked back at the McCarthy hearings and commented: "Nobody can do a great deal of harm as long as [the] fierce light of publicity shines on everything he does, and that I think as much as anything else destroyed people like McCarthy."

Whatever Eisenhower thought of McCarthy, he was willing to take the advice of the liberal-wing Republicans when the chief justiceship of the Supreme Court became vacant. He appointed Governor Earl Warren, who had served as attorney general in California, and was later rumored to have regretted making his choice. In 1954 it was Warren who read the opinion in *Brown v. Board of Education,* a decision that left a permanent mark on the nation by ordering the end of school segregation "with all deliberate speed."

As president, Eisenhower was reluctant to involve his administration in a vigorous follow-up of the *Brown* decision. Generally, Republicans showed little interest in championing further gains in civil liberties for blacks. The old ties of black loyalty to the Republican party had disintegrated during the New Deal, when both city- and farm-dwelling blacks switched parties until 80 percent of the black vote was Democratic by 1944.

Ironically, as blacks reinforced their Democratic loyalty, southern whites abandoned theirs in massive numbers. A coalition of Republicans and southern Democrats evolved during the Eisenhower years and led to filibustering on civil rights issues. Few civil rights laws were passed for another decade.

The exact impact of the *Brown* decision was still being pondered when voters gave control of Congress back to the Democrats in the off-year elections of 1954. In the Senate, the Republicans lost one seat and the Democrats gained one, while the House became more markedly Democratic, 332 to 203. Cooperation between the White House and Congress was easily achieved, however, as moderates in Congress respected the president's popularity and enacted programs of moderate dimensions. One result was that none of the social programs launched by Roosevelt and Truman were dismantled during Eisenhower's tenure.

One sore spot, long festering in the Senate, concerned the ultraconservatives who resented the United Nations covenant on human rights. When the issue was first debated shortly after World War II ended, after a California court decision cited the United Nations charter to strike down a state law on alien ownership of land, the ire of Senator Millikin of Colorado was notable. Then the head of the American Bar Association took aim at the Human Rights covenant, and the ABA went on record as opposed to its ratification by the Senate. Senator John Bricker, returned to the chamber in the 1946 Republican landslide, took up the cause and, first through resolutions and then with a constitutional amendment, sought to restrict the president's power in foreign affairs. From 1951 to 1956, when the "Bricker Amendment" was introduced, various Republican senators wanted to revise drastically the 1936 Supreme Court *Curtiss-Wright* decision giving the president broad powers in foreign affairs. Even though Eisenhower was president, the brunt of the matter was the fear of conservatives that another Franklin Roosevelt might come along. Bricker's 1956 amendment never came to a final Senate vote, and when the senator himself was crushed by a liberal Democrat in the 1958 off-year elections, his effort to restrict presidential power had come to naught.

Although things looked quiet in the Senate chamber, the domestic scene heated up. As school boards across America began to comply with the high court's *Brown* ruling after 1955, much tension developed as the schools were integrated in districts where white leaders made no secret of their disgust with the judicial interpretation. An extreme case was the Virginia county that simply closed its public schools in an angry protest of a federal court decree. In Arkansas, Governor Orval Faubus helped fan the flames of discord with his defiant speeches, and in 1957 President Eisenhower reluctantly ordered federal troops into Little Rock to implement the court order at Central High School. After some forty years, bitter memories of the forced integration of the Little Rock school remain. Eisenhower had reservations about the decision, and once said, "I don't believe you can change the hearts of men with laws or decisions." But, in the Little Rock incident, he did what a president is supposed to do. He enforced the law.

The Little Rock affair came in the aftermath of Eisenhower's second election victory. After a slight heart attack, the president had cut down on his official duties, played more golf, and delegated even more responsibilities to second-level Republican leaders. The only drama of the 1956 campaign was furnished when Harold Stassen, who held a minor post in the Eisenhower administration, announced he was starting a move to dump Richard Nixon from the 1956 ticket. What prompted Stassen to do this? Perhaps he was urged by liberal Republicans who were suspicious of Nixon, but the effort proved abortive when the president told reporters he was satisfied that Nixon had been a good vice president. It may have been a close call, but Richard Nixon was saved again.

In a replay of the 1952 contest, Stevenson was again nominated by Democrats, but enthusiasm was lacking in the summer and fall campaigning. The Republicans held their 1956 convention in San Francisco in August and did endorse the *Brown* decision with a platform plank that said school segregation should be "progressively eliminated." "Parity" farm prices, once a big issue, were mentioned in both party platforms—the Democrats wanted commodities supported at 100 percent of the formulated price, while Republicans favored flexible commodity payments. But the nation's mood was reflected in the lack of fireworks, and businessmen found nothing to quarrel with in Charles Wilson's remark that "what's good for the country is good for General Motors, and what's good for General Motors is good for the United States."

Pollsters were becoming confident again as new techniques sharpened their ability to derive more accurate readings from their statistics. A big Eisenhower win in 1956 was predicted, although Stevenson reminded voters that pollsters were not infallible and his supporters prayed for another upset of 1948 dimensions. Then it was all over. The nation's number-one golfer had won in a landslide, 35.5 million votes to Stevenson's 26 million. The Senate was still only barely Democratic; but in the House, Republicans lost one vote and fell to a minority of 232 to 199. America still liked Ike a whole lot, but they felt more comfortable with Democrats in charge of Congress.

Wall Street, once the whipping boy of the Democrats, had not been much of a factor in the 1956 campaign, which was the first in which television completely dominated both Republican and Democratic planning. No more whistle-stops; no more rallies in huge auditoriums. The networks made time available, and the viewing public obliged by watching a toned-down Stevenson try to pry votes away from Ike, who was now a father figure for the nation.

Television alone, however, was not responsible for the Eisenhower landslide of 1956. Mild prosperity and low inflation kept wage earners happy. The national budget was balanced by the Eisenhower team, and Secretary of Defense Wilson shocked defense contractors when he announced that the 1958 budget for armaments would be limited to a mere $38 billion. *RAND* became a part of the federal dictionary, as Research and Development programs were expanded or substituted for actual hardware for the armed services. And in human terms, research paid off immensely when Jonas Salk revealed his successful vaccine for the dreaded polio virus. Secretary Hobby's insistence that free distribution of the vaccine would be nothing more than "socialized medicine" quickly aroused a spate of negative comments across the country. Hobby lost her job.

Jobs? Most Americans had good jobs during the Eisenhower years. The jobless rate hovered between 3 and 6 percent from 1953 to 1960, inflation was minimal, and low interest rates encouraged a housing boom that sparked a massive exodus from the inner cities by America's middle class. "Suburbia" became a reality as the expanding highway system allowed commuters to travel twenty-five miles to work where once a short streetcar ride had sufficed. The new homes, bought with mortgages at interest rates of 5 and 6 percent, had built-in dishwashers and two-car garages. Detroit's new line of 1957 cars had plenty of chrome and V-8 engines. Americans who had never before gone abroad were taking cruises in the Mediterranean or flying to Europe, where the dollar was strong. Signs of recovery were evident as the Marshall Plan received bipartisan accolades for the surge of prosperity seen in western Europe. Beyond the Iron Curtain, well, nobody wanted to go *there*.

All was not quite perfect, however, as the sudden appearance in the October 1957 sky of the Soviet space satellite *Sputnik* proved. The successful launch of the first globe-circling satellite by the Soviets staggered the national ego as it visibly streaked across America's skies. Accustomed to believing the USSR was a second-rate power crippled by communism, Americans began a binge of soul-searching. What had the country been doing, sleeping at the switch while the Russians were making spaceships? Congress clamored for action, parents were told American educators had neglected science and mathematics and spent too much time on history and English. School boards felt the pressure, and congressmen searched for answers.

Eisenhower, the old soldier, was in no mood to be rushed. Once the excitement over *Sputnik* cooled down, thoughtful scientists and industrialists began piecing together a space program that would do the impossible—place an American on the moon. A timetable could not be established because the price tag was beyond calculating, perhaps a hundred billion dollars, perhaps a trillion? Meanwhile, the cold war strategy of giving Third World countries economic aid rather than arms was reversed. Truman had ordered food and machinery sent to struggling new nations caught in the middle as the two superpowers vied for friends in a polarized world. Under Eisenhower, weapons and military missions were sent out to block "Soviet aggression."

A slight thaw in the cold war was provided by Nikita Khrushchev, who became the Soviet premier when Stalin died in 1953. By 1956 the leadership inside the Kremlin acknowledged the brutality of Stalin's era, and Khrushchev even spoke of "peaceful coexistence" between the communist and capitalist societies. But in the State Department the rhetoric was harsh and grew harsher after Hungarian dissenters were brutally suppressed. "Massive retaliation" was threatened if the Soviets pushed their luck, and the Central Intelligence Agency (CIA) was given a stepped-up role in efforts to increase the nation's military readiness.

American policy in the Middle East also created international shock waves. Egypt shook off its dependence on Great Britain in 1954 and two years later played the two cold warriors against each other in seeking aid for a dam on the Nile River at Aswan.

A petulant threat from Dulles angered the Egyptian leader, who retaliated by seizing the Suez Canal. England, France, and Israel then invaded the canal zone, but President Eisenhower joined with United Nations partners in condemning the military action. England and France withdrew, and Great Britain began a general pullback from the Middle East that soon contributed to the instability of the oil-rich region. Within a year, Eisenhower sent 8,000 American troops to Lebanon to prop up a UN-supported government, but the Pax Britannica imposed in the region since 1919 ended. Would the United States pick up the pieces?

Despite the fact that Democrats dominated Congress through most of Ike's two terms, no legislative stalemate ensued. Senator Lyndon B. Johnson, the majority leader, was the quintessential deal maker—compromise was his middle name. Thus several important social measures, many with a New Deal tinge, passed, and Eisenhower signed them into law. Significantly, for the first time in eighty years Congress passed a civil rights act that liberalized laws dealing with black involvement in jury duty and jury trials. The *New York Times* called the 1957 Civil Rights Act "the most significant domestic action of any Congress in this century." A leading black activist called it "a weak but very important law" because it established a vital precedent.

Throughout the Eisenhower years, however, domestic concerns took a backseat to the cold war with Russia. Clearly, the arms race was heating up as both the USSR and the United States escalated their arms budgets for atomic weapons, intercontinental missiles, and nuclear submarines. Eisenhower still hoped to negotiate cutbacks, and he scheduled a meeting in May 1960 with Khrushchev to discuss arms control. Unfortunately, a U-2 spy plane streaking over the USSR was shot down and the pilot brought to Moscow for public display. At first, the United States claimed the downed airplane was on a meteorological mission, but within a week the president admitted that pilot Gary Powers was on a spying assignment when he was captured.

The U-2 mission, the mishandled first claims of innocence, and the ultimate admission by Eisenhower that the government had told an official lie were shocking to many Americans. Even during wartime, versions of battles and casualties rang true, but here was another casualty of the cold war: truth. An angry Khrushchev used the incident as an excuse to cancel the scheduled summit meeting in Geneva.

Foreign policy was not on the minds of Republicans, however, for 1960 was an election year and they were caught in a trap of their own making—the Twenty-second Amendment that forbade a president more than two terms in office. Passed by the Eightieth Congress as revenge for Roosevelt's four victories, the amendment had slowly wound its way through the ratifying process to become part of the Constitution in 1951. Now it was there as a barricade against a third term for Eisenhower. The president's age (seventy) and health (he'd had another operation) were balanced against Eisenhower's popularity by party chieftains.

Governor Nelson Rockefeller of New York quickly entered the void as the Republican with liberal credentials who had won in the Empire State with a half-million-vote plurality. But Richard Nixon's friends were clamoring for their man as the logical successor to Ike, and their hopes rose when the president finally stopped equivocating and gave Nixon his blessing. Nixon had been aggressive during the last two years of Eisenhower's tenure, first with a televised verbal tiff with Khrushchev at a Moscow trade fair, and then as a mediator in a steel strike early in 1960. Rockefeller's supporters went to Chicago early in July to seek concessions on civil rights and arms control. Puzzled Nixon backers asked their man to talk with Rockefeller. The ensuing meeting seemed to patch up differences between the Republican party center and the liberal stance represented by the New Yorker.

No real threat to Nixon developed, for the eastern liberals eschewed a public brawl. Southern delegates voiced their disapproval of the final wording of a civil rights plank, but its mildness prevailed in party councils. Henry Cabot Lodge of Massachusetts, the Boston blue blood and former senator, was nominated for the vice presidency.

Pitted against Nixon was the Democrat's forty-three-year-old senator from Massachusetts, John F. Kennedy. Kennedy's good looks and schoolboy charm were projected from the Los Angeles nominating convention where Senator Lyndon B. Johnson stumbled but accepted the second place on the ticket.

The next president was going to be one of the youngest ever to hold the office, for Nixon was only forty-seven. Unlike Kennedy, however, Nixon found it hard to be friendly with reporters, and he became convinced the newspapermen were trying to make him look bad. Perhaps to bypass the "liberal press," Nixon had made a convention pledge to visit all fifty states, and he wore himself out flying to remote places while Kennedy joked with supporters at televised rallies and tried to defuse the issue of his Catholic background.

Perhaps misled by an early poll that gave him a six-point margin over Kennedy, Nixon agreed to a series of televised debates with the Democratic challenger. Kennedy's years in the House and Senate had not been crowned with distinction. Indeed, Kennedy's record was mildly liberal, and he had given his name to no piece of major legislation in fourteen years of congressional service. Before joining Kennedy on the ticket, Senator Johnson had suggested his junior colleague might wait "until he has some gray in his hair" before seeking the presidency. Kennedy needed to show voters he was capable of mature judgment and was a bona fide Democrat despite his distinctive Harvard accent.

For his part, Nixon wanted to appear to voters as a man in the Eisenhower tradition, sound on foreign policy and trustworthy on domestic issues. In the first debate, held in Chicago in late September, Nixon was ill prepared. He looked tired, and the television cameras caught his face in an unfortunate light pattern, giving him a "five o'clock shadow." Kennedy seemed tan, relaxed, and in full command of his information. In all likelihood, the election was decided by midnight on September 26, although the full effect of the debates was not confirmed until the day after the election.

During the long campaign, Nixon was uplifted by a tremendous reception on his southern tour. The southern disenchantment with the Democrats was gathering steam, and Nixon was welcomed in major southern cities on podiums crowded with civic leaders, professional men and women, and a host of former Democrats now eager to be identified with the Republican party. Nixon was impressed.

Nixon, to be consistent, had separated himself from the racial controversy involving Martin Luther King a few weeks before the voting. King had been arrested for trying to be seated at a lunch counter in Atlanta. Kennedy seized on the incident and made some well-placed telephone calls to important Democrats in Georgia; King was soon released on bail. The circumstances indicated Kennedy had intervened with local officials; at least, that was the interpretation of black voters. Between the disastrous television debates and the King controversy, Kennedy made it appear that Nixon was ill equipped for leadership and not concerned about the racial tension building up in the country since the *Brown* decision.

Because the race was close, the weak television image joined to the loss of black support over the mishandled King incident may have cost Nixon the election. He lost the big city vote where blacks made a difference, and it was clear that a huge Catholic turnout for Kennedy in the Northeast had offset the southern Protestant vote for Nixon. Early reports of Kennedy's wins in New York and Pennsylvania cheered Democrats' election-night parties, but when Nixon took Virginia, Kentucky, Florida, and Tennessee, a close contest loomed. Doubt persisted until the afternoon following the voting, when the Michigan, Ohio, and Missouri results made Kennedy the winner. In the closest election since 1884 (in popular voting) Kennedy had 49.7 percent of the ballots and Nixon 49.5 percent. The electoral count favored Kennedy, 303 to 219, with 15 votes going to Senator Harry Byrd of Virginia from disgruntled southerners. To his credit, Nixon dismissed charges of voting fraud in some midwestern states and generously conceded to Kennedy. Thus no recounts were sought.

In practical terms, Kennedy's election proved once and for all that a Catholic could be elected president. But the 1960 election also showed that the changing demographic patterns of the 1950s and the backlash over civil rights issues had split the old Confederacy into a two-party region. Nixon had carried four southern states plus Oklahoma and had nearly won in Texas. Senator Barry Goldwater of Arizona, a conservative Republican in good standing, had toured the South on Nixon's behalf and found he enjoyed the campaign so much that he encouraged well-wishers to think of him in 1964. The 1960 race also showed how important presidential primaries had become. Kennedy won in New Hampshire in February and seemed unstoppable well before some last-minute switches made his first ballot nomination probable. Within a decade, the convention process became obsolete. The only business remaining for the delegates was confirmation of decisions already made in the state primaries. At the same time, the growth of television campaigning and contributions from political action committees had caused budgets to spiral into millions of dollars. Indeed, by the 1990s a serious candidate was one who had already amassed around $15 million as he headed into the first presidential primaries.

Long dead was the undertow of support from the party's faithful collection of appointees to federal jobs, for the Hatch Act and legislative supplements since 1939 had knocked that source of money and privilege into a cocked hat. The federal laws granting campaign funds to candidates, an income-tax gimmick that required qualifying percentages, had never replaced the PACs or private donors as sources of influence, as the law's sponsors had hoped.

Ironically, the PACs had come into being as a device to allow labor unions to contribute to candidates. As the power of unions diminished, the vacuum was taken up by giant corporations, which created their own PACs as lobbying devices that could siphon funds to the campaigns of friendly candidates.

Money is power, of course, but the Kennedy presidency showed that one characteristic helpful to a president is beyond price—charisma, or the ability to project a simultaneous sense of power and confidence. Kennedy's charm, coupled with his dazzling sense of humor, was apparent. Despite a foreign policy failure with the aborted invasion of Cuba, the president recovered much confidence in his handling of the Cuba missile crisis of October 1962, which had taken the nation to the very brink of war.

The first American in space became an instant hero, and John Glenn became the first Yank to orbit the planet in 1962. These accomplishments helped soothe the nation's wounded psyche, and the money poured into the space program helped fuel the country's mild prosperity. Critics rankled, however, over the tactics of the president's brother, who served as attorney general, and over the nation's unpreparedness in case of a nuclear attack. Kennedy also seemed to believe in the "trickle-down" theory of tax cuts as a means of stimulating the economy. This appeared to be a Coolidge-like solution in a Democratic test tube. The idea was still working its way through congressional mills when Kennedy traveled to Texas in November 1963.

Except for the surprise election of a Republican senator in Texas in 1961, the Republicans found little to cheer about during most of the Kennedy years. Kennedy's frequent press conferences, televised tours of the White House conducted by the first lady, and glamorous visits to Europe gave the nation a breathtaking view of its young president and his laconic sense of humor. The tragedy in Dallas on November 22, 1963, stunned the world. Recovery was not immediate, and as chilling reality set in, President Lyndon Johnson made it clear that he was no "caretaker president" but meant to be as relentless in the White House as he had been when majority leader in the Senate. He was the first southerner who meant what he said when talking about civil and voting rights for blacks.

Johnson knew the risks he ran but was determined to leave his mark on the presidency even if he hurt his party. After the 1964 Civil Rights Act was passed over the bitter opposition of southern Democrats, Johnson signed the bill and told a friend: "I think we just delivered the South to the Republican party."

Johnson steamrollered his way into the Democratic convention and took as his vice presidential candidate Hubert Humphrey, the first Democrat elected to the Senate by Minnesotans in generations. Frankly, Johnson said he was going to finish the job on civil rights and see that the civil war in Vietnam was brought to a swift conclusion.

A handful of Republicans had other plans. Although Governor William Scranton of Pennsylvania had the backing of the liberal eastern wing of the party, the majority gathering in San Francisco for the nominating convention wanted a conservative on the ticket. Nixon had lost his 1962 race for the governorship in

California and was never considered a factor, except for his good standing among the big contributors who remembered the close 1960 race. Again, the eastern party leaders backed away from a fight, so almost by default Senator Barry Goldwater was the front-runner, cheered on by a gallery full of exuberant Republicans from California and Arizona who came to steamroller their opposition.

Thus encouraged, Goldwater never let up and emerged as the victor. In his acceptance speech, the Arizona senator promised to curb federal power and said his candidacy offered "a choice, not an echo." Congressman William Miller of New York was added to the ticket as the vice presidential candidate. An attempt to censure the right-wing John Birch Society, a move designed to make the party more moderate, was howled down by the delegates before they adjourned.

The campaign had some unpleasantness. Democratic television commercials emphasized Goldwater's swashbuckling attitude toward nuclear weapons, with an atomic cloud pictured while an announcer pronounced Johnson the "peace" candidate. Goldwater's belligerent style led him to say things that frightened timid voters away. "Extremism in the defense of liberty is no vice," he told voters. "Moderation in the pursuit of justice is no virtue."

Television speeches and "sound-bite" commercials dominated the campaign, although Republicans had clever slogans for bumper stickers and a sheriff's badge as a Goldwater campaign button. The bumper sticker bearing the chemical symbols for gold and water—AuH_2O—brought smiles to voters' faces but did not carry much weight in the polling booths. The Johnson-Humphrey ticket won hands down with 61 percent of the popular vote, the most decisive landslide since Roosevelt's 1936 triumph. Johnson won forty-four states and the District of Columbia, Goldwater carried six, and the electoral total showed a 486-to-49 imbalance.

The Eighty-ninth Congress that assembled in January 1965 had a Democratic majority, 68 to 32. In the House, 295 Democrats faced 140 Republicans across the aisle. When President Johnson gave his State of the Union message, he launched his

"Great Society" program that would bring sweeping changes in civil rights legislation, voting patterns, educational endeavors, and the nation's approach to environmental issues.

Vastly outnumbered, Republicans fought rearguard actions on some of Johnson's more extravagant programs, but Medicare for the elderly and Medicaid for the poor were set in place by a complaisant Congress. Social security benefits were expanded, and the Office of Equal Opportunity was established to combat racial bias in the marketplace.

Gradually, however, the civil war in Vietnam crowded its way onto Johnson's agenda. In 1966, $22 billion was spent on the war in Indochina and more American troops were sent into combat, while all of Johnson's "War on Poverty" programs received only $1.2 billion. As costs escalated and casualty lists lengthened, Congress seemed trapped in a maze of confusion. In the summer of 1964 both houses had passed (following reports of attacks on American vessels in the Gulf of Tonkin) a resolution authorizing the president to take "all necessary measures" to repel armed attacks. Johnson interpreted the resolution, which the Senate passed 88 to 2 and the House by a 416-to-0 margin, as a green light for stepping up the American effort.

From 1965 onward Vietnam became a quagmire for American troops trying to fight an almost invisible enemy in steamy jungles and pouring rain. By the end of the year, after Johnson had promised that no American boys would be sent "nine or ten thousand miles away from home to do what Asian boys ought to be doing for themselves," the United States had 190,000 ground troops in Vietnam. Tons of aerial bombs, millions of rounds of ammunition, and napalm dumped on villages created a hell that was covered on nightly television.

In general, Republicans in Congress and on the street supported the Vietnam fighting as part of a global assault on communism. Resistance to the war came from the left rather than from the right. Students who were potential draftees rebelled with threats that they would burn their draft cards, then set obligingly set blazes for the television cameras. For the most part Republicans did not join in the protests, for they apparently feared that dissent in wartime might be branded as disloyal or unpatriotic. When the federal deficit for 1967 jumped to $23 billion, however, the public perceived that the war was costing more in dollars and lives than anyone had reckoned when the first Americans had gone ashore in the Mekong Delta.

The public also grew more skeptical of the military leadership in Vietnam, which kept promising that one more offensive would end the fighting. Johnson finally said no to the generals, and from early 1968 it was clear that the American people were fed up with Vietnam and Johnson. Peace talks between North Vietnamese representatives and American negotiators began in Paris, and in a surprise announcement, Johnson said he would not be a candidate for the presidency in November.

Truly the summer of 1968 was a time of discontent. Not only was the Vietnam War going badly, but racial tensions were also accelerating in urban areas from Boston to Los Angeles. Sometimes the cause was a busing incident; at other times it was a claim of police brutality. But the assassination of Martin Luther King on April 4 in Memphis galvanized dozens of black ghettoes into action. Looting and burning, even in the nation's capital, followed through the day and night as word of King's death spread. On college campuses, near riots occurred in the spring following King's assassination, partly in protest against the draft and also aimed at an amorphous "Establishment" that seemed out of touch with public opinion.

Looking back, older Americans also felt disillusioned. In the summer of 1963 the United States was a superpower with a strong currency, a silver coinage, low inflation, no drugs, no wars, and nearly full employment. A mere five years later the dollar had weakened as the national debt soared, drugs had invaded colleges and schools, a "Beatle" culture of youthful rebellion was spreading rapidly, and the war in Vietnam was out of control.

Two Democrats seemed to sense what was lacking. Senators Eugene McCarthy of Minnesota and Robert Kennedy of New York supplied the opposition Republicans were unable to form. Both announced they would run in presidential primaries, stop the fighting in Vietnam, and restore the confidence of young people in their confused country. But Kennedy was killed by an assassin on the night he defeated McCarthy in the California primary, and the nation went through the trauma of burying another Kennedy martyred by a demented gunman. Meanwhile, Vice President Humphrey, who had entered no primaries but had worked on the delegations, became the Democrats' nominee at their Chicago convention in August 1968. The melee that ensued in Chicago when protesters tried to disrupt the convention, again fully reported on television, gave viewers the impression that anarchy reigned in America's big cities.

All these sights of discontent and disruption were taken by Governor George Wallace of Alabama as a sign that he should enter the presidential race as a third-party candidate. He temporarily stole the limelight from Richard Nixon, but the former vice president entered the primaries and turned back challenges from three governors—Ronald Reagan, George Romney, and Nelson Rockefeller—to win the Republican nomination. Nixon surprised everybody by picking Spiro Agnew, the governor of Maryland, as his running mate.

During the campaign, Nixon spoke of a "silent majority" that was disenchanted with rowdy protesters, drug pushers, and noisy urban demonstrators. This quiet band of voters, Nixon promised, would be rewarded by his election; to add a novel twist to the campaign, Nixon said he had a "secret plan" to end the war in Indochina. All the candidates were wary of a television debate and preferred to spend millions on short television commercials made with the aid of makeup, perfect lighting, and loaded questions from off-camera voices.

The 1968 election was close. White-collar voters were already backing Nixon, but amid the frankly racist appeal of Wallace and Nixon's criticism of the Great Society's social programs, blue-collar workers deserted the Democratic party, North and South, and that wholesale movement by former Democrats accounted for Nixon's victory. Of the 131 "Little Italy" precincts of south Philadelphia, Nixon carried only one in 1960, but Nixon and Wallace between them had a handsome majority in 1968. West of the Mississippi, Nixon carried every state except Hawaii, Minnesota, Texas, and Washington. Nixon also owed a debt to the deep South, where he swept nearly everything that Wallace missed or Humphrey couldn't penetrate. Yet the popular vote favored Nixon by only a slender margin, 31.7 million to 31.2 million. Wallace, the American Independent candidate, drew 9.9 million votes and in the electoral college picked up 46 votes. Nixon's electoral victory was more pronounced, with 301 votes to 191 for Humphrey. Democrats still held control of Congress, however, with a 57-to-43 margin in the Senate and a 243-to-192 margin in the House.

After twenty-two years of politicking, of comebacks and near misses, the man who seemed to thrive on crises had finally achieved the presidency. Supporters spoke of this "new Nixon" who was confident he could pull the nation back together, end the war in Vietnam, and restore domestic tranquillity. A tall order, yes, but Republicans looked ahead to 1969 as a year of revival and restoration.

CHAPTER THIRTEEN

The Nine Lives
of Richard Nixon

Historians and biographers are often poor pundits. They take facts and try to re-create events and conditions, and sometimes they venture an opinion about what all the information and interpretation mean. Then a Richard Milhous Nixon comes along and all the rules are suspended, but the process of judgment is not. In many respects, Nixon's fall is one of the great tragedies of the century. In the year 2050, British and American historians may write about the two most interesting men of the twentieth century, and they probably will be focusing on Winston Churchill and Richard Nixon. One realized all his potential and became a great leader, while the other overreached himself and reeled into a miasma of deceit and failure.

Nixon was capable of being a great president. He came from an impoverished family with a Quaker background. From childhood he was engaged in a struggle for existence and education. Nixon graduated from his hometown college and then went to Duke University's law school. During World War II he served in the navy, and he came home to run against a certified New Deal liberal. A jubilant Nixon won his congressional seat in the 1946 Republican sweep.

The Horatio Alger story has several twists. In his role as the dogged prosecutor of Alger Hiss, Nixon won acclaim in Republican circles for his provable anticommunist stance. Senator McCarthy talked much but produced little in the way of results, while Nixon got his man and Hiss eventually was sent to prison. Then Nixon took on the glamour lady of the New Deal, Helen Gahagan Douglas. Nixon trounced her in a bitter election in which Democrats claimed Nixon smeared the former film actress with a red brush. From there it was only a short leap to the 1952 Republican convention, where party leaders decided a young Californian would help balance the ticket with General Eisenhower.

Life was a series of ups and downs, however. Like the mythical Horatio Alger, Nixon would not accept defeat. For Nixon was almost forced off the 1952 ticket, until his "Checkers" speech, yet one aftermath was that the eastern party leaders never warmed up to the California whiz kid. In 1956 Nixon was again close to being knocked off the ticket, until Ike placed a friendly arm on his shoulder and saved him from party annihilation. His television performance at Moscow seemed to show how deft Nixon could be facing the communists, and in labor negotiations his demonstrated skills indicated Nixon was maturing. Then came the humiliation of 1960, and heaped on that flawed performance was the loss of the California governor's race to an effusive Pat Brown in 1962. But Nixon was not finished.

Always, like a fighter whose managers are about to throw in the towel, Nixon would come out of his corner and keep slugging. After 1962 he worked with a Wall Street law firm, drawing a comfortable salary. Although he practiced little law, Nixon saw and soothed dozens of big contributors, governors, congressmen, and Republicans with influence in presidential primary states. Twenty-five years, some of it in the trenches, some of it in the penthouse, gave Nixon the 1968 nomination despite the appearance of some glamorous candidates who threatened him in the primaries.

Inaugurated on a cold January morning in 1969, Nixon assembled a team of loyalists in the White House, appointed a cabinet that included longtime friend (and lawyer) William Rogers as secretary of state and Henry Kissinger as national security adviser. Early on, Nixon named appeals judge Warren Burger to replace Earl Warren as chief justice. He talked about a "new federalism," which seemed to mean Nixon wanted more power for state governments and a slowing down of regulations from Washington bureaus. The Democratic Congress passed clean air and clean water acts, and Nixon gladly signed them. As he put pen to paper Nixon said: "It is now or never for us to pay our debt to the past by reclaiming the purity of . . . our environment." But when consumer advocate Ralph Nader attacked Nixon for half-measures, the president shook his finger and vowed that the environmental issue would not become a weapon to be used "in a demagogic way, basically to destroy the system."

The conservative senators who wanted Taiwan recognized as the legitimate (if absentee) government of China were all dead or back at home, so Nixon dared to do what no Democrat could have risked. In July 1971 he announced that he intended to visit communist China, and in February 1972, with much ceremony and pomp, he visited the Great Wall and was given red-carpet treatment in Beijing and Shanghai. Diplomatic exchanges would in time lead to the reestablishment of historic ties between the Chinese government and the United States and make China one of America's biggest trade customers.

Thus Nixon did what no Democrat in the White House could have done, because the critics were in Nixon's party and all they could do was applaud this diplomatic coup. Nixon went back to the open-door policy espoused early in the century, and the nation accepted his diplomatic coup with a sense of wonderment, admiration, and possibly some slight suspicion. The turnaround of America's China policy had been *too* easy.

At home, things were a bit more complicated. Inflation persisted, and in August 1971 Nixon told a national television audience he was taking unusual steps to curb price increases on everything from footlockers to Fords. He ordered a ninety-day freeze on prices and wages, and to stabilize U.S. dollars in world trading Nixon said he had ordered Treasury Secretary John Connally "to suspend temporarily the convertibility of the dollar into gold." Thus, with the stroke of a pen, Nixon canceled the Bretton Woods guarantee to offer gold in international exchange for $35 an ounce, an agreement reached with the nation's allies after World War II. The immediate effect was a free-floating currency with a daily price established by market conditions, a system still in place a generation later. Wall Street took Nixon's actions in stride. On the Monday following his announcement, the Dow Jones average was up 32.9 points to 888.95. The president, a stock-market analyst said a few days later, "has unceremoniously pulled us free from the cross of gold." Gold quickly took off and was selling in the free market for $67 an ounce when the Republican convention took place at Miami Beach a year later. "Nixon had created a big splash," historian Stephen Ambrose wrote, "without making many big waves."

The same can be said for Nixon's push to negotiate a Soviet-American treaty on strategic arms limitations. He visited Moscow early in the election year of 1972 and started in motion the tortuous process that led to ratified SALT treaties.

In domestic affairs and diplomatic maneuvers Nixon was acting like a strong leader, but he was never able to shake off the tar baby that Vietnam had become by 1969. First, Nixon tried secret raids in Cambodia; when the public learned of them, a firestorm of protest erupted. The killing of four young people at Kent State University on May 4, 1970, threw a damper on any enthusiasm left for the Vietnam mess. The confused American policy of that time is clearer since the diary of Nixon's chief aide, H. R. Haldeman, has revealed that some of Nixon's closest advisers thought continuance of the war would enhance his chances of reelection.

The Democrats made it easy for Nixon. They adopted rules for their nominating convention that replaced the smoke-filled room with a coalition of blacks, women, single-issue groups, war protesters, and very few old-time professional politicians. This conglomerate nominated Senator George McGovern as the Democratic presidential candidate after front-runner Edmund Muskie's campaign was torpedoed by Nixon loyalists through "dirty tricks" that smeared the Maine senator.* Forthwith the National Democratic Committee rented a suite in the swank

---

*The "dirty tricks" involved a spurious letter that falsely accused Muskie of slurring a raft of "Canucks."

Watergate complex near downtown Washington for its message center. Reports of a break-in there were printed in the *Washington Post* that summer but seemed inconsequential in an inept Democratic campaign that was going nowhere.

Another threat to Nixon's hold on the presidency was removed that spring when George Wallace, campaigning in Maryland, was struck by a bullet and paralyzed. Until this tragedy, Wallace had been building strength in industrial states and was wooing both blue- and white-collar workers with his claim that "there's not a nickel's worth of difference between the two parties—neither one of them cares about the little man any more." With Wallace out of the way, Nixon attracted working folks who resented the implications of government programs giving job opportunities to minorities. After the Watts riots not a few whites believed they were being penalized in order to keep the lid on tension in the black communities.

Blue-collar Americans and Nixon may have been soul mates because he had long resented the power of the eastern elite in his own party. Although his hero was Theodore Roosevelt, and he had the Rough Rider's portrait placed prominently in the White House, Nixon was no admirer of the eastern blue bloods— Scranton, Rockefeller, and other Republicans with their silver-spoon origins in such strong contrast to his own. Deep down, Nixon may have thought that the Republican party could survive only if it got rid of the eastern mandarins and directed its appeal to the Baptists and Methodists who knew how to work hard and saved their dollars in a sugar bowl. Yet Nixon's enemies insisted that he was an ego-driven run-of-the-mill politician with a touch of paranoia.

The voters saw things differently. Pollsters spoke with confidence in September 1972. Nixon would win "big"; the only question was, "how big?" Returns on election night confirmed the predictions, for Nixon captured 61 percent of the popular vote, and the dismal McGovern effort produced electoral-college votes for the Democrats from only Massachusetts and the District of Columbia. It was 1964 all over again except that, this time, the Republicans had achieved a landslide of historic proportions. Disturbing news, but not talked about at the election-night parties, was the relatively small turnout of only 55 percent of the eligible voters and the Democrats' continued hold on Congress. The ongoing Republican coalition with southern Democrats was working well, however, so the statistics were misleading. (To help southerners vote Republican, Nixon had hired a feisty speechwriter, Pat Buchanan, to give his campaign speeches the same twist that George Wallace had used to lure angry blue-collar workers into polling places.)

By all accounts, the Ninety-second Congress was to be one Nixon could work with harmoniously. And so it might have been, except for the dreaded specter of Watergate. The full dimensions of the scandal did not surface until after a peace accord—mainly saving face for the United States but condemning South Vietnam to a communist takeover—was signed in Paris in January 1973. American troops withdrew, but the civil war went on, and the flow of refugees would vastly increase after all South Vietnamese resistance ended in 1975. By that time, Watergate was history.

With the gift of hindsight, Nixon's confidant Haldeman recalled the White House atmosphere in the spring of 1970 and thought the troubles started then. "Kent State," Haldeman ventured, "marked a turning point for Nixon, a beginning of his downhill slide toward Watergate." The sordid unfolding of the Watergate arrests, the secret White House tapes, the "Saturday Night massacre," and the firing of Haldeman and John Ehrlichman are among the darkest chapters in the annals of the Republican party. The president's complicity in what amounted to a "third-rate burglary attempt" was never questioned by his inner circle, but his effort to obstruct the legal process became an impeachable offense. The testimony of one Nixon aide that a $400,000 slush fund had been created for hush money shocked the nation, and as the hearings proceeded through the spring and summer of 1973, most Republicans came to realize their titular leader was dissembling when he said, "I am not a crook." When seven House Republicans voted with the Democratic majority on three articles of impeachment, the die was cast. The *coup de grâce* came when Senator Goldwater, once a staunch ally, told the president he knew of only fifteen senators who would stay with him to the end.

Unable to admit responsibility for the debacle, Nixon told a national television audience on the night of August 8, 1974, that he would resign on the morrow. Watergate was not mentioned, but Nixon implied that the reason for his resignation—the first in American history by a president—was the unworkable relationship between the executive branch and Congress.

Nixon had handpicked veteran congressman Gerald Ford for the vice presidency in 1973 after Spiro Agnew was forced to resign or face a jail term because of misconduct as governor of Maryland. As he took over the office of president, Ford told the nation, "The long nightmare is over," and both Republicans and Democrats prayed silently that the new president's statement was true. The public was almost numb by the time Nixon boarded the helicopter that would whisk him away into history.

But not into obscurity, for within a month after Ford took office he seemed to exonerate Nixon of all crimes he had committed with a "full, free, and absolute" pardon. Cynics cried that Ford was carrying out his part of a bad bargain, but no evidence of any collusion was ever presented. Thereafter, Ford insisted he had acted solely to speed up the nation's healing process.

No doubt Ford was telling the truth. The Watergate saga went on without the principal, but two dozen men who had served in the Nixon cabinet or on the White House staff spent terms in federal prisons. By then, Congress had passed the Fair Practices Act, which limited campaign expenses and called for strict accounting of receipts and expenditures. Although Nixon was gone, his three appointees to the Supreme Court often swung the balance in crucial decisions involving abortion, law enforcement, and racial integration. Harry Blackmun and William Rehnquist had been easily confirmed, as was Lewis Powell Jr. after Nixon's first two southern nominees were rejected by a resentful Senate.

President Ford chose Nelson Rockefeller as his vice president, but the choice was not popular in conservative circles and the Senate hearings were stormy before Rockefeller's final confirmation. A petroleum shortage caused long lines at filling stations, the price of gasoline shot up when the Middle East oil-producing states cut down on exports, and inflation became a topic on nightly news broadcasts as it reached 12 percent in the fall of

1974. Ford also drew blame for a recession in 1975 that tightened the pinch of inflated prices for food and clothing.

Few breaks came Ford's way. He kept Henry Kissinger on as secretary of state, but the American effort to make more progress on arms control stalled. The shah of Iran, whom anti-Western Iranians claimed to be an American puppet, was backed by the Ford administration, although his support at home was eroding. On a trip to Japan, President Ford was shown stumbling on the steps of Air Force One, and television reporters intimated the miscue was typical of Ford's ineptness.

In one sense, the criticism of Ford as a "nice guy who is not big enough for the job" had a universal ring. What distinguished Ford from Theodore Roosevelt, or Franklin Roosevelt? Clearly, Americans tend to judge their presidents under a microscope and expect too much of men who have landed in the White House, with or without extraordinary effort. The most ambitious are condemned for their lust for power, but when all of the forty-one men holding office between 1789 and 1996 are considered, the majority have been gentlemen of modest intellectual ability, unable to laugh at their foibles, and acutely sensitive to criticism. Nearly all have distrusted the press.

The pall cast by Watergate fell over the 1976 election. The Democrats had weakened their national organization and the number of state primaries had reached thirty when the former governor of Georgia, James Earl Carter Jr.—he preferred "Jimmy"—ran as an anti-Washington candidate and surprised reporters, television commentators, and perhaps his mother by winning in the key states. Ford was conceded the Republican nomination, for the party was not as enamored as Democrats were with the idea of a broad ethnic representation at its convention, and the state chairmen and congressional delegations merged behind Ford. But it was closer than anyone expected, because Governor Ronald Reagan of California entered the primaries, and suddenly it was a race. At the August convention, Ford prevailed, however, although Reagan was thanked for adding excitement to a rather dull contest. Ford picked Senator Robert Dole of Kansas for second place on the ticket to replace Nelson Rockefeller.

There was little for Republicans to laugh about, but humorist Art Buchwald took a mythical trip to the Rockefeller household after Ford dumped his handpicked vice president:

> In the last few months the Rockefellers have been throwing party after party to introduce everyone to the new vice presidential residence on Massachusetts Avenue, and it cost them a pretty penny. I'm certain they wouldn't have gone to that expense if they had any idea that President Ford was going to push Rocky off the ticket in 1976. As a matter of fact, I wouldn't have wanted to have been in Rocky's shoes the night he came home and broke the news to Happy. . . .
>
> "How could he do this to you? You've worked so hard and been so loyal."
>
> "That doesn't count when you're vice president. Jerry's worried about his own job, and he figures if he gets rid of me, the Republican board of directors will get off his back."*

As is often the case, words written in jest have the ring of truth. Buchwald was onto something. The western chairmen were said to be dead-set against placing Rockefeller on the ticket. Dole was not a far westerner, but he wasn't considered a liberal either.

The polls soon had Ford losing. The trouble was hard to pin down, but most of the shifting voters either were upset about the pardon of Nixon or thought Ford had not shown a fair modicum of executive ability since he took over in 1974. Carter was not a great speaker, but in the televised debates that Ford agreed to, the president made a tremendous blunder when he asserted that Poland was not a part of the communist eastern bloc. Viewers wondered if they needed to adjust their sets. Had their hearing been impaired? "Ford's mistake disrupted the momentum of his campaign and brought an abrupt halt to his improved showing in the polls," historian Burton Kaufman noted. From that point on, Ford's campaign went downhill fast, even though Dole tried a rescue effort that made some observers say the campaign might have been better off if the roles of Dole and Ford had been reversed.

Election night was no solace to Republicans, who hoped the polls were prejudiced or just plain wrong. Carter won 41 million

---

*Art Buchwald, *Washington Is Leaking* (New York: G. P. Putnam's Sons, 1976), 30.

votes to 39 million for Ford, although in electoral votes the count was not outlandish. Carter had 297 to 240 for Ford, but the race was closer on analysis than it looked in Wednesday morning's newspapers. Carter had won by running against Washington, without much help from his national organization. No wonder David Broder and other political columnists soon were writing obituaries for the two-party system.

Carter took office in January 1977 with Democrats in control of Congress, but the honeymoon was brief. Since he ran as an outsider, Carter had difficulty dealing with a Congress that was loaded with seniority and resentment. For four years Carter never quite figured out how to move around in the maze of Washington power bases. Carter was a southerner, but he had not cultivated the senior political figures from his region, and soon it became apparent that the Speaker of the House, Thomas "Tip" O'Neill, was probably the most influential Democrat in Washington. A series of domestic problems, ranging from inordinately high interest rates (reaching 16 percent in 1980) to 12 percent inflation in 1979 caused Carter to turn his attention to foreign affairs. In his meeting with the leaders of Egypt and Israel at Camp David, a historic accord was reached, but Americans were feeling pressure in their pocketbooks and perceived Carter as less than effective on worrisome issues in his own backyard.

Disaster struck when the Iranian dissenters seized control of their country, ousted the shah, and on November 4, 1979, imprisoned sixty American hostages from the United States Embassy in Teheran. Despite frantic negotiating, the Americans were still captives as the 1980 election year opened.

Events smothered Carter. The Soviets invaded Afghanistan, a grain embargo of the Soviet Union and then of the Olympic Games in Moscow managed to anger farmers and young athletes, but Carter won the primaries and came from the Democratic convention ready to tackle the best Republicans could offer.

Republicans finally gave Ronald Reagan his chance. After disappointments in 1972 and 1976, Reagan charmed his way through the primaries, clashed with George Bush, and then magnanimously placed his former adversary on the ticket. The Reagan-Bush ticket appeared to have a head start, for the candidates' home bases in California and Texas had—for openers —a whopping 65 electoral votes. Meanwhile, Carter's military advisers talked him into a rescue effort for the hostages in April. Helicopters crashed, mistakes by the commanders abounded, and instead of a triumph of American military might the rescue mission turned into a gigantic fiasco. Naturally, Carter was held accountable.

By late autumn voters were ready to blame anybody for the plunge in national morale. Reagan, still Hollywood handsome and always ready with a quip, entered the television debates exuding confidence. When Carter disputed his points, Reagan simply said: "There you go again, Jimmy." Audiences loved Reagan's style, and when he asked voters "Are you better off today than you were four years ago?" a silent studio audience implied the answer.

A maverick Republican congressman from Illinois, John Anderson, tried to capitalize on voter despair and ran an independent campaign. Anderson was adored by a far-left group of Republican liberals but had little general support once the campaign shifted into high gear.

The election-night broadcasts from the two parties' victory celebrations told viewers more than any thousand-page volume could capture. Reagan and his California friends were exuberant; Carter and his coterie were in shock. The Reagan landslide gave the Republican 50.7 percent of the popular vote and 489 electoral votes. Carter trailed badly with 41 percent of the vote but only 49 electoral ballots. Anderson was a poor third, with 6 percent of the vote. Reagan and his vice president, George Bush, would confront a mixed Congress, however, when they got down to business in January 1981. The Republicans had a 53-to-47 edge in the Senate, but the House remained in Democratic hands.

Previous presidents had been political animals, mostly governors or congressmen or senators. Ronald Reagan had been governor of California, but his life had been spent on film studio lots, playing roles chosen by studio bosses. As Reagan rode down Pennsylvania Avenue on January 20, 1981, the cheering throngs knew that he had a new role, and a new boss: the people of the United States.

CHAPTER FOURTEEN

The Reagan "Revolution"— and Beyond

No president, not even Theodore Roosevelt, enjoyed his White House tenure as much as did Ronald Reagan. Happily, the Iranian hostage crisis was defused almost on the day Reagan took office, as an exchange was negotiated to end the crisis. Reagan modestly took no credit, but the public gave him the laurels anyway. At sixty-nine, he was the oldest president ever to take office, and when he left eight years later he was the oldest to have ever held the office; but he looked ten years younger and knew how to use his age or how to forget it. When reporters shouted questions, Reagan would pretend he couldn't hear and not answer. When he was shot by a would-be assassin in 1981, he joked with doctors as he lay on the operating table, saying he hoped they were all Republicans.

Yet Reagan let everybody know how he felt about the Soviet Union, which he called "an evil empire" early on, and he urged Congress to pass record budgets for defense spending. Awed by the president's popularity, Democratic Congresses gave Reagan most of what his cabinet members asked for. Californians were part of his cabinet, starting with Attorney General Edwin Meese and Defense Secretary Caspar Weinberger, and his press conferences, though not frequent, were full of quips and repartee that had been missing from the Washington scene since John Kennedy's day. On occasion, Reagan picked up the telephone and called Richard Nixon for advice.

Reagan never pretended that he was an expert on taxation, defense, or any government program except perhaps the National Endowment for the Arts. Advisers guided Reagan into his plan for tax cuts that would eventually lead to a general rise in prosperity, the "voodoo theory of economics" condemned by George Bush when they were rivals in 1980. A pliable Congress went along, passing laws that gave tax benefits to upper-income citizens out of proportion to cuts at lower-income levels. Reagan resumed production of the expensive B-1 bomber program that Carter had canceled and gave the green light to a mobile missile program. Congress occasionally balked, particularly in the sacred areas of Medicare and Social Security benefits, but in general Democrats went along with the Reagan proposals and thus share the blame for the huge deficits that began mounting in 1982. When Carter left office, the national debt hovered around $800 million. In 1984 it had risen to $1.4 trillion and was moving upward with the momentum of a runaway Mack truck.

Still, Reagan's popularity glossed over the business recession of 1982 and allowed the Republicans to gain two Senate seats in the off-year elections. A suicide bomber in Lebanon killed 241 American servicemen sent there on a peacekeeping mission in October 1983. The American Marines were soon pulled out, and thereafter Reagan was reluctant to send military missions abroad.

Reagan weighed the odds and sent troops into Grenada, supported the right-wing "Contras" in Nicaragua, and insisted that the Soviet Union was sending arms into Latin America to prop up leftist regimes. His hard-line approach to negotiations with the USSR on arms control resonated well in conservative Republican circles, where the chant "We're Number One" loosened wallets at fund-raising dinners. With his Hollywood ties, Reagan welcomed an entourage of film stars to Washington, led by singer Frank Sinatra (who, like Reagan, had once professed to be a Democrat), for gala entertainments in Washington's glittering Kennedy Center.

Democrat Walter Mondale, who had been vice president in the Carter administration, entered the 1984 primaries and settled in as Reagan's chief challenger. Republicans saw no opposition to Reagan surfacing, so the primaries became a Democratic free-for-all and a Republican cakewalk. At their convention the Democrats chose Mondale for president and broke tradition by nominating a woman, Representative Geraldine Ferraro, as their vice presidential candidate.

On television the seventy-three-year-old Reagan never looked better. Whether talking in the Rose Garden at the White House or speaking on network television, Reagan was the symbol of confidence. Thus the septuagenarian put the fifty-six-year-old Mondale on the defensive. The Democrat suggested the soaring deficit probably would force a tax increase, an idea that was immediately ridiculed even by Democrats. Mondale recanted and fell victim to another Reagan landslide. Reagan received 54 million votes and overpowered Mondale in the electoral college, 525 to 13. Voters gave the Republican president an overwhelming vote of confidence, as Mondale carried only his home state of Minnesota and the District of Columbia. (Indeed, it seemed that the District had become the Democrats' "rotten borough," for voters there rejected Reagan by a wide majority—180,000 votes for Mondale, 29,000 for Reagan.)

The 1984 results demonstrated the power of a rising element in the Republican ranks—evangelical southern white voters. Led by a group of Protestant ministers with television followings, a "Christian Coalition" actively supported Reagan and Republican candidates generally. When Reagan beat Carter, these conservative Christians gave him 65 percent of their votes. Against Mondale, Reagan's 69 percent showed how remarkably Republicans had broken down old prejudices in the South. As historian Kevin Phillips had predicted, the flag burnings and drug scenes of the 1960s had alienated voters "who were Democrats largely because a century earlier their families had worn Confederate gray." Reagan gave them an excuse to leave their Democratic moorings behind.

In other surveys of voting patterns perhaps the most notable statistics were those concerning young Americans going to the polls for the first time. Since 1932, beginning voters had been filing pell-mell into the Democratic ranks; but Reagan attracted first-time voters in great droves. In 1984 Reagan also demolished the loyalty of labor unions to Democrats and confirmed the trend in evidence since 1968 as middle-class whites—wearing collars blue, white, or even starched—voted for the Republican ticket in overwhelming numbers.

The new alliance between small-town and rural America and the Republican party branched out by 1984. If anything, Atlanta, Miami, Birmingham, Knoxville, Memphis, Dallas, Houston, and Oklahoma City had become rock-solid Republican strongholds and sent congressmen back to Washington to prove it. A few Democrats, such as Phil Gramm of Texas, switched parties and joined in the Reagan barbecue by running, and winning, on the Republican ticket. The bright young Texan who went to law school in Austin decided he could no longer make his reputation as a Democrat. By 1984, if he wanted a future in southern politics, he would have to be a Reagan Republican. Senator Newland's remark about former Democrats becoming Republicans when they had $50,000 was still applicable seventy years later, only the ante had gone up tenfold. Inflation and politics seem to go hand in hand.

For all his personal popularity, Reagan could not help all the Republicans hoping to go to Congress. As during the Eisenhower years, the Democrats kept their House majority (253 to 182), even though Republicans still held the Senate (53 to 47). For what it was worth, a poll taken in 1984 indicated most voters thought a division of power between the executive and legislative branches was a good idea.

Reagan's second term proved how agile the aging president could be. After years of railing against the Soviet Union, he accepted an invitation to visit Moscow and there turned his charm on a student audience at the state university. Suddenly there was talk of a "detente" or winding down of Soviet-American friction. The new Soviet premier, Mikhail Gorbachev, unlike his predecessors, favored finding a way to end the arms race, and significant disarmament treaties were accomplished in this new atmosphere of cordiality.

Congress also voted for change in the 1986 Tax Reform Act, which overhauled the tax code drastically, closing loopholes to bring in $300 billion in revenue lost under the old rules. The radical bill also raised corporate taxes, levying new rates that brought in over $100 billion in a five-year span.

One of the few specks on Reagan's record was the threatened scandal of 1986 concerning arms sales to Iran as part of an effort to secure the release of American hostages in Lebanon. The murky details barely hint that Reagan may have illegally approved deals that violated the Boland Amendment (a federal statute specifically forbidding the government from sending aid to the Nicaraguan Contras). Congressional investigations led to the trial of a Marine colonel for contempt of Congress, but underlings insisted that Reagan never approved any arms swap or violated any laws. Reagan simply said he didn't remember any details of the so-called Iran-Contra negotiations, and rather than pursue a trail possibly leading to impeachment, Congress dropped the matter in 1987.

The Iran-Contra mess proved that everything Reagan touched did not necessarily turn to gold. He appointed two associate justices to the Supreme Court and elevated William Rehnquist to the chief justice's job. But Reagan lost the Midas touch when he sent Robert Bork's name to the Senate for confirmation to a high-court seat. Bork's long-standing battle against judicial activism allowed Democrats to pick at his past until it was clear Bork was not going to make it. Conservative columnists pilloried the Democrats as "mindless liberals," but Bork was denied the appointment in one of the rare slaps Congress made at Reagan during his eight-year tenure.

Probably the most amazing development in Reagan's last years as president was the public apathy toward the soaring federal deficit. Heavy arms spending, low taxes, and mounting interest payments brought the national debt into the $3 trillion range, yet concern on Capitol Hill was limited to a few archconservatives who talked about introducing a balanced-budget amendment to the Constitution, but never did.

The closest they came was the 1985 Gramm-Rudman Balanced Budget Act, which had a 1991 target date. As its opponents had predicted, the law had so many loopholes it turned out to be a temporary Band-Aid and not the drastic surgery its sponsors had promised. Frustrated Democrats complained that Reagan was somehow granted special status by conservatives who had almost made careers out of criticizing federal fiscal policy, but congressmen became part of the applauding audience under Reagan's spellbinding defense programs.

A second gray area was foreign trade. Americans began buying Japanese automobiles in record numbers, forcing the nation into a debtor status as the trade imbalance between Japan and the United States soared to over $85 billion annually. Not since World War I had America maintained debit balances abroad, but the strong dollar made the lure of trouble-free automobiles irresistible to American motorists. In technology, particularly the growing market for computers, America was still a world leader. And the stock market did not seem to mind the excesses of spending and borrowing until October 19, 1987, when Wall Street almost fell apart. The Dow Jones industrial average dropped over 500 points in one day, frightening the timid with reminders of an earlier October market plunge that heralded the Great Depression.

No bone-crunching economic disaster was imminent, however. The stock market shrugged off the bears in short order, and America looked prosperous as Republicans placed "We're Number One" stickers on bumpers in anticipation of the 1988 presidential election. But the inner-core cities had pockets of real resistance to prosperity. Budget cuts in mental health programs threw thousands of homeless citizens onto the streets, where they slept in cardboard boxes near major thoroughfares. Drug-enforcement laws cost millions but seemed to produce little in the way of tangible results as black dealers went to the ever-expanding prisons while affluent whites held "coke" parties unmolested. An epidemic of AIDS brought a new threat to a permissive society, but again, mainstream America preferred to look the other way.

Industrial America was full of good news and bad news. Corporate profits in basic industries such as steel and oil fell, but the new market for high-technology equipment exploded in the 1980s to make millionaires out of boy wonders who had experimented with electronic devices in their garages. New names crowded onto *Fortune* magazine's elite "500 Top Corporations" list, such as Hewlett-Packard and Microsoft, but old-line corporations cut their workforces drastically, and a few, such as troubled asbestos-maker Johns-Manville, sought refuge in bankruptcy.

What would Republicans do to keep the country prosperous? Would the defense budget be cut, now that the cold war was thawing? Would the trade imbalance decline as American automakers improved their products? Would high-tech jobs be created to replace those lost by layoffs in antiquated factories? All of these questions and more came out at the town meetings held early in 1988 as Vice President George Bush entered presidential primaries by the carload. His chief challenger proved to be Senator Robert Dole, with television preacher Pat Robertson and Representative Jack Kemp also making challenges—mainly from the right wing of the party.

Bush won the primaries, after condemning "voodoo economics" and promising to rein in federal spending. The big surprise came toward the end of the Republican nominating convention, when Bush picked Senator Dan Quayle of Indiana for the vice presidential spot. Surprised by Bush's choice of a relatively unknown lawmaker, Senator Alan Simpson of Wyoming sheepishly confessed that the handsome Quayle represented "a cross between Robert Redford and Donald Duck." Money from Republican loyalists poured into the campaign coffers, for the television budget alone was calculated at $40 million for network time, not counting the projected debates.

The Democrats huffed and puffed and came out of their convention with the governor of Massachusetts, Michael Dukakis, as their candidate. Senator Lloyd Bentsen of Texas was added to the ticket for geographical, if not ideological, balance.

Bush, with his Yale and New England background, had become a naturalized Texan in the 1960s. He served in Congress, became head of the CIA briefly, was a diplomat in China, and had a commendable record as a Navy pilot in World War II. Dukakis, the son of Greek immigrant parents, claimed he had turned around the economy of his home state and offered liberal credentials on such important issues as abortion and prison reform. The campaign was fought mainly on television, with Bush the clear winner as he exploited the pollution in Boston harbor and utilized the slogan "Read my lips—no new taxes." The criminal record of a paroled killer from Dukakis's backyard was also thrust into television commercials that made the Democratic candidate appear ineffectual. The lackluster debates probably changed few voters' minds.

No Bush landslide was in prospect, but in August the Democrats lost any momentum they had earlier, and by November they were soundly defeated. Bush captured 54 percent of the popular vote and 426 electoral votes; Dukakis had 111 electoral votes and had lost many former Democratic strongholds such as Chicago and Philadelphia. Bush carried most of the South but lost Iowa and Minnesota, both once counted as 100-percent-safe Republican states.

The Bush cabinet was not a collection of Reagan holdovers but represented a new team, headed by Secretary of State James Baker. Secretary of Defense Richard Cheney was also close to the president, as was Budget Director Richard Darman. Darman's role became vital when the sudden collapse of scores of savings and loan associations turned into a scandal of major portions. Reckless lending practices and the collapse of the real estate boom caught hundreds of savings and loans short on cash and loaded with bad loans in the aftermath of the deregulation enacted during Reagan's administration. The buzzards came home to roost with a vengeance, and the final bill for taxpayers who bailed out the ailing institutions was calculated at over $200 billion. Several congressmen who had been friendly with one of the biggest losers, Charles Keating, quickly distanced themselves from the former millionaire as his paper empire vanished and he was sent to jail.

Republicans were somewhat relieved when the Supreme Court in 1989 limited the impact of the 1973 *Roe v. Wade* decision, which held that a woman had a constitutional right to obtain an abortion. In the *Webster* ruling the high court allowed states to impose some restrictions on abortions. Other conservative rulings in the same vein followed. Bush's Supreme Court nomination of Clarence Thomas, a conservative black with no previous courtroom experience, ran into difficulty when a former employee accused Thomas of sexual harassment. A Senate hearing produced sensational testimony and brought claims from feminist groups that the Republican senators had in turn harassed the female witness. Thomas was confirmed on a close vote and soon proved to be one of the most conservative of the nine sitting justices.

Further industrial layoffs created more unemployment in 1989 and 1990, making a business downturn seem likely. As the cold war evaporated in the goodwill emanating out of Moscow, defense contracts were canceled and military bases closed. California was hit hard by the change in priorities, and in its by-elections two women Democrats were elected to the Senate.

Domestic problems mounted, but President Bush turned his attention to the Middle East. Without provocation, Iraq invaded its neighbor, the oil-rich kingdom of Kuwait, early in August 1990. Apparently the CIA knew nothing of the impending invasion, but Bush reacted quickly and pushed for a United Nations Security Council resolution condemning Saddam Hussein, the Iraqi leader, and calling for an immediate withdrawal from Kuwait. Americans were told Hussein was a cut below Hitler but came out of the same base cloth. After the United Nations gave the go-ahead, Bush ordered U.S. troops to the combat area. When Iraq ignored an ultimatum, UN forces 150,000 strong (mostly American, and all well equipped) demolished the opposing Iraqi forces in a forty-two-day "war" that saw virtually no American blood spilled.

Unfortunately, Bush had made a great point of toppling Saddam Hussein. Muslim solidarity was challenged, and Hussein's Arab brothers seemed to be in no hurry to help "Uncle Sam" carry out extravagant promises. When U.S. forces finally left the region, after the mission was declared "accomplished," Bush shared the spotlight with Generals Colin Powell and Norman Schwartzkopf, the leaders of "Operation Desert Shield." But Hussein was still in power in 1996.

American morale needed a boost, and Desert Shield had provided it by the ton. Television coverage was extensive, hometown heroes were created overnight, and the small casualty rate (less than 150 for the whole operation) proved that this was no

Vietnam but a clear-cut, effective display of American firepower. A gleeful George Bush told the nation: "We've kicked the Vietnam Syndrome once and for all." Polls gave the president a 90 percent approval rating, the highest for a president since Franklin Roosevelt's heyday. Coupled with the capture of the Panamanian despot in December 1989 by American commandos, the Iraq venture seemed to prove that U.S. forces, not draftees but all volunteers, were as good as any soldiers in the world.

Bush inspected the battlefields and came home to find his detractors few, his admirers everywhere. A columnist in the *New York Times* predicted Bush's popularity had frightened away the opposition, so that only a foolhardy Democrat would try to turn him out of the White House in 1992. Bush's popularity was so palpable, James Reston wrote in May 1991, that "most observers have assumed his [certain] re-election." At his Maine vacation home in the summer of 1991 Bush quashed the gossip that he would replace Quayle on the 1992 ticket with a Republican "heavyweight." Quayle was on his team to stay, Bush said.

There were a few signs that Bush did not have Reagan's ability to rise above the cracks in his political wall. The deficit would not go away, and during the Persian Gulf war it reached nearly $4 trillion. The Congress elected that fall was once again Democratic in both houses, 56 to 46 in the Senate, 267 to 167 in the House. An increase in income taxes appeared to be the only way to stop runaway deficits, so Bush swallowed his "Read my lips" promise and signed legislation that raised taxes just enough to slow down the rise of the deficit, if not decrease it.

The fact was that Bush was fairly comfortable with the Democratic Congress. He vetoed 44 bills, far short of the 78 vetoes by Reagan, and a mere dab compared to Eisenhower's 181 vetoes when he had to deal with Democratic congresses. Still, Bush had made so much of his no-new-taxes promise that reneging undercut his credibility. Perhaps in his own mind Bush balanced the Middle East success and the warming relations with China and the Soviet Union into a winning formula for 1992, even though the domestic economy was ailing.

One Democrat who thought differently was William J. Clinton, the two-time governor of Arkansas, who leaped into the presidential primaries where others feared to tread. Insisting that he was just plain "Bill," Clinton attacked the Bush administration's economic program, denounced the rising deficit as a Republican contraption, and appealed to the jobless, the blacks, and first-time voters as a "new Democrat." Clinton outdistanced his come-lately opposition, and to stress his party's youthful image he chose Senator Al Gore of Tennessee for the vice presidential place on the ticket. Clinton was forty-three and Gore was forty-four as they began their campaign in earnest.

Republicans saw no reason to abandon Bush and every reason to renominate a Bush-Quayle ticket. Bush easily brushed aside the conservative Pat Buchanan, a former Nixon teammate, and was soon endorsed by the Christian Coalition. When stories of Clinton's alleged marital infidelity surfaced, Republicans heard a great deal about "family values" from Bush and Quayle. Right-wing groups also attacked Hillary Rodham Clinton, the president's lawyer-wife, with barbs not unlike those thrown at Eleanor Roosevelt fifty years earlier. Mrs. Clinton should go home, the critics said, after the candidate's wife said she wasn't interested in staying in the kitchen and baking cookies.

The 1992 campaign was more of a tug-of-war than a shouting match. Democrats said that President Bush was ignoring the plight of workers laid off by "heartless" corporations, and Republicans cast aspersions aplenty on Clinton's failure to serve during the Vietnam War. "Want a Draft Dodger? Vote for Clinton," was one of the kinder bumper stickers. Retaliating, Democrats replayed television footage of President Bush in a supermarket, where the Republican president seemed more bewildered than amused by the electronic checkout stands.

Neither candidate commanded the loyalties of yesteryear when voters were eager to claim kinship with a Roosevelt or a Reagan. On the day before the election, a supermarket customer was asked by a television interviewer how she saw the two contestants. "Well," the lady said, "I'd say it is a case of choosing the lesser of two evils." Millions in the viewing audience apparently agreed.

Lesser or greater, Clinton won, but not by any landslide. The "wild card" had been the candidacy, off and on, of Ross Perot.

The billionaire Texan had run as an independent, spent $40 million of his own money to campaign, and was on the ballot in all fifty states. Perot won 19.7 percent of the vote, enough perhaps to have ensured the election of Clinton because of the number of voters who deserted Bush to support Perot. But this is only conjecture. Whatever the reason, Bush had 39 percent of the vote to Clinton's 43 percent. Thus Clinton, like Lincoln, was elected with less than a majority of the votes; and the comparison can end there. Bush carried the South and took all the states between North Dakota and Texas, but Clinton took all from Minnesota to Louisiana and much of the West, including California. Moreover, Clinton would have a Democratic Congress after his inauguration in January 1993. The Democratic margin in the House was 256 to 178, while that in the Senate was 56 to 44.

Clinton promised to reinvent government for the people and by the people, but he soon was bogged down with his imprudent pledge to open the military forces to homosexuals, an issue that alienated mainstream America. His call for deficit reduction included tax increases and required some courage, but nominal Democrats threatened to prevent passage of that legislation as well as Clinton's proposed North American Free Trade Agreement bonding Mexico and Canada with the United States in a duty-free market. A handgun-control bill came out of committee, named after Reagan's press secretary Jim Brady, who had been critically wounded in the 1981 assassination attempt. These measures passed, sometimes with only one vote to spare. The tax measure, however, was opposed by *every* House Republican. Nobody in Washington could remember when the Republicans had been so unified.

Republicans also dragged their feet on Clinton's call for a ban on assault weapons and talked about a constitutional amendment to allow prayers in public schools; as Minority Leader Newt Gingrich told reporters, "We don't want to do anything to make Clinton look good." Here was a partisan admission that might disturb a citizen who believed the duty of Congress was to serve the best interests of the whole nation. But Gingrich and Robert Dole, the Senate minority leader, were in no mood to cooperate.

They appeared to believe that Clinton was a political accident who deserved neither their respect nor their cooperation. The bipartisanship of the 1940s was in the same category as the dodo bird—extinct.

When Clinton and his wife came to Congress with a plan for universal health care in 1994, the sharp knives were unsheathed. Aided by a $200 million advertising campaign financed by medical groups and pharmaceutical companies, opponents of the president's overlong plan ridiculed it on television as a bulky but watered-down version of "socialized medicine." Mrs. Clinton's role in promoting the proposal was ridiculed, and after six months of public debate, the attempt to give coverage to 37 million citizens who had no medical insurance was also in the dodo bird category. Dead, dead, dead.

Liberal critics asked if Republicans were simply negative and trying to embarrass the president. Not so, said Gingrich and his congressional staff. There were certain sacred cows that could not be touched, such as the National Rifle Association and its 3 million members who were enraged by the assault-weapons ban. By the time the 1994 by-elections came around, Gingrich had formulated a platform of sorts, which he called "A Contract with America." Gingrich gave highest priority to a tax cut but also had room for cutbacks in social programs as well as proposed amendments for a mandatory balanced budget and limits on congressional terms. Moreover, Gingrich's promise was that if Republicans won in November 1994, he would see that these ideas became law during the first hundred days of the 102d Congress. His allusion harked back to the famous "hundred days" of 1933, when most of Franklin D. Roosevelt's social programs were sent to Congress over a three-month period. By 1994, it was safe for a Republican as partisan as Gingrich to say good things about the New Deal!

No reporter, columnist, think-tank seer, or even Gingrich himself could have predicted the landslide victory that occurred in the November 1994 by-elections. After forty years of Democratic domination, Republicans swept both the House and the Senate. The numbers were not overwhelming, but a Republican majority of 230 to 204 in the House, and of 53 to 47 in the Senate, grew when two Senate Democrats switched parties early in 1995. Also surprising was the defeat of two Democratic incumbents from Tennessee, both replaced by Republicans making their first try for office.

The victory of every single Republican incumbent running for reelection to the House or Senate was remarkable in itself. Add to that the reelection of incumbent governors, and the dimension of the Republican victory grows significantly. A total of 177 Republicans asked to be reelected and were, a circumstance not likely to be repeated again for centuries. The election of Republican governors in California, Texas, and New York gave special significance to the statehouse elections, for in these states the GOP challengers faced entrenched incumbents (Ann Richards in Texas and Mario Cuomo in New York) or an opponent with impressive credentials (Kathleen Brown's father and brother had both been governor of California).

Perhaps the Republican sweep of 1994 was proof that the GOP had again become the majority party in the United States, breaking the long hold on voter affection cultivated by Democrats from FDR through Kennedy. Since 1968 the signs of a major shift were apparent, but the dramatic changes affected the North as well as the South. The South became a Republican bastion, but New England voters veered away from the GOP along with those in the upper midwestern states as environmental issues and global trade policies drew attention from citizens once fiercely loyal to Republicans. On the other side, a latent isolationism and lack of enthusiasm for trade pacts or gun-control laws moved many former Democrats into the Republican fold across the nation.

Another indicator of shifting political sands was the issue of capital punishment. Revival of the death penalty, once outlawed by the Supreme Court, was a smoldering issue, and from Virginia to Texas state legislatures restored capital punishment, and for good measure enacted "old frontier" laws that permitted citizens to carry concealed weapons as a deterrent to street crime.

Public attitudes on endangered species and America's role in the United Nations thus worked a minor miracle in the nation's political topography in the six decades after 1936. Republican bastions in Massachusetts, Minnesota, the Dakotas, and the

Pacific rim states were tilting Democratic in 1996, while Alabama, Mississippi, and Texas sent Republicans to the U.S. Senate and appeared to be firmly in the GOP column for generations to come.

Still, there was no proof that the 1994 election returns meant Clinton was already a "lame duck" waiting to fade away after 1996. Certainly the pro-gun lobby had poured millions into the campaign to defeat congressmen and senators who favored the assault-weapons ban. But one issue does not a campaign make, and in most instances the margins in the House and Senate were still close enough to deny Republicans complete comfort. Angry as the voters had been, that fury could boomerang and strike again if the Republican promises were broken. In the Senate, more than one Republican promise had already miscarried. The balanced budget amendment was sidetracked by Senator Mark Hatfield, a Republican, and another Republican, Senator Pete Domenici, suggested that budget balancing had a higher priority than tax cuts on his 1995 agenda.

Meanwhile, early in 1995 Senators Dole, Gramm, and Arlen Specter of Pennsylvania said they would enter the 1996 presidential primaries, as did Representative Robert Dorman of California and columnist Pat Buchanan. And where was the perennial mock-candidate, Harold Stassen? Fund-raising dinners helped fill campaign chests, and the faintest odor of "eau d'1948" wafted on the air as Republican hopefuls seemed to believe that the party nomination was tantamount to election in 1996. When the smoke cleared, Dole emerged as the GOP candidate. In November, voters would determine whether Clinton was an easy target.

A few warning shots crossed the Republican bow. One was fired by former Senator Warren Rudman, who believed the budget strain was going to be the central issue in 1996. "If there is not a substantial reversal of this [deficit] trend," Rudman predicted, "you will see a third party in 1996, and it will be a broadly based third party."* Prognostications about third parties are usually

---

*Quoted in Kevin Phillips, *The Boiling Point: Democrats, Republicans, and the Decline of Middle-Class Prosperity* (New York: HarperCollins, 1994), 245.

wrong, but Rudman's attempt to wake up his own party may be significant.

Finally, there was the old image that the Republican hierarchy was still a millionaire's club. "The rich enjoy a certain moral prestige in the Republican party," a *New Yorker* reporter observed. "Republican ideology glorifies private enterprise over public service. The successful business executive is the beau ideal."* The number of dirt farmers registered as Republicans is a moot point, but the preponderance of bankers, lawyers, doctors, and corporate executives in the GOP ranks is beyond doubt.

To say 1994 was a watershed year for the Republicans, heralding a resurgence that will restore the glory of old, is to risk derision. Equally dangerous is the strategy of calling the Democrats "liberals" and then dismissing the ideas and issues that are part of the Democratic party's long history. The Republican party came into being because it represented a moral position that proved to be unassailable. No such clear-cut issue as slavery exists today, so the Republicans must sort and choose. If the great problem in 1996 and beyond is the budget deficit, then an honest approach will demand taxes—not demagoguery. If the decay of inner cities is a major concern, the nation cannot spend billions on a nuclear submarine and battle social decay with a pittance. If drugs and sexual promiscuity are a cancerous growth eating the vitals of America, all the prisons in the world will not solve the problem, and the Republicans must acknowledge the need for some solution other than incarceration.

Over time, the so-called watershed years simply fade into the general scheme of history. There are early warning signs for major trends, but even revolutions rarely bring overnight reversals in conduct or governments. Indeed, the revered Constitution is structured to prevent rapid change. That more than 400 amendments have been offered to the Constitution and only 26 ratified tells us something about whether the system works or not. The whole of American history is full of checks and balances, constitutional and otherwise.

*Hendrik Hertzberg, "Banana Republican," *New Yorker,* February 19, 1996, p. 52.

Republicans earned their right to be a vital force in that history in 1860 and have been in control of the nation's political destiny much of the time over a span of more than 135 years. The tariff, silver coinage, and colonialism issues are all dead and must be replaced with a fresh vision of what America will become in the next century. A republic dedicated to expanding human freedom and protecting the planet from destruction? Perhaps. Our two-party system, like our Constitution, is not faultless. But there is nothing better on the horizon, and we know the two-party system works.

Let us not forget, a decent respect for the opposition, a certain kind of civility in politics, is necessary when all the political rhetoric fades after an election. As the late Richard Hofstadter reminded us, "The two-party system, as it has developed in the United States, hangs on the common recognition of loyal opposition; each side accepts the ultimate good intentions of the other." It is important to remember that neither party has produced many saints.

Martin Luther King spoke of his dream. Republicans can be dreamers, too. They can dream of an America "with liberty and justice for all." Such was Lincoln's vision in 1860, and it is still a goal worth pursuing in the century ahead. To further "the blessings of liberty" for the entire nation will be the ongoing challenge facing Republicans in the twenty-first century.

Bibliographical Note

Laymen and undergraduates, the people for whom this book is intended, will find that party histories tend to appear at least once every decade, or have since Arthur N. Holcombe's *The Political Parties of Today* (New York: Harper and Row, 1924). Wilfred E. Binkley, in *American Political Parties: Their Natural History* (New York: Knopf, 1966), broke new ground and even had a touch of humor in his tracking of the major parties. Another political scientist, Clinton Rossiter, helped explain the peculiarities of the American two-party system with his *Parties and Politics in America* (Ithaca: Cornell University Press, 1960). Critical of both parties for their failure to accept reforms is Leon D. Epstein, *Political Parties in the American Mold* (Madison: University of Wisconsin Press, 1986). More recently, A. James Reichley's *The Life of the Parties: A History of American Political Parties* (New York: Free Press, 1992) provided a balanced account with some nostalgia for the demise of city machines and smoke-filled rooms.

Almost thirty years ago, Kevin P. Phillips brought out his optimistic work, *The Emerging Republican Majority* (New Rochelle, N.Y.: Arlington House, 1969), which foresaw the switch of the South into a solid Republican majority. Less fortunate as a forecaster of events was Theodore J. Lowi, whose *The End of the Republican Era* (Norman: University of Oklahoma Press, 1995) was finished prior to the 1994 Republican sweep of Congress and saddled with the comment that "Conservatism can never govern America because its view of authority is contrary to democracy"!

American historians have been so close to the statistics they have sometimes forgotten how peculiar our undisciplined party system can appear to outsiders. Foreigners since de Toqueville's time have been acute observers of our political spectrum, and sometimes not too forgiving. Take Denis Brogan's remark: "The fact that all Republicans claim to be democrats and all Democrats [claim] to be republicans, makes the confusion of party names nearly complete" (*Politics in America* [New York: Harper and Brothers, 1954], 47).

Broad-brushed histories of the party are helpful for readers hoping to understand the philosophical foundations of our parties. Malcolm Moos, in *The Republicans: A History of Their Party* (New York: Random House, 1956), surveyed the party's growth up to the Eisenhower administration with the optimistic conclusion that GOP gains in suburbia and with blue-collar voters boded well for the party's future prospects. In another general history, *The Republican Party, 1854–1964* (New York: Oxford, 1964), George H. Mayer saw much growth for the party in the South but was concerned that "most of the [southern] recruits were militant advocates of white supremacy" who had left the Democratic party. More restricted is William E. Gienapp, *The Origins of the Republican Party, 1852–1856* (New York: Oxford, 1987). For the party's role during the 1920s, John D. Hicks's *Republican Ascendancy, 1921–1933* (New York: Harper and Row, 1960) is a brilliant synthesis.

Biographies of the leading Republicans are also useful for comprehending how parties have shaped our history. David Herbert Donald's magisterial biography, *Lincoln* (New York: Simon and Schuster, 1995), is the best one-volume work on the party's first president ever to appear. But close behind is Mark E. Neely Jr., *The Last Best Hope: Abraham Lincoln and the Promise of America* (Cambridge: Harvard University Press, 1993). I also recommend David M. Potter, *Lincoln and His Party in the Secession Crisis* (New Haven: Yale University Press, 1942), which is another classic. Not to be overlooked, either, is Merrill Peterson, *Lincoln in American Memory* (New York: Oxford, 1994).

Vice presidents often are ignored, but H. Draper Hunt's *Hannibal Hamlin of Maine: Lincoln's Vice President* (Syracuse: Syracuse University Press, 1969) has merit. For an insider's view of the Lincoln and Johnson administrations, Gideon Welles's *The*

Diary of Gideon Welles, Secretary of the Navy under Lincoln and Johnson (3 vols., Boston: Houghton, Mifflin and Co., 1911) is a vital resource.

Reconstruction, both as a process and as an era, has attracted many scholars. A revisionist view is found in Harold M. Hyman, ed., *The Radical Republicans and Reconstruction 1861–1870* (Indianapolis: Bobbs-Merrill Co., 1967). An earlier work, still good reading, is Matthew Josephson, *The Politicos, 1856–1896* (New York: Harcourt, Brace and Co., 1938). To see how the fortunes of a party are sometimes moving like a yo-yo, read Stanley P. Hirshson, *Farewell to the Bloody Shirt: Northern Republicans and the Southern Negro 1877–1893* (Bloomington: Indiana University Press, 1962). For the full impact of the corruption after 1866, see Richard N. Current, *Those Terrible Carpetbaggers* (New York: Oxford, 1988). Martin E. Mantell, in *Johnson, Grant, and the Politics of Reconstruction* (New York: Columbia University Press, 1973), found flaws in the Republicans' reconstruction aims, as did Richard H. Abbot in *The Republican Party and the South, 1855–1877* (Chapel Hill: University of North Carolina Press, 1986). For the Gilded Age, Mark W. Summers's *The Era of Good Stealing* (New York: Oxford, 1993) offers a perspective on the corruption in both parties that shocked Americans and left the reputations of many congressmen in disarray.

U. S. Grant the general and Grant the president seem to be two different persons in many scholarly works. The best modern biography of the ill-starred eighteenth president is William S. McFeely, *Grant: A Biography* (New York: Norton, 1981).

Except for Grant, few of the Republican presidents elected between 1868 and 1896 have deserved extensive study, but I found Thomas C. Reeves's *Gentleman Boss: The Life of Chester Alan Arthur* (New York: Knopf, 1975) to be well researched and sympathetic to a much-maligned president—the only incumbent Republican never renominated by his party convention for a second term. Theodore Roosevelt has had a plethora of biographers, including Nathan Miller, *Theodore Roosevelt: A Life* (New York: Morrow, 1993). Still valuable is John Morton Blum's influential work, *The Republican Roosevelt* (Cambridge: Harvard University Press, 1954). Worth reading, too, are William

Harbaugh's *The Life and Times of Theodore Roosevelt* (New York: Oxford, 1975) and Edward Cadenhead's neglected work, *Theodore Roosevelt: The Paradox of Progressivism* (Woodbury, N.Y.: Barron's Educational Service, 1974). *The Warrior and the President: Woodrow Wilson and Theodore Roosevelt* by John Milton Cooper (Cambridge: Belknap Press of Harvard University Press, 1983) has a different and provocative twist.

Harding is a tragic figure in everybody's book, but Wesley M. Bagby, in *The Road to Normalcy: The Presidential Campaign and Election of 1920* (Baltimore: Johns Hopkins University Press, 1962), has provided a fascinating account of how Harding landed in the White House. Robert H. Ferrell's *The Strange Deaths of President Harding* (Columbia: University of Missouri Press, 1996) examines the suspicions about Harding's death and argues that his reputation has been unfairly devalued by scholars.

With the passage of years, Calvin Coolidge has faded into the dimmest memory, but William A. White's *A Puritan in Babylon* (New York: Macmillan, 1938) has considerable charm because White was a Republican insider for decades. More recently, Donald R. McCoy's *Calvin Coolidge: The Quiet President* (New York: Macmillan, 1967) is a work of insight and intelligence. A revival of interest in Herbert Hoover has prompted scholars to refocus attention on the Iowa-born Quaker. These include Martin L. Fausold, who edited *The Hoover Presidency: A Reappraisal* (Albany: State University of New York Press, 1979), and David Burner, whose *Herbert Hoover: A Public Life* (New York: Knopf, 1979) encompasses Hoover's career as a public servant. Joan Hoff Wilson, in *Herbert Hoover: Forgotten Progressive* (Boston: Little, Brown and Co., 1975), sees a different president from the man most historians have studied. No important biography of Alfred M. Landon has appeared, but Mary E. Dillon's *Wendell Willkie* (Philadelphia: J. B. Lippincott, 1952) explains the rise of the 1940 standard-bearer as an outsider with good connections.

For the post–New Deal years, Richard Norton Smith's *Thomas E. Dewey and His Times* (New York: Morrow, 1992) is a useful study in political failure, showing not only that Dewey lost an election he should have won, but also that he let his party slip into a philosophical crevice that he had long opposed.

A study in hero worship is Stephen E. Ambrose's *Eisenhower: Soldier and President* (New York: Touchstone Books, 1991). Fred I. Greenstein's *The Hidden-Hand Presidency: Eisenhower as Leader* (Baltimore: Johns Hopkins University Press, 1994) shows how a crusading biographer can cause the public to revise its view of a presidency.

The Nixon era has been examined with an outpouring that may never cease. H. R. Haldeman's *The Haldeman Diaries: Inside the Nixon White House* (New York: Putnam, 1994) is a vital source of information as committed to memory by one of Nixon's closest lieutenants. Perhaps a generation must pass before a fair assessment of Nixon's impact on history will be available. Meanwhile, *Breach of Faith: The Fall of Richard Nixon* by Theodore H. White (New York: Atheneum, 1975) has merit, as does Herbert Parmet's *Richard Nixon and His America* (Boston: Little, Brown and Co., 1990).

Gerald Ford, the only president never elected to serve in the executive branch, still occupies an undefined place in history. See Jerald F. tenHorst's *Gerald Ford and the Future of the Presidency* (New York: Third Press, 1974) to understand the dilemma. I found merit in Ronald Reagan's own story—*An American Life* (New York: Simon and Schuster, 1990)—a sentimental journey into presidential politics that focuses on the White House years. Garry Wills, in *Reagan's America: Innocents at Home* (New York: Doubleday, 1987), takes a more somber view of the Reagan presidency.

Not to be overlooked is the excellent American Presidential Series from the University Press of Kansas. As the 1996 election approached its list was almost complete. Volumes on Grant, Coolidge, Nixon, Reagan, and Bush are yet to come, but there are exhaustive and perceptive accounts of all the other Republican presidents; my personal favorites in the series are by Lewis L. Gould on McKinley (1980) and Theodore Roosevelt (1991).

Also useful for its plethora of vital information is *The Encyclopedia of the American Presidency,* edited by Leonard W. Levy and Louis Fisher (4 vols., New York: Simon and Schuster, 1994), a singular reference work of compounded scholarly value. *Political Parties in American History,* edited by Wilfred E. A. Bernhard,

Felice A. Bonadio, and Paul A. Murphy (3 vols., New York: G. P. Putnam's Sons, 1974) is a collection of essays by experts, with volume 3, *1890–Present,* being the most helpful for insights on modern Republicanism.

Finally, some notice is due the Ripon Society for its publications program. A frankly partisan group with adequate financial backing, the society is "dedicated to the principle of making the Republican party a more enlightened institution" through "the stimulation of controversy and excitement in a party that might otherwise appear stodgy and dull." Most libraries hold some of the group's publications, and I recommend Clifford W. Brown Jr., *Jaws of Victory* (Boston: Little, Brown and Co., 1973), which looks beyond the tragedy of Watergate and warns that a "managerial party" such as that which Nixon controlled had "technical competence" but lacked a soul and deserved no permanence.

Index

Index

Index

Index

Index

Index

About the Author

Robert Allen Rutland is author or editor of numerous books, including *The Democrats: From Jefferson to Clinton* (University of Missouri Press), *The Presidency of James Madison, James Madison: The Founding Father,* and *James Madison and the American Nation.* Editor-in-Chief of *The Papers of James Madison* from 1971 to 1987, Rutland is Emeritus Professor of American History at the University of Virginia.